OHIO

ENVIRONMENTAL LAW HANDBOOK

Fifth Edition

by the law firm of

Porter Wright Morris & Arthur LLP

Editor

Daniel J. Prater

Authors

Andrew S. Bergman
Robert L. Brubaker
Katerina M. Eftimoff
Michael D. Heintz
J. Jeffrey McNealey
David E. Northrop
Daniel J. Prater
Robert J. Schmidt
Christopher
Martin S.

Government Institutes
Rockville, Maryland

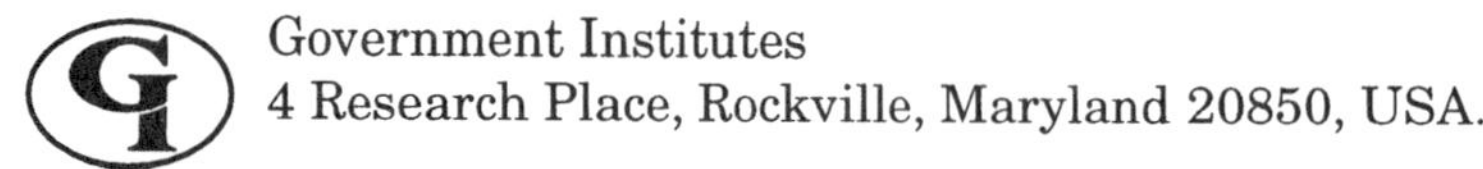
Government Institutes
4 Research Place, Rockville, Maryland 20850, USA.

07 06 05 04 5 4 3 2 1

ISBN: 0-86587-976-1

Printed in the United States of America

OHIO ENVIRONMENTAL LAW HANDBOOK

Fifth Edition, 2004

TABLE OF CONTENTS

Chapter III: AIR POLLUTION CONTROL 35

PREFACE

Our goal in writing this 5th Edition of the *Ohio Environmental Law Handbook* was to provide an updated and easy reference for those who want a comprehensive, introductory guide to environmental law in Ohio.

We want users to understand how Ohio's unique historical, political, economic, cultural, and philosophical perspectives impact the federal-state partnership for regulating environmental quality in the state. Because these perspectives are constantly evolving, a primary objective is to help users understand the changes in the way that Ohio deals with major environmental issues and how those changes affect the regulated community. Some of the more substantive changes covered in the 5th Edition address the following:

- storm water regulations,
- isolated wetlands, TMDL programs, and sludge management,
- corrective action requirements for both hazardous waste management and underground storage tank sites,
- site investigation and remediation requirements,
- the Voluntary Action Program's new MOA track, and
- tort claims by a purchaser of real property against the seller.

In addition, we have completely rewritten the chapters on environmental considerations in real estate transactions and insurance coverage for environmental liability to reflect significant changes in the marketplace over the last several years.

The biggest change in this edition as compared to the *Handbooks* we wrote in 1990, 1992, 1994, and 1997, however, is our acknowledgement and use of the vast resources available through the Internet. All the statutes, regulations, and judicial decisions we discuss are available at agency and court web sites. In addition, the Ohio EPA materials that we appended in earlier versions – *e.g.*, organizational charts and maps, permitting forms, and guides – now may be downloaded from the agency's various web sites in their most current versions. In each case we provide an appropriate web address for readers to use.

Because of the dynamic nature of environmental law, as well as the ready availability of constantly updated information on the web sites of administrative and regulatory bodies, we encourage users to be alert to continuing changes in the law and to the many and varied formats in which those changes will be made available to the public.

* * * * * * *

The editor and authors acknowledge the support of Porter Wright Morris & Arthur LLP for this 5th Edition and thank Claudia Ruggles for her outstanding services in preparing the manuscript.

ABOUT THE AUTHORS

ANDREW S. BERGMAN

Mr. Bergman counsels clients on Clean Air Act issues and other environmental matters, and provides defense in environmental enforcement actions. Prior to joining Porter Wright, he was an Assistant Ohio Attorney General in the Environmental Enforcement Section, a member of the OAG Chief Counsel's Staff, and an Assistant State Solicitor. While with the OAG's Office, he was co-counsel on a number of U.S. Supreme Court cases and helped lead a coalition of states in challenges to federal rulemaking in the U.S. Court of Appeals for the D.C. Circuit. Mr. Bergman is a 1986 *cum laude* graduate of the University of Minnesota Law School. He received a bachelor's degree with honors from Grinnell College and a master's degree from the Humphrey Institute of Public Affairs at the University of Minnesota. He has served as Adjunct Professor of Environmental Law at Capital University Law School.

ROBERT L. BRUBAKER

Mr. Brubaker practices environmental law, concentrating on Clean Air Act legislation, rulemaking, permitting, and litigation. He represents manufacturers, utilities, small businesses, trade associations, and public sector clients on matters involving the Clean Air Act and other environmental issues. Mr. Brubaker has argued numerous Clean Air Act cases in the U.S. Courts of Appeals for the D.C. and Sixth Circuits and has defended clients in Clean Air Act enforcement actions and citizen suits. He is vice chair of the Environmental Committee of the American Bar Association Public Utility Section, a member of the National Coal Council, and past chair of the East Central Section and Southwest Ohio Chapter of the Air and Waste Management Association. A 1972 graduate of the University of Chicago Law School, he holds a bachelor's degree from Earlham College. He is a frequent lecturer and writer on environmental law issues.

KATERINA M. EFTIMOFF

Ms. Eftimoff's practice focuses on Clean Air Act and Superfund issues. She is experienced in matters of cost recovery under CERCLA and regulation under EPCRA. She graduated *summa cum laude* in 1994 from the Capital University Law School, where she served as Executive Articles Editor of the Capital University Law Review and was elected to both the Order of the Curia and the Order of the Barristers. She received a bachelor's degree from The Ohio State University College of Engineering. Ms. Eftimoff chairs the Air Subcommittee of the Environmental Litigation Committee of the American Bar Association Litigation Section, and serves on the ABA Standing Committee on Environmental Law. She is Assistant Editor of Litigation News, the Litigation Section's newsletter, and a Fellow of the ABA Young Lawyers' Division.

MICHAEL E. HEINTZ

Mr. Heintz practices in all areas of environmental law, including environmental litigation and zoning. He is a graduate of Indiana University-Bloomington, where he received both his law degree, in 2003, and a master's degree in environmental science. In law school, Mr. Heintz was the Senior Notes and Comments Editor of the Federal Communications Law Journal and a winner in the Sherman Minton Moot Court Competition. He holds a bachelor's degree in natural resources and environmental sciences from Purdue University.

J. JEFFREY MCNEALEY

Mr. McNealey practices environmental, general corporate, and zoning law. He has served as lead counsel in major air, water, and Superfund cases, and has handled issues related to wetlands, brownfield redevelopment, and environmental assessments. He also has counseled on constitutional taking issues related to private development. Mr. McNealey was founding chair of the Ohio State Bar Association Environmental Committee and is a member of the environmental committees of various other professional organizations. A graduate of

The Ohio State University College of Law in 1969 and Cornell University, he lectures frequently on environmental and development issues.

DAVID E. NORTHROP

Mr. Northrop has practiced environmental law both in the public sector as an Assistant Ohio Attorney General and in private practice. At Porter Wright, he focuses on client counseling and litigation in Clean Air Act, Clean Water Act, solid waste, and hazardous waste matters. His practice also includes environmental aspects of real estate transactions and Superfund defense. Mr. Northrop is a 1972 *summa cum laude* graduate of The Ohio State University College of Law and holds a bachelor's degree from Allegheny College.

DANIEL J. PRATER

Mr. Prater is an environmental policy analyst. He received a master's degree with emphasis in public policy from the University of Kentucky in 1974 and holds a bachelor's degree from that institution. He has researched and written numerous articles on environmental regulation for various publications and was a contributing editor of the *NPDES Permit Handbook* (Government Institutes, Inc., 1989).

ROBERT J. SCHMIDT, JR.

Mr. Schmidt's practice focuses on a wide range of environmental issues, including the Clean Water Act, underground storage tanks, Superfund, and the defense of civil enforcement actions. He also represents clients in local zoning and health code-related matters. Prior to joining Porter Wright, he was an Assistant Ohio Attorney General in the Environmental Enforcement Section. A 1993 graduate of the University of Virginia School of Law, he received an LL.M. in international environmental law from the University of Washington and holds a bachelor's degree from the University of Virginia.

CHRISTOPHER R. SCHRAFF

Mr. Schraff practices in the areas of environmental law and public utilities regulation. He has worked on matters involving environmental litigation as well as the permitting and licensing of manufacturing and energy facilities. He has extensive experience in the defense of administrative and judicial enforcement actions involving RCRA, CERCLA, the Clean Air Act, the Clean Water Act, and comparable state statutes. He also practices before the Ohio Power Siting Board in proceedings involving the siting of new electric generation and transmission facilities and natural gas transmission lines. An Adjunct Professor of Law at the Capital University Law School, Mr. Schraff is co-author of *RCRA and Superfund: A Practice Guide With Forms* (Shepards-McGraw Hill, 1990). He received his law degree, *cum laude*, from the University of Notre Dame in 1972, and a bachelor's degree, *magna cum laude*, from John Carroll University.

MARTIN S. SELTZER

Mr. Seltzer's practice is in environmental law, with special emphasis on issues relating to solid and hazardous waste, toxic substances, water issues, and brownfield redevelopment. He has performed numerous environmental assessments on behalf of lenders in connection with business and real estate transactions, and has represented industrial and governmental clients in obtaining federal and state environmental permits. Mr. Seltzer is General Counsel to the Ohio Chemistry Technology Council, past co-chair of the Ohio EPA Public Advisory Group on Solid and Hazardous Waste, and former chair of the Columbus Bar Association Environmental Law Committee. He received his law degree from The Ohio State University College of Law in 1977. He also holds a doctorate in engineering from Yale University and a bachelor's degree from New York University. He is a frequent presenter at seminars and other forums.

Chapter I

OVERVIEW OF
OHIO ENVIRONMENTAL LAW

1.0 OHIO ENVIRONMENTAL STATUTES

1.1 Environmental Protection Agency: Chapter 3745

In the early 1970s, the Ohio General Assembly created new administrative agencies to manage and regulate Ohio's environment and natural resources. Previously, the Ohio Water Pollution Control Board, Ohio Air Pollution Control Board, and local Boards of Health had the major responsibility for overseeing environmental concerns. However, with the enactment of SB 397 in 1972, the Ohio Environmental Protection Agency ("Ohio EPA") and the Environmental Board of Review (now known as the Environmental Review Appeals Commission) came into being. Under Chapter 3745 of the Revised Code, Ohio EPA administers the major regulatory programs pertaining to air and water pollution, public water supply, and solid and hazardous wastes.

1.2 Air Pollution Control: Chapter 3704

The Director of Ohio EPA is authorized to adopt and maintain a program for the prevention, control, and abatement of air pollution that is consistent with the federal Clean Air Act, and to obtain financial assistance and delegation of powers from the U.S. Environmental Protection Agency ("U.S. EPA") to administer this program. Emission limits necessary to meet National Ambient Air Quality Standards are prescribed by regulation, and permits are required to install and operate air contaminant emission sources.

1.3 Water Pollution Control: Chapter 6111

In conformity with the federal Clean Water Act and Safe Drinking Water Act, the Director of Ohio EPA is authorized to develop plans and programs to regulate new or existing sources of pollution of the waters of the State, including the adoption of water quality standards and effluent limitations to enable the use of Ohio's waters for public water supplies, industrial and agricultural needs, propagation of fish and aquatic life, and recreational purposes. The Director also may issue, revoke, modify, or deny permits for the direct or indirect discharge of sewage, industrial waste, or other wastes into Ohio's waters.

1.4 Solid And Hazardous Wastes: Chapter 3734

The Director of Ohio EPA has the authority to regulate solid waste facilities in the State. It is the Director's responsibility to inspect and issue permits for the installation or modification of all solid waste facilities in order to assure that these facilities will be located, maintained, and operated in a sanitary manner so as not to create a nuisance or health hazard, or contribute to water pollution. The Director is empowered to seek appropriate legal or equitable remedies against any violator who poses a substantial threat to the public welfare or whose actions result in air or water pollution. However, the Director may delegate authority to the local Boards of Health to provide for the annual inspection, licensing, and enforcement of sanitary standards for solid waste facilities.

These provisions do not apply to: (1) single-family residential premises; (2) the temporary storage of solid wastes other than hazardous wastes prior to their collection; or (3) the collection of solid wastes by persons holding a franchise or license from a political subdivision of the State.

The Director also is granted authority to administer and enforce Ohio's program for the regulation of the generation, transportation, storage, treatment, and disposal of hazardous wastes. The program must be consistent with, and equivalent to, the national program enacted by Congress in the Resource Conservation and Recovery Act. Hazardous wastes are defined as those that have hazardous characteristics, as set out in regulations promulgated by the Director, and those that are listed as wastes in the regulations. Facilities that store, treat, or dispose of hazardous wastes may be constructed and operated only as authorized by permits issued by the Hazardous Waste Facility Board.

1.5 Sewer Districts And Related Provisions

1.5.1 Chapter 6112: Private Sewer Systems

The Director of Ohio EPA, with certification by the appropriate Board of County Commissioners, has the responsibility for approving applications made by private entities for the construction and installation of sewage disposal systems.

1.5.2 Chapter 6113: Ohio River Sanitation Compact

"The Ohio River Valley Water Sanitation Compact" was established by the states of Illinois, Indiana, Kentucky, New York, Ohio, Pennsylvania, Tennessee, and West Virginia to deal with the pollution of the Ohio River. The Compact's goals and duties include:

(1) the guiding principle that pollution by sewage or industrial wastes originating within a signatory state shall not injuriously affect the use of the interstate waters;

(2) a survey of the territory included within the district, a study of the pollution problems of the district, and a comprehensive report for the prevention or reduction of stream pollution; and

(3) the issuing of orders to entities to stop the discharge of sewage or waste into the river.

1.5.3 Chapter 6115: Sanitary Districts

The Revised Code also provides for the establishment of sanitary districts and their organizational structure. Upon a hearing, every district declared to be a sanitary district becomes a political subdivision and a public corporation of the State. Districts may be created for any of the following purposes:

(1) to prevent and correct the pollution of streams;

(2) to clean and improve stream channels for sanitary purposes;

(3) to regulate the flow of streams for sanitary purposes;

(4) to provide for the collection and disposal of sewage and other liquid wastes;

(5) to provide a water supply for domestic, municipal, and public use within the district;

(6) to reduce populations of biting arthropods and abate their breeding places;

(7) to collect and dispose of garbage; and

(8) to collect and dispose of any other refuse that may become a menace to health.

While the Director of Ohio EPA must approve the plans for a district's improvement, the Board of Directors of a sanitary district is chiefly responsible for the construction and maintenance of improvements to the sanitation and water supply.

1.5.4 Chapter 6117: Sewer Districts / County Sewers

Sewer districts may be established by Boards of County Commissioners for the purpose of preserving and promoting the public health and welfare. Upon establishment of a sewer district, the Board must have the county sanitary engineer prepare a plan of sewerage and sewage disposal for the district. After the plan's approval, a series of hearings are granted in which objections from all interested parties are heard. The improvement resolution will be passed if no objections or appeals are raised.

1.5.5 Chapter 6119: Regional Water And Sewer Districts

Under the Revised Code, any area situated in an unincorporated part of one or more contiguous counties or in one or more municipal corporations, or both, may be organized as a regional water and sewer district. The purpose of such a district may be for either or both of the following reasons:

(1) to supply water to users within and without the district;

(2) to provide for the collection, treatment, and disposal of wastewater within and without the district.

1.6 Drinking Water And Water Supply Provisions

1.6.1 Chapter 6103: County Water Supply Systems

The Board of County Commissioners for a particular area, with the assistance of the county sanitary engineer, is the principal body for ensuring that the public water supply or waterworks system in a county is properly acquired, constructed, maintained, and operated. Municipal ownership of a public utility, such as a waterworks system, is generally free from the restriction imposed by the Ohio Revised Code. However, the Board has the authority to levy assessments and to maintain and operate any water supply improvements that it provides within a municipal corporation.

The Director of Ohio EPA may order improvements when unsafe water supply conditions exist. Upon a written complaint by the Board of Health or a legislative authority, the Director is required to investigate and notify the Board of his findings. It is then the Board's responsibility to comply with any orders that the Director proposes.

1.6.2 Chapter 6109: Safe Drinking Water

The Director of Ohio EPA regulates the public water systems and ensures that the systems are in compliance with the federal Safe Drinking Water Act. Any plans for the construction or installation of a public water system must meet the approval of the Director.

1.7 Pollution Control Financing And Related Provisions

The Ohio Air Quality Development Authority, created in Chapter 3706 of the Revised Code, oversees all phases in the construction, maintenance, and operation of air quality projects and facilities in the State. Under Chapter 6121 of the Revised Code, the Ohio Water Development Authority has similar statutory powers. It is responsible for not only water development projects but also projects involving solid waste and energy resource development. Both authorities have the power to make loans and grants to governmental agencies and/or private entities for the acquisition or construction of projects in their respective areas as well as to issue bonds and notes for such projects.

1.8 Statutes Concerning The Ohio Department Of Natural Resources

1.8.1 Chapter 1502: Recycling And Litter Prevention

Following the repeal of Revised Code Sections 1502.01 to 1502.05 and 1502.07 (effective June 30, 1993), there was created, within the Department of Natural Resources, a Division of Recycling and Litter Prevention that has the principal responsibility for establishing and implementing a comprehensive statewide recycling and litter prevention program.

1.8.2 Chapter 1505: Division Of Geological Survey

The Division of Geological Survey is responsible for the collection, study, interpretation, and dissemination of all information pertaining to the geomorphology, stratigraphy, paleontology, mineralogy, and geologic structure of the State of Ohio.

1.8.3 Chapter 1509: Oil And Gas

The Division of Oil and Gas issues, denies, and modifies permits, and issues notices and enforcement orders related to the drilling, plugging, and abandonment of oil and gas wells in the State.

1.8.4 Chapter 1531: Division Of Wildlife

The Division of Wildlife has responsibility for the general care and supervision of fish and wildlife in Ohio, including the protection, preservation, propagation, and management of wild animals and their sanctuaries and refuges.

1.8.5 Chapter 1541: Division Of Parks And Recreation

The Division of Parks and Recreation determines the policies and programs for the State's parks system. It has extensive powers in the control and management of all the lands and waters dedicated and set apart for State park purposes since it is responsible for their protection, maintenance, and repair.

1.9 Underground Storage Tank Regulation: Chapter 3737

The State Fire Marshal, with the assistance of the Petroleum Underground Storage Tank Advisory Committee, has the principal responsibility for the implementation of the underground storage tank ("UST") program and corrective action program for releases from petroleum USTs as established by the federal Resource Conservation and Recovery Act. In order to implement the program, the Fire Marshal has a wide range of powers for achieving his objectives – *e.g.*, he may require annual registration of USTs and issue citations and orders to enforce those rules.

In addition, the Revised Code has provided for the establishment of a Petroleum Underground Storage Tank Financial Assurance Fund for the purpose of reimbursing owners and operators of petroleum USTs for the costs of corrective actions and compensation paid to third parties for damages caused by the release of petroleum from the tanks. The Petroleum Underground Storage Tank Release Compensation Board is charged with administering the moneys in the Fund.

1.10 Power Siting Law: Chapter 4906

The Revised Code creates the Ohio Power Siting Board and sets out the State's power siting law for the regulation of major utility facility siting. A central feature of the law is the requirement for a certificate of environmental compatibility and public need that calls for an assessment of the environmental impact of major utility facilities such as electric power plants, electric transmission lines, and natural gas transmission lines.

1.11 Confined Animal Feeding Facilities: Chapter 903

In 2000, the General Assembly created a new program for the environmental regulation of confined animal feeding facilities by the Department of Agriculture. Facilities that have a design capacity of more than 1,000 "animal units" are regulated. An "animal unit" is defined differently for each type of farm animal. Regulated facilities must obtain both permits to install, authorizing the construction or modification of a facility, and permits to operate. To obtain a permit, the facility must submit, and obtain approval of, plans for the management and disposal of manure and the control of insects and rodents. The plans must confirm to "best management practices" established by rules promulgated by the Director of

Agriculture. The Director is also authorized to administer the National Pollutant Discharge Elimination System permit program for such facilities.

1.12 Enacting New Environmental Legislation

In 1995, the Ohio General Assembly passed legislation imposing new requirements on the enactment of measures dealing with "environmental protection."[1] Set out in Chapter 121 of the Revised Code, the new law defines environmental protection as:[2]

(1) protection of human health or safety, biological resources, or natural resources by preventing, reducing, or remediating the pollution or degradation of air, land, or water resources or by preventing or limiting the exposure of humans, animals, or plants to pollution;

(2) appropriation or regulation of privately owned property to preserve air, land, or water resources in a natural state or to wholly or partially restore them to a natural state;

(3) regulation of the collection, management, treatment, reduction, storage, or disposal of solid, hazardous, radioactive, or other wastes; and

(4) plans or programs to promote or regulate the conservation, recycling, or reuse of energy, materials, or wastes.

When proposed legislation dealing with environmental protection is referred to a committee of the General Assembly (other than a committee on rules or reference), the sponsor of the legislation is required to submit to the committee members a written statement that identifies either the documentation that is the basis of the legislation or the federal requirement(s) with which the legislation is intended to comply. If the legislation is not based on documentation or has not been introduced in order to comply with federal requirements, the sponsor's statement must include that information.[3]

At the time of the first committee hearing on the proposed legislation, a statewide organization that represents businesses in the State and that elects a board of

---

1 HB 106, 121st General Assembly (Eff. Mar. 5, 1996).

2 ORC § 121.39(A).

3 ORC § 121.39(B).

directors may submit to the committee a written estimate of the costs to the regulated community of complying with the legislation, if enacted.[4] In addition, at any hearing on the legislation before the committee, a representative of any state agency, environmental advocacy group, consumer advocacy group, or any private citizen may present documentation containing an estimate of the monetary and other costs to public health and safety and the environment, and to consumers and residential utility customers, and the effects on property values, if the legislation is not enacted.[5]

Until the sponsor presents the written statement to the committee, the legislation shall not be reported by that committee. This requirement does not apply, however, if the component of the legislation dealing with environmental protection is removed from the legislation or if two-thirds of the committee members vote to report the legislation.[6]

The new requirements do not apply if the proposed statute is procedural or budgetary in nature or if it governs the organization or operation of a State agency and will not affect the substantive rights or obligations of any person other than a State agency, its employees, or its contractors.[7] In addition, the insufficiency, incompleteness, or inadequacy of a statement, information, or documentation submitted to the committee in connection with a proposed statute shall not be grounds for invalidating the statute.[8]

2.0 OHIO ENVIRONMENTAL AGENCIES

2.1 Ohio Environmental Protection Agency

The Ohio Environmental Protection Agency ("Ohio EPA") is headed by the Director of Environmental Protection.[9] Under the Director's supervision, the Agency administers all the laws pertaining to:

(1) chemical emergency planning, community right to know, and toxic chemical release reporting;

---

[4] *Id.*

[5] *Id.*

[6] ORC § 121.39(C).

[7] ORC § 121.39(E).

[8] ORC § 121.39(F).

[9] *See* http://www.epa.state.oh.us.

(2) prevention, control, and abatement of air and water pollution;

(3) public water supply;

(4) comprehensive water resource management planning; and

(5) disposal and treatment of solid waste, hazardous waste, sewage, industrial waste, and other wastes.

Ohio EPA is responsible for issuing, denying, modifying, revoking, or renewing permits, licenses, and variances designed to prevent and control pollution of the environment. In carrying out these actions, the Director is required to follow the administrative procedures outlined in Chapter 119 of the Revised Code. In some cases – *e.g.*, revocation or denial of a permit – the Director must issue the action as proposed, rather than as final, to allow interested parties the opportunity to request an adjudication hearing or, in the case of rulemaking, a public hearing.

Another important function of the Ohio EPA Director is to investigate verified complaints alleging the violation of environmental laws. Depending upon the Agency's findings, the Director may enter an order prohibiting the violation, commence legal proceedings, or dismiss the complaint.

2.2 Hazardous Waste Facility Board

The Hazardous Waste Facility Board has primary responsibility for the approval or disapproval of hazardous waste facility permit applications and certain permit modifications. Members include the Ohio EPA Director, who serves as chair, the Director of the Ohio Department of Natural Resources, and the chair of the Ohio Water Development Authority – or their respective designees – a chemical engineer, and a geologist. The latter two members, who must be employed by a State university, are appointed by the Governor, subject to Senate approval, for terms of two years.[10]

[10] ORC § 3734.05(D)(1).

2.3 Environmental Review Appeals Commission

The role of the Environmental Review Appeals Commission ("ERAC"), formerly the Environmental Board of Review, is to oversee the actions of the Director of Ohio EPA. The three-member Commission is appointed by the Governor, with the advice and consent of the Senate, on the basis of the members' extensive experience in pollution control and abatement technology, ecology, public health, environmental law, economics of natural resource development, or related fields.

The ERAC has exclusive original jurisdiction to vacate or modify a final action of the Ohio EPA Director or a local Board of Health. If an adjudication hearing was not conducted by Ohio EPA, the Commission is authorized to conduct *de novo* hearings. Section 3745.04 of the Revised Code sets forth the procedural requirements for filing an appeal. Parties adversely affected by an ERAC order may appeal to the Franklin County Court of Appeals or to the court of appeals of the district where the alleged violation of a law or regulation occurred.

2.4 Power Siting Board

The Ohio Power Siting Board ("Board") is composed of the Chairman of the Public Utilities Commission, the Directors of Agriculture, Development, Environmental Protection, Health, and Natural Resources, and a representative of the public who is an engineer appointed by the Governor. The Board also includes four legislative members who fully participate in all deliberations but who may not vote. The Board conducts hearings on applications for certificates for the construction of all proposed major utility facilities in Ohio.

2.5 Department Of Natural Resources

The Department of Natural Resources is the primary authority for the regulation and management of Ohio's natural resources, including programs for recycling and litter prevention, forestry, geological survey, shore erosion, oil and gas, soil and water conservation, surface mining, natural areas and preserves, endangered species, recreational trails, water, wildlife, parks and recreation, parkways, watercraft and waterways, and energy and civilian conservation.[11]

2.6 State Fire Marshal

The State Fire Marshal ("SFM") has responsibility for administering and enforcing both the underground storage tank ("UST") program and the corrective action program for petroleum UST releases.[12] The SFM is given authority to promulgate rules, to designate areas as being sensitive for the protection of human health and the environment, and to certify installers of UST systems.

2.7 State Emergency Response Commission

Created in 1987 pursuant to the requirements of the federal Emergency Planning and Community Right-to-Know Act of 1986 ("EPCRA"), the State Emergency Response Commission ("SERC") is responsible for promulgating rules that conform to the scope, content, and coverage of EPCRA. It is comprised of nine ex officio members, two nonvoting members of the General Assembly, and ten members appointed by the Governor.

2.8 Attorney General

The Attorney General of Ohio is the chief law officer for the State and all its departments, and thus is responsible for prosecuting, on behalf of Ohio EPA, both civil and criminal actions for violations of Ohio's environmental laws.[13] In addition, the Attorney General has responsibility for conducting background investigations pursuant to Ohio's disclosure statement statute, which requires any person seeking a permit or license for an off-site waste facility to file a statement with Ohio EPA and the Attorney General that discloses, among other things, the applicant's experience and credentials, and a history of civil and criminal prosecutions.

---

[11] *See* http://www.dnr.state.oh.us.

[12] *See* http://www.com.state.oh.us/ODOC/sfm.

[13] See http://www.ag.state.oh.us.

2.9 Department Of Agriculture

In 2000, the Department of Agriculture[14] was authorized to regulate confined animal feeding facilities exceeding a design capacity of one thousand "animal units". Facilities must obtain permits to install and permits to operate from the department requiring compliance with "best management practices" for the disposal of manure and the control of insects and rodents. Facilities also may not discharge pollutants to waters of the State except as authorized by a permit issued by the department.

[14] *See* http://www.ohioagriculture.gov.

Chapter II

OHIO ADMINISTRATIVE LAW

1.0 INTRODUCTION

The Ohio General Assembly has the authority to create administrative agencies to carry out legislatively specified purposes. An Ohio administrative agency is permitted to exercise only such jurisdiction and powers as are conferred upon it by the statute that created it or vested it with such power. The powers of an Ohio administrative agency are thus limited to those specifically granted; the agency cannot expand those powers.

Administrative agency powers are implemented by two primary mechanisms: rulemaking and adjudication. The distinctions between these functions and acts of a ministerial nature are important when considering the procedures that an agency must follow and when determining the availability and scope of judicial review of agency actions.

This chapter discusses the Ohio Administrative Procedure Act ("Act"), Chapter 119 of the Ohio Revised Code, which governs Ohio administrative procedures in general, as well as the statutory procedures specifically applicable to Ohio EPA.

2.0 RULEMAKING

2.1 Definition

Rulemaking can be described generally as an administrative action that resembles legislation. The rulemaking power of an agency is the power to prescribe, within the limits of the law governing the agency, standards having a general and uniform application. A rule, in turn, is defined in the Act as:[1]

> any rule, regulation, or standard, having a general and uniform operation, adopted, promulgated, and enforced by any agency under the authority of the laws governing such agency, ... [but it] does not include any internal management rule of an agency unless the ... rule affects private rights and does not include any guideline adopted pursuant to section 3301 of the Revised Code.

As long as administrative rules are consistent with the statutes enabling their adoption, they constitute judicially enforceable law.[2] A properly adopted administrative rule is as binding on the agency that created it as it is on anyone else.[3]

An Ohio administrative agency must follow specific rulemaking procedures set out in the Act, as discussed below. If the agency attempts to impose a standard of uniform operation without following the procedural requirements of the Act and the agency's specific statute, such a standard will be struck down by the courts as illegal rulemaking. For instance, sludge management guidelines used by Ohio EPA were determined to be rules improperly adopted by the agency. The "rules," which took the form of agency guidelines or policy, were struck down on judicial review.[4]

2.2 Adoption, Amendment, Or Rescission Of Rules

Revised Code Sections 119.03 and 119.04 establish the procedures that agencies must follow in adopting, amending, and rescinding rules. If an agency fails to comply with these procedures, the rule is susceptible to invalidation upon proper judicial review.

---

[1] ORC § 119.01(C).

[2] *See, e.g.*, Kroger Grocery & Baking Co. v. Glander, 149 Ohio St. 120, 77 N.E.2d 921 (1948), *overruled on other grounds,* Gen'l Mills v. Limbach, 35 Ohio St.3d 256, 520 N.E.2d 218 (1988).

[3] *See, e.g.*, Cleveland Electric Illuminating Co. v. Williams, 55 Ohio App.2d 272, 380 N.E.2d 1342 (Franklin Cty. 1977), *cert. denied,* 439 U.S. 865, 99 S.Ct. 189, 58 L.Ed.2d 175 (1978).

[4] Jackson Cty. Env. Comm. v. Schregardus, 95 Ohio App.3d 527 (1994).

2.2.1 Consultations And Considerations

If the rule to be adopted or amended deals with environmental protection, the agency proposing the rule or amendment must first consult with organizations that represent political subdivisions, environmental interests, business interests, and other persons affected by the proposed rule or amendment.[5] "Environmental protection," as used here, is defined as:[6]

> (1) protection of human health or safety, biological resources, or natural resources by preventing, reducing, or remediating the pollution or degradation of air, land, or water resources or by preventing or limiting the exposure of humans, animals, or plants to pollution;
>
> (2) appropriation or regulation of privately-owned property to preserve air, land, or water resources in a natural state or to wholly or partially restore them to a natural state;
>
> (3) regulation of the collection, management, treatment, reduction, storage, or disposal of solid, hazardous, radioactive, or other wastes; and
>
> (4) plans or programs to promote or regulate the conservation, recycling, or reuse of energy, materials, or wastes.

In addition to consulting other affected organizations and entities, the agency proposing the rule or amendment must consider documentation relevant to the need for, the environmental benefits or consequences of, and the technical feasibility of the proposed rule or amendment.[7] The agency must identify whether the proposed rule is being adopted or amended in order to obtain or maintain approval to administer and enforce a federal environmental law or to participate in a federal environmental program. The agency also must identify whether the proposed rule or amendment is more stringent than its federal counterpart and, if so, the reasons therefor.[8]

---

[5] ORC § 121.39(D)(1).

[6] ORC § 121.39(A).

[7] ORC § 121.39(D)(2).

[8] ORC § 121.39(D)(3).

2.2.2 Notice Procedures

At least thirty days prior to the date set for a hearing under Section 119.03 of the Revised Code, the rulemaking agency must give reasonable notice to the public. This notice must include:[9]

(1) a statement of the agency's intention to consider adopting, amending, or rescinding a rule;

(2) a synopsis of the proposed rule, amendment, or rule to be rescinded or a general statement of the subject matter to which the proposal relates;

(3) a statement of the reason or purpose for adopting, amending, or rescinding the rule; and

(4) the date, time, and place of a hearing on the proposed action; the hearing must not be earlier than thirty-one nor later than forty days after the proposed rule, amendment, or rescission is filed.

In 1999, the Ohio General Assembly adopted amendments to the Ohio Administrative Procedure Act that were designed to create a single repository for the collection of information on proposed rules.[10] Starting in April 2002, all administrative agencies are required to provide notice of proposed rules via electronic media accessible on the Internet.[11] The Legislative Service Commission ("LSC") must publish the text of the public notice, draft rule, and fiscal analysis in the *Register of Ohio*, an electronic publication that functions as a gazette.[12] In addition, the LSC is required to maintain printed versions of the public notice, proposed rule, and fiscal analysis. The administrative agency must file the public notice, proposed rule, and fiscal analysis at least sixty-five days before issuing the order adopting the rule.[13] The public notice, proposed rule, and fiscal analysis must be

---

[9] ORC § 119.03(A).

[10] SB 11, 123rd General Assembly (Eff. Sept. 15, 1999 and July 1, 2000).

[11] ORC § 103.051 - .054.

[12] *See* http://www.registerofohio.state.oh.us.

[13] *See* ORC § 119.03(A), (B).

available to the public for inspection at least thirty days prior to the public hearing on the proposed rule.[14]

2.2.3 Preparation Of A Rule Summary And Fiscal Analysis

The rulemaking agency must prepare a complete and accurate summary and fiscal analysis of each proposed rule that it files. That summary includes:[15]

(1) the name, address, and telephone number of the rulemaking agency, as well as that of the person within the agency designated as responsible for the coordination of information regarding the proposed rule;

(2) the Ohio Administrative Code rule number of the proposed rule;

(3) a brief summary of, and the legal basis for, the proposed rule, including citations to the statute prescribing the rulemaking procedure, the statute authorizing the agency to adopt the proposed rule, and the statute the agency intends to amplify or implement by adopting the proposed rule;

(4) an estimate of the amount by which the proposed rule would increase or decrease revenues or expenditures during the current biennium;

(5) a citation to the appropriation that authorizes each expenditure that would be necessitated by the proposed rule;

(6) a summary of the estimated cost of compliance with the rule to all directly affected persons;

(7) the reasons the rule is being proposed;

(8) if the rule has a fiscal effect on school districts, counties, townships, or municipal corporations, an estimate of the cost of compliance and an explanation of the ability of the agency and local government's ability to pay the costs; and

---

[14] ORC § 119.03(A).

[15] ORC § 127.18(B). Similarly, Section 121.24(B) provides that if an agency intends to adopt a rule and reasonably believes that the proposed rule, if adopted, is likely to affect individuals, small businesses, or small organizations, the agency must prepare a fiscal analysis that estimates the dollar amount of the increase or decrease in revenues or expenditures caused by the rule.

(9) any other information necessary to make the proposed rule or the fiscal effect of the proposed rule more fully understandable.

This rule summary and analysis must accompany the proposed rule when it is filed with the General Assembly's Joint Committee on Agency Rule Review ("JCARR").[16] JCARR will not accept any proposed rule for filing unless a rule summary and fiscal analysis are included.[17]

If the proposed rule or amendment pertains to "environmental protection," as defined in Revised Code Section 121.39(A), the agency also must identify whether the rule is being adopted or amended to enable the State to obtain or maintain approval to administer and enforce a federal environmental law.[18] When the proposed rule or amendment is more stringent than a federal rule it is designed to adopt, is an amendment to an existing rule that makes the rule more stringent, or is otherwise related to environmental protection, the agency must submit to JCARR information demonstrating the need for, environmental benefits or consequences of, and technological feasibility of the proposed rule or amendment.[19] These requirements do not apply in the case of an emergency rule adopted pursuant to Revised Code Section 119.03(F), or a proposed rule or amendment that is procedural or budgetary in nature that governs the organization or operation of a State agency or that otherwise will not affect the substantive rights or obligations of any person other than a State agency or its employees or contractors.[20]

2.2.4 Filing A Proposed Rule

The rulemaking agency must file the full text of the proposed rule, amendment, or rule to be rescinded, together with the public notice, the rule summary and fiscal analysis, and, if the rule pertains to environmental protection, any required information related to the need for, environmental benefits or consequences of, or technological

[16] *See* http://www.jcarr.state.oh.us.

[17] ORC § 127.18(C).

[18] ORC § 121.39(D)(3).

[19] ORC § 121.39(D)(4).

[20] ORC § 121.39(D)(4), (E).

feasibility of the proposed rule or amendment with the Secretary of State, the Director of LSC, and JCARR.[21]

The proposed rule, amendment, or rescission and the public notice must be filed at least sixty-five days before the agency issues an order adopting the proposal. Substantive revisions in the text of the proposal shall be filed promptly with the Secretary of State, the Director of LSC, and JCARR.[22]

Copies of the proposed rule are to be available at the agency's offices for at least thirty days prior to the hearing and shall be provided free of charge to any person affected by the proposal.[23] In addition, the Director of LSC must electronically publish the public notice, proposed rule, and fiscal analysis in the *Register of Ohio*.[24]

2.2.5 Comment And Hearing

The agency must conduct a public hearing on the proposed action at the date, time, and place specified in the public notice. Affected persons and their representatives may appear at the hearing and present their positions orally or in writing, offer and examine witnesses, and present evidence to show that the proposed rule, amendment, or rescission, if adopted, will be unreasonable or unlawful.[25]

Although the agency determines the admissibility of evidence at the hearing, the affected person may object and proffer evidence ruled inadmissible. Such evidence must be made a part of the hearing record. It is the responsibility of the agency to make a stenographic record of the proceedings, including all testimony and rulings.[26]

At these hearings, the agency often is represented by several staff members who are most familiar with the subject area in question and who are given the opportunity to question the witness. The Ohio Supreme Court has stated in *dictum* that the "offer and

---

[21] ORC §§ 119.03(B), (H), 121.39(D)(4).

[22] ORC § 119.03(B), (H).

[23] ORC § 119.03(B).

[24] ORC § 103.051. *See* http://www.registerofohio.state.oh.us.

[25] ORC § 119.03(C).

[26] Although Chapter 119 uses the term "evidence" in the context of rulemaking, it is not the same as evidence in a trial-type hearing. "Testimony" and "comments" are used interchangeably to describe real statements made at a rulemaking hearing. Such statements typically are not made under oath and are not subject to cross-examination, although the presiding agency representative may ask informal questions to clarify the record.

examine" language of Revised Code Section 119.03(C) grants no right to cross-examine witnesses.[27]

2.2.6 Legislative Review Of Rulemaking

JCARR may recommend the adoption of a concurrent resolution invalidating part or all of any proposed rule, amendment, or rescission if it finds that:[28]

(1) the agency has exceeded the scope of its statutory authority in proposing the action;

(2) the proposal conflicts with another rule, amendment, or rescission adopted by the same or a different rulemaking agency;

(3) the proposal conflicts with the legislative intent of the applicable statute; or

(4) the agency failed to prepare a complete and accurate summary and fiscal analysis of the proposal.

While JCARR has the authority to recommend a concurrent resolution from the General Assembly invalidating a proposed rule, amendment, or rescission, the committee itself has little independent authority. JCARR is authorized to suspend a rule that was adopted by an administrative agency only if the final rule differs from the proposed rule filed with JCARR; the final rule exceeds the agency's authority, conflicts with another rule, or is inconsistent with the legislative intent; or the agency has not filed a summary and fiscal analysis of the rule. The suspension is effective only until the time for legislative review expires unless the General Assembly adopts a concurrent resolution invalidating the rule.[29]

The General Assembly may then adopt a concurrent resolution invalidating all or part of any proposed rule, amendment, or rescission.[30] Chapter 119 of the Revised Code makes it clear that the Legislature's failure to invalidate a proposed rule, amendment, or rescission is not to be interpreted as a ratification of either the lawfulness or reasonableness of the proposal, or the validity of the procedure by which the proposal was adopted.

---

[27] Sterling Drug, Inc. v. Wickham, 63 Ohio St.2d 16, 406 N.E.2d 1363 (1980).

[28] ORC § 119.03(I).

[29] ORC § 119.031.

If the General Assembly adopts such a resolution, the agency may not, during the same legislative session, adopt any version of the invalidated rule unless the General Assembly adopts a concurrent resolution allowing the agency to conduct or continue rulemaking proceedings.[31]

2.2.7 Promulgation Of Final Rule

If the General Assembly does not adopt a resolution to invalidate a proposed rule within the statutorily allowed time, the agency may issue an order adopting the rule, but no sooner than sixty days after the initial filing of the proposal. At that time, the agency must specify an effective date, which must be at least ten days after the final form of the proposed rule is filed.[32] Revised Code Section 119.04 prescribes the requirements for filing the final rule with the Secretary of State.

Before the rule, amendment, or rescission becomes effective, the agency is statutorily required to make a reasonable effort to inform those persons affected and to have available for distribution the full text of the rule as adopted or amended.[33]

The Chairman of JCARR must compare the final rule as filed with the original proposal. If the final version contains a substantive revision from the proposed rule, the Chairman must notify the agency, the Secretary of State, and the Director of LSC. JCARR again must review the rule and may suspend all or any part of the rule during this supplemental review. Within the same time frame as for a proposed rule, calculated from the date of filing in final form, the General Assembly may adopt a concurrent resolution invalidating the rule or any part of it. The action or inaction of the Legislature has the same effect as if taken with respect to a proposed rule.[34]

---

[30] ORC § 119.03(I).

[31] ORC § 119.03(I)(1)(d). To date, JCARR has invalidated a relatively small number of agency rules. However, the JCARR review process has resulted in many proposed rules being withdrawn or revised to avoid confrontation over controversial or infirm features.

[32] ORC § 119.03(D).

[33] *Id.*

[34] ORC § 119.031.

2.2.8 Ongoing Administrative And Legislative Rule Review

Under legislation enacted in 1996,[35] each agency that adopts or amends a rule that is subject to JCARR review must assign to the rule a review date that is no later than five years after the rule's effective date.[36] If no review date is assigned, or if the date assigned exceeds the five-year limit, the review date is five years after the effective date.[37] This requirement does not apply to the Department of Taxation, State colleges or universities, community or technical colleges, emergency rules, internal management rules, rules of the Ohio Student Aid Commission that comply with a federal law or rule, rules that must be adopted verbatim by an agency pursuant to a federal law or rule (to become effective within sixty days of adoption, in order to continue the operation of a federally reimbursed program), and certain rules relating to workers' compensation, banks, savings and loan associations, and credit unions.[38]

For rules already in effect at the time this review requirement became effective, the legislation required agencies to assign review dates to provide for review of all existing rules within five years following the enactment of the requirement.[39]

This ongoing review process is intended to determine whether the rule should be continued without amendment, amended, or rescinded. The review should take into consideration the purpose, scope, and intent of the statute under which the rule was adopted; whether the rule needs amendment or recision to give more flexibility at the local level or to eliminate unnecessary paperwork; and whether the rule duplicates, overlaps, or conflicts with other rules. In performing the review, the agency is required to consider the continued need for the rule, any complaints or comments received concerning the rule, and any relevant changes in the subject matter affected by the rule.[40]

At least ninety days before the designated rule review date, the agency that adopted the rule must notify JCARR that it has reviewed the rule. The notice must indicate

---

[35] HB 473, 121st General Assembly (Eff. Sept. 26, 1996).

[36] ORC §§ 111.15(B), 119.04(A)(1), 4141.14(B)(1).

[37] ORC § 119.04(A)(1).

[38] ORC §§ 111.15(D), 119.03(H).

[39] ORC § 119.032(B).

[40] ORC § 119.032(C) - (D).

the agency's determination concerning the need for the rule to be amended or rescinded, provide an accurate rule summary and fiscal analysis, and designate a new review date no later than five years following the most recent review date. JCARR must give public notice of the agency's determination regarding the rule for four consecutive weeks following receipt of the agency's notice.[41]

Following the expiration of the four-week public notice period, but during JCARR's ninety-day review period, JCARR may, by a two-thirds vote of members present, recommend the adoption of a concurrent resolution invalidating the rule if JCARR determines that the agency improperly applied the criteria in reviewing the rule and recommending its continuance without amendment or recision, or that the agency failed to file proper notice with JCARR regarding the rule. If JCARR does not take such action, the rule continues in effect, without amendment, and must be reviewed by JCARR by the date designated in the agency notice.[42]

If the agency determines that the rule needs to be amended or rescinded, the agency must file the amended or rescinded rule with JCARR at least ninety days before the rule's review date, in accordance with the applicable provisions of Sections 111.15, 119.03, or 4141.14 of the Revised Code.[43]

If the agency fails to conduct the required review or fails to provide notice to JCARR by the rule review date, JCARR may recommend, by a majority vote of members present, the adoption of a concurrent resolution invalidating the rule. JCARR may not adopt such a recommendation, however, until it has given the agency an opportunity to appear before it and show cause why JCARR should not recommend the adoption of such a resolution.[44]

2.2.9 Emergency Rulemaking

If the Governor, upon the request of an agency, determines that an emergency requires the immediate adoption, amendment, or rescission of a rule, the Governor shall issue

---

[41] ORC § 119.032(E).

[42] ORC § 119.032(F).

[43] ORC § 119.032(E)(5).

[44] ORC § 119.032(F).

a written order, suspending the rulemaking procedure. The agency may then immediately adopt an emergency rule, amendment, or rescission. Such a rule becomes effective on the date that copies of the final action are filed with the Secretary of State, the Director of LSC, and JCARR. An emergency rule, amendment, or rescission is valid for only ninety days. Before the ninety days expire, the agency may adopt the emergency rule, amendment, or rescission as a nonemergency action by complying with the procedure for adopting nonemergency rules. However, the agency may not use the emergency rulemaking procedure to reenact an emergency rule for an additional ninety-day period.[45]

3.0 ADJUDICATION

3.1 Definition

The Ohio Administrative Procedure Act defines an adjudication as:[46]

> the determination by the highest or ultimate authority of an agency of the rights, duties, privileges, benefits, or legal relationships of a specified person, but does not include the issuance of a license in response to an application with respect to which no question is raised, nor other acts of a ministerial nature.

Whether a particular agency action is classified as an adjudication is a key determination for purposes of procedural safeguards and judicial review. The Ohio Supreme Court has differentiated between rulemaking and adjudication, determining that Article IV of the Ohio Constitution gives the court of common pleas jurisdiction to review the quasi-judicial, but not the quasi-legislative, actions of an agency.[47] An adjudication is a quasi-judicial action, while rulemaking is quasi-legislative. Thus, absent a statutory provision to the contrary, a determination of an agency in an adjudication may be appealed to a court.

---

[45] ORC § 119.03(F).

[46] ORC § 119.01(D).

[47] *See, e.g.*, Rankin-Thoman, Inc. v. Caldwell, 42 Ohio St.2d 436, 329 N.E.2d 686 (1975); Burger Brewing Co. v. Liquor Control Comm'n, 34 Ohio St.2d 93, 296 N.E.2d 261 (1973); Fortner v. Thomas, 22 Ohio St.2d 13, 257 N.E.2d 371 (1970); Zangerle v. Evatt, 139 Ohio St. 563, 41 N.E.2d 369 (1942). These cases apply to rulemaking appeals to the court of common pleas. Ohio EPA rules, however, can be appealed to the Environmental Review Appeals Commission ("ERAC"), and then to the Franklin County Court of Appeals. See Section 4.0 of this chapter; for further discussion, see Chapter XII of this Handbook.

3.2 Requirement For Adjudication

Generally, an agency adjudication order is not valid unless an opportunity for hearing is afforded. There are, however, three types of adjudication orders that are effective without a hearing:[48]

(1) orders revoking a license pursuant to the judgment of a court;

(2) orders suspending a license pursuant to a statute specifically permitting the suspension without a hearing; and

(3) orders pursuant to a rule of the agency or a statute specifically allowing an appeal to a higher authority and giving the appellant a right to a hearing on such appeal.

If a statute does permit the suspension of a license without a prior hearing, the agency taking such action must afford the affected person a hearing upon request.[49]

3.3 Adjudication Hearing

3.3.1 Notice

In the absence of an applicable exception under Revised Code Section 119.06(C), if a hearing is required prior to the issuance of an order, the agency must notify the affected parties of the right to a hearing. This notice shall be given by registered mail and must inform the affected parties of the charges or other reasons for the proposed action, the law or rule directly involved, and the entitlement to a hearing upon a request for such hearing within thirty days of the mailing of the notice. Further, the notice must inform the parties of the right to appear in person, to be represented by an attorney or other person permitted to practice in front of the agency, or to present their position in writing. At the hearing, parties may present evidence and examine witnesses. Failure to give proper notice for any hearing invalidates an order entered pursuant to such hearing.[50]

---

[48] ORC § 119.06. Because the ERAC is a higher authority to which Ohio EPA actions may be appealed, Ohio EPA has the option, which it generally uses, of issuing permits and other adjudicatory determinations without a prior hearing.

[49] ORC § 119.06.

[50] ORC § 119.07.

3.3.2 Hearing Procedures

Although the agency determines the admissibility of evidence in an adjudication hearing, a party may object to such rulings at the time they are made. If the agency refuses to admit the evidence, the party nevertheless may proffer the evidence and the proffer becomes a part of the record. The agency or party may call any person to testify under oath as upon cross-examination and issue subpoenas to compel attendance at hearing.[51]

In required adjudications, the agency may appoint a referee or examiner to conduct the hearing. This examiner must submit a written report to the agency detailing the findings of fact and conclusions of law, as well as a recommendation of the action to be taken by the agency. The affected party must be provided a copy of this report within five days of the date it is filed and has ten days from the date of receipt within which to file written objections. The agency must consider these objections before ruling on the recommendation. The agency may approve, modify, or disapprove the finding of the examiner, but it must provide reasons for modification or disapproval. Upon entering an order, the agency must provide the party with a certified copy of the decision.[52]

3.4 Judicial Review Of Administrative Action

Appeals of the orders of most agencies, not including Ohio EPA, are governed by Section 119.12 of the Revised Code. "Any party adversely affected by any order of an agency issued pursuant to an adjudication denying an applicant admission to an examination, or denying the issuance or renewal of a license or registration of a licensee, or revoking or suspending a license, or allowing the payment of a forfeiture …" may appeal the order to the common pleas court in the county in which the licensee's place of business or residence is located.[53] Any party adversely affected by any order of an agency issued pursuant to any other adjudication may appeal to the Franklin County Court of Common Pleas.[54]

---

[51] ORC § 119.09.

[52] *Id.*

[53] ORC § 119.12. Certain agencies – *e.g.*, Ohio EPA and the Public Utilities Commission of Ohio – have special appeal procedures in lieu of those generally specified in Section 119.12. For a discussion of Ohio EPA administrative procedures, see Section 4.0 of this chapter.

[54] ORC § 119.12.

Generally, within fifteen days of the mailing of the notice of the agency's order, the party seeking review must file a notice of appeal with the agency and the court, setting forth the order appealed from and the grounds for appeal. This filing does not serve to suspend the agency's order. The court, however, may grant such a suspension if it determines that execution of the order would result in unusual hardship to the appellant.[55]

The agency is accorded thirty days after the receipt of a notice of appeal to prepare and certify the complete record of the proceedings in the case. Unless otherwise provided by law, the court is confined to this record. However, upon request, the court may admit additional information when satisfied that such evidence is newly discovered and could not have been ascertained prior to the hearing before the agency. Counsel may be heard on oral argument, briefs may be submitted, and evidence may be introduced if the court has granted a request for the presentation of additional evidence. If the court finds that the agency's order is supported by reliable, probative, and substantial evidence, it must affirm the order. Otherwise, the court may reverse, vacate, or modify the order, or make such other ruling as is supported by reliable, probative, and substantial evidence.[56]

Appeals of common pleas court decisions proceed in the same fashion as appeals of civil actions.[57]

4.0 ADMINISTRATIVE PROCEDURES OF OHIO EPA

While Chapter 119 of the Revised Code provides general administrative procedures for State agencies, Ohio EPA is subject to special statutory procedural requirements that supplement and supersede certain provisions in Chapter 119.

4.1 Ohio EPA Rulemaking

Ohio EPA conducts its rulemaking according to Revised Code Section 119.03, as described above. Proposed rules are noticed in the *Ohio EPA Weekly Review*, the *Register of Ohio*, newspapers of large circulation, and mailings to interested parties. The Director adopts rules as a final action, appealable to the Environmental Review Appeals Commission

---

[55] *Id.*

[56] *Id.*

[57] *Id.*

("ERAC") (formerly the Environmental Board of Review ("EBR")).[58] An entity is permitted to participate in the rulemaking process, but it must appear, submit evidence, or otherwise participate in the proceeding in order to attain the necessary standing to challenge the resulting administrative rules at ERAC.[59] Under a ruling by the Franklin County Court of Appeals, Ohio EPA is not required to provide a new comment period if the final adopted rules differ substantially from the proposed rules.[60]

4.2 Actions By The Director

The Director of Ohio EPA issues permits or orders as proposed, draft, or final actions.[61] Rule 3745-47-05 of the Administrative Code provides for the issuance of draft or proposed actions and, in Division (A), instructs the Director to issue Agency actions as proposed actions. A proposed action, by definition, gives an indication of the Director's proposal to act in a certain manner.[62] The proposed action may bear a date upon which it will become effective as a final action. There is a thirty-day period from the date of issuance of the proposal in which any aggrieved or adversely affected party may request an adjudication hearing on the proposal. In the absence of a hearing request, the Director issues the proposed action as final on the date specified.[63] The Ohio Supreme Court has held that a permit or license denial must be issued first as a proposed action so as to allow an adjudication hearing as required by Chapter 119 of the Revised Code; however, the court stated that there is no requirement that a proposed action be issued when a permit or license is granted.[64]

Unlike a proposed action, a draft action – defined as a written statement that gives the Director's intention on a certain matter – does not entail a right to an adjudication

---

[58] For further discussion, see Chapter XII of this Handbook.

[59] New Boston Coke Corp. v. Tyler, 32 Ohio St.3d 216, 513 N.E.2d 302 (1987).

[60] City of Middletown v. Nichols, 9 Ohio App.3d 135, 458 N.E.2d 886 (Franklin Cty. 1983).

[61] OAC 3745-47-05.

[62] OAC 3745-47-03(M).

[63] OAC 3745-47-05(A) - (B). The effective date must not be prior to the deadline for filing comments, the deadline for requesting public meetings, or the deadline for filing adjudication hearing requests and objections. *Id.* at (A)(1) - (3).

[64] Gen'l Motors Corp. v. McAvoy, 63 Ohio St.2d 232, 407 N.E.2d 527 (1980).

hearing.[65] It does, however, give rise to the right to public comment and eventually to ERAC review.

The Director is permitted to issue a draft action in any instance in which he would be permitted to issue a final action without a hearing.[66] Such instances are described as follows:[67]

> [T]he director may issue a final action without first issuing a proposed action where the statutes pertaining to the agency specifically give a right to appeal to the [EBR] and also give the appellant a right to a hearing on such appeal in accordance with Chapter 119. of the Revised Code, and where no statutory provision or regulation prohibits such action from being effective before persons permitted by statute or rule to participate in an adjudication hearing have been afforded an opportunity for a hearing.

The EBR invalidated this provision, finding that it denies a hearing guaranteed by Section 119.06 of the Revised Code. The Franklin County Court of Appeals reversed the EBR's decision, but the Ohio Supreme Court then reversed the lower court and dismissed the appeal because there were no facts involved in the challenge to the definition of "draft action."[68] Thus, by reversing the decision and dismissing the appeal, the Supreme Court left intact as good law the EBR's original decision invalidating the provision. Nevertheless, the definition of "draft action" in Rule 3745-47-03(E) remains a part of the Administrative Code.

While Rule 3745-47-13(E) states that a party that does not request an adjudication hearing on a proposed action is "deemed to have consented to the proposed action" and to have "waived all rights to a hearing," the Franklin County Court of Appeals has found this provision invalid to the extent that it declares that a person who does not request an adjudication hearing consents to a proposed action becoming a final order.[69] Even a party that does not request a hearing on a proposed action still has the statutory right to

---

[65] OAC 3745-47-03(E).

[66] OAC 3745-47-05(C).

[67] OAC 3745-47-05(E). The rule has not been amended to refer to the ERAC but, instead, still references the EBR.

[68] White Consolidated Industries v. Nichols, 15 Ohio St.3d 7, 471 N.E.2d 1375 (1984).

[69] Campbell v. Maynard, 19 Ohio App.3d 41, 482 N.E.2d 990 (Franklin Cty. 1984).

appeal to the ERAC, with the appeal limited to the record before Ohio EPA at the time the decision was made.

Final Ohio EPA actions issued after an adjudicatory hearing may be appealed to the ERAC. A final action may be issued pursuant to the Section 119.06(C) exception with no opportunity for a prior adjudication hearing. Such an action becomes final immediately upon issuance and is appealable within thirty days to the ERAC, which then provides for a hearing *de novo.*[70]

4.3 Adjudication Hearings Before Ohio EPA

Ohio EPA adjudication hearings are governed by Rule 3745-47-21, which provides that the hearing examiner must admit "all relevant and material evidence, except evidence that is unduly repetitious, even though inadmissible under the rules of evidence applicable to judicial proceedings."[71] The discovery involved in an adjudication hearing should be conducted in the same manner and to the same extent as prescribed in the Ohio Rules of Civil Procedure.[72]

The weight accorded evidence is to be determined by its reliability and probative value.[73] If evidence is ruled inadmissible, the party offering it may make an offer of proof, consisting of a brief statement of the nature and substance of the evidence, to be included in the transcript. If the Director finds that the hearing examiner's exclusion of the evidence was erroneous, the hearing may be reopened to permit the taking of the evidence, or the Director may evaluate the evidence and proceed to a final decision.[74]

The burden at all hearings with respect to applications, permits, licenses, variances, and certificates shall be upon the applicant to prove entitlement to the permit, license, variance, or certificate.[75] Ohio EPA, however, bears the burden of proof at all

---

[70] For further discussion, see Chapter XII of this Handbook.

[71] OAC 3745-47-21(A). While the adjudicatory procedure is based on oral testimony, Ohio EPA also has a "modified procedure" for hearings that allows an adjudication hearing to be conducted through written testimony. OAC 3745-47-31.

[72] OAC 3745-47-20(A). *See* Ohio R. Civ. Pro. 26-37.

[73] OAC 3745-47-21(A).

[74] OAC 3745-47-21(D).

[75] OAC 3745-47-23(A)(1).

adjudication hearings relating to proposed modifications initiated by the agency, proposed revocations, proposed orders, and findings and notices of hearing.[76]

After a hearing is concluded, the hearing examiner submits a written report to the Director detailing the findings of fact, conclusions of law, and recommendations of the action to be taken. This report must be filed within forty-five days of the filing of the adjudication hearing transcript by the hearing clerk, unless a post-hearing briefing schedule has been established, in which case the report must be filed within forty-five days of the completion of briefing. Each party is provided a copy of the report and may file written objections within ten days.[77] The Director then has sixty days after the submission of objections in which to take action upon the report.[78] Final orders are appealable to the ERAC.

4.4 Ohio EPA Policies

Ohio EPA has a longstanding practice of issuing policies, which are "written clarification[s] or explanation[s] of a statute or rule that [are] initiated by the Environmental Protection Agency [but do] not include any educational guideline[s], suggestion[s], or case stud[ies] regarding how to comply with a statute or rule or any document[s] or guideline[s] regarding the internal organization or operation of the agency, including matters regarding administration, personnel, or accounting." These policies, which do not go through the rulemaking process, do not have the force or effect of law.[79]

The Ohio General Assembly passed legislation in 1996 that clarifies the role of policies in the regulation of environmental matters and imposes several new requirements on Ohio EPA.[80] Subsequent revisions to Chapter 3745 of the Revised Code require that policies comply with statutes and rules in existence at the time the policy is established, and create no new requirements. In addition, policies are to be created only at the Central Office of Ohio EPA. The first page of every policy must bear the following statement, in uppercase

---

[76] OAC 3745-47-23(A)(2).

[77] OAC 3745-47-24.

[78] OAC 3745-47-26(A).

[79] ORC § 3745.30(A).

[80] HB 106, 121st General Assembly (Eff. Mar. 5, 1996).

letters: "THIS POLICY DOES NOT HAVE THE FORCE OF LAW."[81] Proposed policies must be advertised in the *Ohio EPA Weekly Review.*

Any person may file a complaint at any time with the Director alleging that a policy established by Ohio EPA does not comply with these requirements. The Director shall review the policy within ninety days of receiving such a complaint and shall issue a determination as to whether the policy complies. The Director's determination is not a final action that is appealable to the ERAC.[82]

Ohio EPA is required to compile copies of all its policies and keep the compilation at the Central Office. The compilation shall be kept current and made available for public inspection and copying.[83] The Agency is required to review its published policies every five years and prepare written documentation certifying that it has done so.[84]

---

[81] ORC § 3745.30(B).

[82] ORC § 3745.30(D).

[83] ORC § 3745.30(F).

[84] ORC § 3745.30(C).

Chapter III

AIR POLLUTION CONTROL

1.0 OHIO'S AIR POLLUTION REGULATORY SCHEME

The Ohio Air Pollution Control Act, Chapter 3704 of the Ohio Revised Code, is designed to provide for an air pollution control program in the State that meets the requirements of the federal Clean Air Act. In 1993, the Ohio air law was extensively amended to authorize a new Title V operating permit program and to conform to other provisions in the federal Clean Air Act Amendments of 1990.

Ohio's air program is administered by the Director of Ohio EPA, who has the authority to promulgate regulations, grant or deny permits and variances, issue orders, and refer cases to the Ohio Attorney General for enforcement. The Division of Air Pollution Control within Ohio EPA interacts with U.S. EPA; provides centralized policymaking, planning, engineering, and technical support for the air pollution control program; and oversees the air program functions of the five Ohio EPA District Offices and seven local air pollution control agencies (which are delegated authority to carry out permitting, inspection, and monitoring functions on behalf of Ohio EPA).[1]

In general, Ohio's air program consists of rules that prescribe allowable emissions for specified sources or categories of sources, that require a permit to operate an air contaminant source, and that require an installation permit prior to building a new source or modifying an existing source. Installation permits typically include limits on allowable emissions that are determined on a case-by-case basis.

---

[1] *See* http://www.epa.state.oh.us/dapc/general/dolaa.html.

When the Ohio Air Pollution Control Act was revised in 1971 to conform to the landmark federal Clean Air Act Amendments of 1970, certain distinctive features of the pre-existing State law were retained. As a consequence, the scope of Ohio air law has remained significantly more expansive than the scope of federal air law. Whereas federal air law applies to only a finite number of specific regulated air pollutants (fewer than twenty before the 1990 Amendments, and just over 200 afterward), Ohio air law applies to all "air contaminants," defined broadly to include "particulate matter, dust, fumes, gas, mist, smoke, vapor, or odorous substances."[2] Federal air law applies almost exclusively to designated categories of sources or to sources above a certain size threshold, while Ohio air law extends to any "air contaminant source," which is defined as "each separate operation or activity that results or may result in the emission of any air contaminant."[3]

Ohio's air program is, to a large degree, the product of hundreds of State and federal rulemakings since 1971, many of which are exceedingly lengthy and complicated. Most, but not all, of Ohio EPA's emission limit regulations and permitting requirements are included in the State Implementation Plan ("SIP") approved by U.S. EPA pursuant to the federal Clean Air Act.[4]

Since Ohio's air pollution control scheme has been shaped predominantly by the requirements of the federal Clean Air Act, a brief overview of its most relevant provisions, as amended in 1990, is presented below.[5]

2.0 OVERVIEW OF THE FEDERAL CLEAN AIR ACT

In 1970, Congress enacted far-reaching amendments to the Clean Air Act ("Act")[6] and created a federal-state "partnership" in a command-and-control approach to limiting air pollution at its source. The cornerstone of the Act is the set of National Ambient Air Quality

---

[2] ORC § 3704.01(B).

[3] ORC § 3704.01(C). Ohio's definition of an "air contaminant source" is similar to U.S. EPA's definition of an "emissions unit." *See, e.g.* 40 CFR 52.21(b)(7). U.S. EPA normally uses the term "stationary source" to mean a whole plant or facility, *see, e.g.*, 40 CFR 52.51(b)(5), but there are exceptions to this general rule. For a discussion of U.S. EPA's varied interpretations of the term "source," see the preamble to the Agency's proposed General Provisions for hazardous air pollutants, 58 *Fed. Reg.* 42764 (Aug. 11, 1993).

[4] *See* 40 CFR Part 52, Subpart KK, 52.1870 *et seq.*

[5] For a more complete discussion of the federal Clean Air Act, see F. William Brownell et al., *Clean Air Handbook*, Government Institutes, Inc. (3d ed. 1998).

[6] 42 USC §§ 7401 - 7642.

Standards ("NAAQS"), which are nationally uniform maximum "safe" concentrations of "criteria" pollutants[7] established to protect the public health and welfare with an adequate margin of safety.[8] U.S. EPA promulgates NAAQS for each criteria pollutant. The states then have the responsibility to prepare SIPs to regulate individual sources of criteria pollutant emissions to the degree necessary to attain and maintain the NAAQS.[9] Air quality modeling[10] is typically used to calculate emission levels from existing sources that will not violate the NAAQS; these emission levels are in turn expressed as emission limits in the state rules to be included as part of the SIP. A SIP or SIP revision submitted to U.S. EPA must demonstrate timely attainment of the NAAQS and meet other criteria specified in Section 110(a)(2) of the Clean Air Act. Once approved, a SIP can be enforced in federal courts by U.S. EPA, or by "any person" under the "citizen suit" provision of the Act,[11] in addition to being enforceable under state law.

Except for certain provisions applicable to mobile sources and nonferrous smelters, the Clean Air Act expressly preserves the authority of states and political subdivisions to adopt and enforce air pollution control requirements that are not less stringent than those in effect under the federal Act.[12] Ohio law, however, precludes the Director of Ohio EPA from adopting ambient air quality standards that are more stringent than the NAAQS in effect under the Act.[13]

The Clean Air Act requires significant new or modified emission sources to meet nationally uniform, technology-based new source performance standards ("NSPSs").[14]

---

7 "Criteria" pollutants, so named because the scientific knowledge about them is published in U.S. EPA "criteria documents" pursuant to Section 108 of the Act, are pollutants that, in the judgment of the Administrator, "cause or contribute to air pollution which may reasonably be anticipated to endanger public health or welfare," and "the presence of which in the ambient air results from numerous or diverse mobile or stationary sources." 42 USC § 7408. There are currently six "criteria" pollutants regulated under the Act: sulfur oxides (SO_2); Particulate matter (PM, PM_{10}, or $PM_{2.5}$); carbon monoxide (CO); ozone (O_3); nitrogen oxides (NO_x); and lead (Pb). *See* 40 CFR Part 50.

8 42 USC § 7409; 40 CFR Part 50.

9 42 USC § 7410(a); 40 CFR Parts 51, 52.

10 Computer models simulate the dispersion of air pollutants from their point of release to their points (or areas) of impact on ground level "ambient" air beyond plant fencelines. *See* 56 *Fed. Reg.* 7694 (Feb. 25, 1991) (notice of U.S. EPA's March 19, 1991, Fifth Conference on Air Quality Modeling).

11 *See* 42 USC § 7604. Sixty-days prior notice must be given to U.S. EPA and to the alleged violator before a citizen suit may be commenced.

12 *See* 42 USC § 7416.

13 ORC § 3704.03(D).

14 42 USC § 7411.

Accordingly, U.S. EPA has promulgated NSPSs for dozens of different source categories.[15] Ohio EPA has been delegated authority by U.S. EPA to administer NSPS requirements in the State.[16]

When the Clean Air Act was amended in 1977, Congress added provisions that essentially codified programs administratively fashioned by U.S. EPA in the mid-1970s to deal with prevention of significant deterioration ("PSD") of air quality in areas classified "attainment" for the NAAQS, and for regulating persistent pollution in "nonattainment" areas.[17] The PSD program is designed to prevent excessive degradation of air quality that is already better than the NAAQS concentration levels and requires a permit prior to the commencement of construction of a major new or modified facility.[18]

In order to obtain a PSD permit, the applicant must monitor the "baseline" air quality; demonstrate the protection of the NAAQS and PSD increments for sulfur dioxide, particulates, and nitrogen oxides, using U.S. EPA-approved models; employ "best available control technology" ("BACT"); demonstrate protection of pristine "Class I" areas; and analyze impacts on soils and vegetation.[19] For nonattainment areas, Part D of the Act requires SIP revisions to demonstrate "reasonable further progress" toward timely attainment of the NAAQS, the "implementation of all reasonably available control measures ["RACM"] as expeditiously as practicable," and the implementation of restrictions on emissions from major new and modified facilities.[20] Nonattainment area new source review ("NSR") requires that the new or modified facility comply with the "lowest achievable emission rate" ("LAER") and obtain reductions from nearby existing source allowable emissions to more than offset the new emissions in question.[21] Ohio EPA has fully approved authority to

---

[15] 40 CFR Part 60.

[16] 49 *Fed. Reg.* 28713 (July 16, 1984).

[17] *See* Clean Air Act, Title 1, Parts C, D.

[18] The determination of what constitutes a "major modification" is complicated and problematic. *See, e.g.*, Wisconsin Electric Power Co. v. Reilly, 893 F.2d 901 (7th Cir. 1990). *See also* 57 *Fed Reg*. 32314 (July 21, 1992). U.S. EPA recently issued revisions that affect how the determination is made. *See* 67 *Fed. Reg.* 80186 (Dec. 31, 2002), 68 *Fed. Reg.* 61247 (Oct. 27, 2003).

[19] 42 USC § 7475(a).

[20] 42 USC § 7502(c).

[21] 42 USC § 7503.

administer both the PSD program and the nonattainment NSR program in the State.[22] The PSD program remains in effect without any significant change by the Clean Air Act Amendments of 1990. The nonattainment area NSR program has been made more rigorous by a number of important provisions in the 1990 Amendments.[23]

The PSD program does not apply to "hazardous air pollutants" ("HAPs").[24] The Clean Air Act provides a separate mechanism for the regulation of HAPs[25]. Whereas the Act originally regulated HAPs using the health-based pollutant-by-pollutant scheme of establishing National Emission Standards for Hazardous Air Pollutants ("NESHAPs"),[26] the Clean Air Act Amendments of 1990 replaced the NESHAP approach with a two-tiered scheme of: (1) technology-based standards for specified industry categories (maximum achievable control technology, or "MACT," standards); followed by (2) health-based "residual risk" standards if health risks remain too high after implementation of the MACT standards.[27] Preconstruction review of new, modified, or reconstructed major HAP sources is required by Section 112(g) of the Clean Air Act.[28] In December 1996, U.S. EPA issued a final regulation implementing certain provisions in Section 112(g) of the Clean Air Act as amended in 1990.[29] Under the new rule, all owners and operators of major HAP sources that are constructed or reconstructed are required to install MACT unless specifically exempted. When no applicable MACT standard has been promulgated for a proposed new or reconstructed source, Section 112(g) requires the permitting authority to determine a MACT

---

[22] *See* 68 *Fed. Reg.* 2909 (Jan. 22, 2003), 66 *Fed. Reg.* 51570 (Oct. 10, 2001) (PSD); 68 *Fed. Reg.* 1366 (Jan. 10, 2003) (Nonattainment NSR).

[23] In 1996, U.S. EPA proposed extensive changes to "reform" the PSD and nonattainment NSR rules. *See* 61 *Fed Reg.* 38250 (July *23,* 1996). A portion of those reforms was finalized on December 31, 2002 (67 *Fed. Reg.* 80186). Additional reforms were finalized on October 27, 2003 (68 *Fed. Reg.* 61247). Those revised federal regulations are not effective in Ohio until Ohio adopts, and U.S. EPA approves, revisions to Ohio's SIP.

[24] 42 USC § 7412(b)(6).

[25] The 1990 Amendments to the Act included in Section 112(b)(1) an initial list of 189 pollutants to be regulated as "hazardous," and provided in Section 112(b)(2) and (3) for revisions to the list of hazardous pollutants.

[26] 40 CFR Part 61 sets forth NESHAPs promulgated by U.S. EPA for more than twenty source categories emitting eight hazardous pollutants.

[27] For a brief U.S. EPA summary of the new program for regulating HAPs, see the preamble to the General Provisions for hazardous air pollutants, 59 *Fed. Reg.* 12408 (Mar. 16, 1994).

[28] 42 USC § 7412(g).

[29] 61 *Fed. Reg.* 68384 (Dec. 27, 1996).

emission limitation on a case-by-case basis ("case-by-case MACT").[30] The Section 112(g) case-by-case MACT does not apply to modifications of existing air pollution sources.

The Clean Air Act Amendments of 1990,[31] with eleven titles totaling over 800 typewritten pages in length, became law on November 15, 1990. Most of the provisions of the 1970 and 1977 amendments were retained, while a number of significant new programs were added, including: (1) as noted above, a drastic change to the regulation of HAPs, with 189 listed HAPs being subject to source-category, technology-based standards developed by U.S. EPA in accordance with a tight statutory schedule, with follow-up regulation if necessary, to prevent unreasonable residual risk;[32] (2) a national air operating permit program that states can administer with U.S. EPA's approval, which is funded by annual permit fees and requires self-monitoring and self-reporting of violations; (3) a market-based, national acid rain control program for the reduction of sulfur dioxide emissions by ten million tons below 1980 levels; (4) mandatory elimination and substitution of chlorofluorocarbons and other chemicals that deplete stratospheric ozone levels; and (5) significantly expanded civil and criminal liability and penalties, with new enforcement powers for both the federal government and private citizens.

Other changes made by the 1990 Amendments include: (1) gradations of severity for ozone, particulate matter, and carbon monoxide nonattainment areas, with more restrictive control requirements applying to the nonattainment areas of greater severity; (2) lower "major" source thresholds in nonattainment areas classified as serious, severe, or extreme that increase the scope of operating permit and new source permit program requirements; and (3) new U.S. EPA authority to disapprove or selectively approve SIP submittals and to

---

[30] 42 USC § 7412(g)(2).

[31] Pub. L. 101-549 104 STAT. 2399 (1990).

[32] Section 112(r) of the Clean Air Act establishes a program for the prevention and detection of accidental releases of hazardous pollutants from stationary sources. Sources at which a regulated substance is present in more than a threshold quantity as defined by the regulations must prepare and implement a risk management plan to detect and prevent or minimize accidental releases of the substance. The sources also must provide a prompt emergency response to such releases in order to protect human health and the environment. 42 USC § 7412(r). U.S. EPA promulgated final Section 112(r) risk management program rules in 1996. *See* 61 *Fed. Reg.* 31668 (June 20, 1996). Ohio EPA's regulations for the administration of a delegated Section 112(r) risk management program in Ohio are found at OAC Chapter 3745-104. Facilities subject to the risk management program were required to submit initial risk management plans by June 21, 1999, three years after the date on which a regulated substance is first listed under 40 CFR Part 68 (which is incorporated into Rule 3745-104-04 of the Administrative Code), or before the date on which a regulated substance is first present above a threshold quantity in a process. OAC 3745-104-38(B).

unilaterally redesignate areas from attainment to nonattainment, thus subjecting them to more stringent regulation.

In July 1997, U.S. EPA promulgated controversial revisions to the NAAQS for particulate matter and ozone.[33] Ozone limits were tightened from 0.12 ppm as a one-hour average to 0.08 ppm over an eight-hour period and, although the NAAQS for PM_{10} was retained, a new standard applicable to particles with a diameter of 2.5 microns or less ("$PM_{2.5}$") was added. The new standard for ultra-fine particles was set at an annual limit of fifteen micrograms per cubic meter, and a twenty-four-hour limit of sixty-five micrograms per cubic meter. Numerous judicial appeals to overturn the new standards were filed, but the standards were ultimately upheld.[34]

Although enforcement is discussed in more detail in Chapter XIII of this Handbook, one air-pollution-specific rule published by U.S. EPA should be noted here. In early 1997, U.S. EPA promulgated the "credible evidence" rule.[35] This rule makes sweeping changes to the methods that can be used to "prove" violations of virtually every emission limit that had previously been established under the Clean Air Act. Before the rule, noncompliance for most emission limits was determined through prescribed "reference method tests" prescribed by rule and conducted under "representative" standardized operating conditions.[36] Under the new credible evidence rule, however, any "credible evidence or information" can be used as the exclusive basis for establishing a violation of NSPSs, NESHAPs, or SIP emission limits. Criticism of the rule has been widespread, and numerous petitions for review were filed with the U.S. Court of Appeals for the D.C. Circuit, alleging that the rule is illegal. Among the allegations were charges that U.S. EPA lacks statutory authority to establish such a rule and that the rule constitutes an unlawful revision of substantive standards.[37] The D.C. Circuit Court of Appeals declined to decide the issues, saying they were unripe for review.[38]

---

[33] 62 *Fed. Reg.* 38762, 38856 (July 18, 1997).

[34] American Trucking Associations, Inc. v. EPA, 175 F.3d 1027, *aff'd*, 195 F.3d 4 (D.C. Cir. 1999); Whitman v. American Trucking Associations, 121 S.Ct. 903 (2001)

[35] 62 *Fed. Reg.* 8314 (Feb. 24, 1997).

[36] *See* Michael G. Dowd & Michael H. Levin, *By Any Credible Means*, 148 N.J.L.J. 1376 (1997); Michael H. Levin, *EPA's Indefensible "Credible Evidence" Rule: A Critical Analysis*, Washington Legal Foundation, Critical Legal Issues, Working Paper Series No. 76 (1997).

[37] Clean Air Implementation Project v. EPA, 150 F.3d 1200 (D.C. Cir. 1998).

[38] *Id.*

3.0 OHIO'S AIR POLLUTION STATUTE

The Ohio Air Pollution Control Act[39] was revised in 1971 to enable the State to administer a federally approved air pollution control program in conformity with the then-new federal Clean Air Act as signed into law in 1970. Following amendments to the federal Act in 1977 and 1990, the General Assembly made major revisions to the State statute in 1980 and 1993.

The purposes of the Ohio statute include protecting and enhancing the quality of the State's resources and enabling Ohio to adopt and maintain a program for the prevention, control, and abatement of air pollution that is consistent with the federal Act.[40]

Authority to administer Chapter 3704 of the Revised Code is vested with the Director of Environmental Protection. Among other things, Section 3704.03 of the Revised Code authorizes the Director to:[41]

(1) adopt air quality standards for the State that are no more stringent than counterpart federal standards;

(2) adopt emission standard rules necessary to meet those standards in light of the consideration of certain criteria set forth in Section 3704.03(E);

(3) adopt rules requiring installation permits from the Director as a prerequisite to constructing new sources of air pollution;

(4) adopt rules requiring permits prohibiting the operation of air contaminant sources without either a permit to operate in compliance with applicable rules or a variance issued by the Director;

(5) require operators of pollution sources to monitor emissions or air quality, and to provide such reports as the Director prescribes;

(6) enter upon private or public property for the purpose of making inspections, taking samples, and examining records or reports

---

[39] ORC Chapter 3704.

[40] *See* ORC § 3704.02.

[41] *See* ORC § 3704.03.

to ascertain compliance with air pollution statutes, regulations, or orders;

(7) delegate enforcement and monitoring powers to city or general health districts or political subdivisions; and

(8) issue orders requiring the abatement of emissions that violate applicable standards or other requirements.

Section 3704.04 requires that the Director comply with the procedural requirements of Chapter 119[42] and Chapter 3745 of the Revised Code for rulemaking actions and actions on permits and variances.

4.0 THE 1993 AMENDMENTS TO THE OHIO AIR POLLUTION CONTROL ACT

In response to the federal Clean Air Act Amendments of 1990, the Ohio General Assembly enacted legislation in 1993[43] enabling Ohio EPA to develop and administer a federally approved air pollution operating permit program that meets the requirements of Title V of the federal Clean Air Act Amendments of 1990 and U.S. EPA's Title V regulations set forth at 40 CFR Part 70. The guiding philosophy of the legislation, according to its sponsor, was to provide for the absolute minimum program necessary for federal approval, "and not one dot more." The text of the bill left no doubt that it indeed was intended to restrict the scope of Ohio's Title V permit program as much as possible. SB 153 precluded Ohio's Title V permit program from being more stringent than necessary to meet the minimum federal requirements, and mandated the maximum operational flexibility for facilities covered by the new program.[44] By law, Title V permits cannot impose new substantive requirements beyond existing federally enforceable requirements.[45]

SB 153 called for a uniform annual emission fee of $25 per ton (adjusted for inflation after 1989) of actual emissions of the five relevant criteria pollutants (particulate matter, sulfur dioxide, nitrogen oxides, organic compounds, and lead), with the fees to be used solely

[42] Ohio Administrative Procedure Act.

[43] SB 153, 120th General Assembly (Eff. Oct. 29, 1993). Technical amendments to SB 153 were contained in a budget corrections bill, HB 715, that became effective April 22, 1994.

[44] *See* ORC § 3704.036(A) - (B).

[45] ORC § 3704.036(K).

to fund the Title V permit program.[46] The legislation also required a biennial audit of Title V program revenues and expenditures by an independent certified public accountant, beginning in 1997.[47]

As a result of SB 153, there are two kinds of air operating permits in Ohio: State-only permits and Title V permits.[48] A traditional permit to operate ("PTO") is required for facilities with emissions below the major source threshold – *e.g.* "minor" facilities. PTOs are not federally enforceable, with one exception: they may include a federally enforceable cap on the "potential to emit" for the purpose of making the source a "synthetic minor"[49] source and thereby exempt from federal requirements that apply exclusively to major sources, including Title V permitting.[50] All major sources in Ohio – those with the plantwide potential to emit 100 tons per year ("tpy") or more of any one regulated pollutant, ten tpy or more of any one hazardous air pollutant, or twenty-five tpy or more of any combination of hazardous air pollutants – are required to have a Title V permit. Title V permits have two basic components: federally enforceable provisions and State-only provisions. State-only provisions must be clearly identified as "not federally enforceable," and a source covered by a Title V permit is not required to have a traditional PTO.[51]

U.S. EPA's Title V regulations require that Title V permits cover all emissions of regulated air pollutants from a facility that is "major" for any one pollutant, except for "insignificant activities and emissions levels" listed by the State and approved by U.S. EPA. Accordingly, SB 153 required Ohio EPA to adopt regulations that include in the list of insignificant activities and emission levels all sources exempt from permit to install ("PTI") and PTO requirements, and all sources emitting less than twenty percent of an applicable major source threshold and less than five tpy of any nonhazardous pollutant.[52]

---

[46] *See* ORC § 3745.1(C), (C)(2). The fee does not apply to emissions in excess of 4,000 tons per year of any one pollutant from a single facility, ORC § 3745.11(C).

[47] ORC § 3745.112.

[48] *See* ORC § 3704.036(A).

[49] "Synthetic minor" is a concept derived from the NSR program, and refers to a source that would be classified as "major" *but for* the imposition of a federally enforceable cap on allowable emissions.

[50] ORC § 3704.03(G).

[51] ORC § 3704.036(A).

[52] ORC § 3704.036(B)(4).

In addition, SB 153 provided an "application shield" that protects against liability for failure to have a Title V permit if a complete and timely application is pending.[53] There are specific criteria for application completeness and strong procedural safeguards to protect against premature or arbitrary incompleteness determinations. The Director is required to notify the applicant in writing and offer to meet informally with the applicant before making a final determination that an application is incomplete. If the matter is not resolved informally, a final incompleteness determination does not become effective until twenty days after it is mailed to the applicant. If the applicant appeals to the Environmental Review Appeals Commission ("ERAC") and applies for a stay, the incompleteness determination is automatically stayed until the ERAC rules on the merits of the motion for stay.[54]

There is also an explicit "permit shield" to protect against claims of liability for any violation of the Clean Air Act that can be "shielded" by Title V permits.[55] Title V permit applicants have the right to request an Ohio EPA determination of whether or not a given Clean Air Act requirement is applicable to the facility in question and can thereby broaden the scope of the permit shield.[56]

Title V permit applicants are given the option of proposing alternative emission limits to supersede existing SIP emission limits adopted to attain and maintain NAAQS.[57] If the Director determines that the proposed alternative limits are equivalent to the SIP limits and are quantifiable, accountable, enforceable, and based on replicable procedures, they must be included in the Title V permit in lieu of the SIP limits. Title V permits are required to accommodate "multiple operating scenarios and anticipated changes in emissions" that are not prohibited by federally enforceable requirements.[58] Ohio EPA is authorized to issue "general permits" covering numerous similar facilities or air contaminant sources[59] and is required to adopt regulations that provide for minor modifications and operational flexibility that minimize administrative burdens on a source and ensure maximum operational

---

[53] ORC § 3704.05(K).

[54] *See* ORC § 3704.036(D). For a discussion of the ERAC, see Chapter XII of this Handbook.

[55] ORC § 3704.036(E).

[56] ORC § 3704.036(G).

[57] *See* ORC § 3704.03(E)(3), .036(K).

[58] ORC § 3704.036(H).

flexibility consistent with the Clean Air Act.[60] The Director has authority to provide for emissions trading, marketable permits, auctions of emission rights, and economic incentives that would reduce the cost or increase the efficiency of achieving a specified level of environmental protection.[61]

SB 153 also established a small business technical and environmental assistance program and an independent small business ombudsman pursuant to Section 507 of Title V.[62] Eligibility for the small business assistance program is restricted to businesses that employ 100 or fewer individuals, do not emit more than fifty tpy of any one regulated air pollutant or seventy-five tpy of any two or more regulated air pollutants, are not major sources, and are small business concerns as defined in the federal Small Business Act.[63]

Ohio EPA is required to formulate and implement a "tiered permitting system" that categorizes, prioritizes, and expedites action on non-Title V air permits.[64] The tiered permitting system is to include PTI and PTO exemptions, Registration Status, permits-by-rule, and general permits to cut down on the amount of case-by-case review needed for nonmajor emission sources.

There is also a statutory *de minimis* exemption for any individual air contaminant source with potential emissions of ten pounds per day or less. Sources with potential emissions greater than ten pounds per day but with actual emissions of ten pounds per day or less also can be designated *de minimis*, provided records are kept to verify the source's actual emissions.[65] Sources of HAP emissions are exempt as *de minimis* if their potential annual emissions or adequately documented actual emissions are less than one tpy of all HAPs combined.[66] These exemptions do not apply if federal or state rules specifically regulate emissions more restrictively. Any person may petition the Director for source category PTI

---

59 ORC § 3704.036(I).

60 ORC § 3704.036(B), (M).

61 ORC § 3704.03(V).

62 *See* ORC §§ 3704.18 -.19, 3706.19. U.S. EPA approved Ohio's small business program effective October 16, 1995; *see* 60 *Fed. Reg.* 42042 (Aug. 15, 1995).

63 15 USC §§ 631 *et seq.*

64 ORC § 3704.037.

65 ORC § 3704.011.

66 ORC § 3704.011(C).

and PTO exemptions; the Director is required to accept or reject such petitions within 180 days.[67]

The Director has authority to grant hardship exemptions to the requirement for a PTI if all applicable emission limits and Clean Air Act requirements will be met and the source will not adversely affect public health or safety or the environment.[68] SB 153 also implemented a new requirement that PTIs constitute a PTO for a period not to exceed one year from the commencement of operation.[69] A new definition of "best available technology" ("BAT") is designed to prevent PTIs from requiring technology that is not adequately proven or not cost-effective.[70]

5.0 OHIO TITLE V AND RELATED AIR REGULATIONS

Following the enactment of SB 153, Ohio EPA promulgated a comprehensive set of regulations to implement the Ohio Title V permit program and to make other changes to Ohio's air permitting rules consistent with the new legislation. These rules became effective April 20, 1994.

The Title V permit program rules, which are set out in Rules 3745-77-01 through 3745-77-10 of the Administrative Code, track the requirements of U.S. EPA's Title V permit program rules in 40 CFR Part 70[71] and the directives of SB 153. The Ohio Title V permit program applies only to major sources unless and until U.S. EPA mandates otherwise, but allows nonmajor sources the option of obtaining a Title V permit.[72] Applicants are given the option of applying for a single Title V permit or multiple Title V permits for a given facility.[73] Emission sources in Ohio are obligated to obtain either a Title V permit or a traditional PTO, but not both. Title V permits include "applicable requirements" that are federally enforceable terms and conditions, and separate State-only terms and conditions that

---

[67] ORC § 3704.037(B).

[68] ORC § 3704.03(W).

[69] *Id.*

[70] ORC § 3704.01(F).

[71] *See* 57 *Fed. Reg.* 32250 (July 21, 1992).

[72] OAC 3745-77-02. Ohio's Title V Permit Program was approved by U.S. EPA effective October 1, 1995; *see* 60 *Fed. Reg.* 42045 (Aug. 15, 1995).

[73] OAC 3745-77-03(B).

are expressly designated as not being federally enforceable.[74] Title V permits can be used to establish alternative emission limits to supersede SIP limits designed to achieve NAAQS.[75]

An application shield authorizes operation of a source subject to the Title V permit program during the pendency of an application, provided that the application is complete and timely.[76] During the transition period while initial Title V permit applications are pending, applicants must remain in compliance with the terms and conditions of any and all applicable PTOs regardless of their expiration date.[77]

Concurrent with the promulgation of the Title V permit program rules, Ohio EPA amended existing PTI and PTO rules to provide more streamlined procedures for creating synthetic minor sources. Synthetic minor sources are those that would be classified as major in the absence of enforceable restrictions on emission rates, hours of operation, or production rates. A source classified as minor is not subject to the Title V permit program or to the federal new source permitting requirements under Parts C and D of the Act. Rule 3745-31-02(A)(2) of the Administrative Code allows the owner or operator of an air contaminant source to voluntarily limit the amount or type (such as hazardous versus nonhazardous) of allowable emissions from the source. Such a voluntary cap on emissions is available upon request (without requiring any physical or operational change to the source). The requirements for BAT and consideration of social and economic impacts that normally apply to PTIs do not apply to PTIs issued pursuant to Rule 3745-31-02(A)(2). Rule 3745-35-07 establishes a similar mechanism to cap the potential to emit of a source with federally enforceable PTO terms and conditions. U.S. EPA has approved Ohio's PTI and PTO processes; they are currently viable ways to create a synthetic minor source.[78]

The air permitting rules that became effective April 20, 1994 also include recordkeeping and other provisions related to the *de minimis* source exemption provided in Section 3704.011 of the Revised Code,[79] a provision that grants a PTO exemption for all

---

[74] OAC 3745-77-07(B), -10.

[75] OAC 3745-77-07(A)(1)(c).

[76] OAC 3745-77-06.

[77] OAC 3745-77-04.

[78] 59 *Fed. Reg.* 53586 (Oct. 25, 1994); 60 *Fed. Reg.* 55200 (Oct. 30, 1995).

[79] OAC 3745-15-05.

sources that are covered by permanent PTI exemptions,[80] provisions for implementing the emission fee requirement added by SB 153 to Section 3745.11,[81] and provisions to implement the small business assistance program established by SB 153.[82]

6.0 APPROVAL / DISAPPROVAL STATUS OF THE OHIO SIP

There is no coherent "master copy" of the Ohio SIP. Rather, the SIP is an accumulation of various administrative actions since 1971, some of which are federally promulgated rules, some of which are delegations of authority from U.S. EPA, and the majority of which are U.S. EPA rulemaking actions on SIP revisions submitted by Ohio EPA (virtually all of which incorporate by reference regulatory requirements that have not been published in the *Federal Register* or in the *Code of Federal Regulations*).

The Ohio SIP is set forth at 40 CFR 52.1870 *et seq.*, also referred to as "Subpart KK." Most of Ohio's emission limitations for criteria pollutants or their precursors (particulate matter, sulfur dioxide, nitrogen oxides, volatile organic compounds, carbon monoxide, and lead) have SIP approval status. Ohio's PTI rules are conditionally approved.[83] The PTO rules were not designed to be, and have not been, included in the SIP.[84]

Useful summaries of Ohio SIP history are included in the preamble to several *Federal Register* notices relating to the Ohio SIP.[85]

7.0 PROHIBITIONS

The prohibitions in the Ohio Air Pollution Control Act are set out in Section 3704.05 of the Revised Code. The most basic prohibitions can be summarized as: "Do not install,

---

[80] OAC 3745-35-02(A)(2).

[81] OAC 3745-78-01 to -05.

[82] OAC 3745-79-01 to -03.

[83] *See* 61 *Fed. Reg.* 17669 (Apr. 22, 1996).

[84] An exception to the non-SIP status of the PTO rules is the provision for a federally enforceable cap to be included in a PTO in order to limit the potential to emit of a source, as provided in Section 3704.03(G) of the Revised Code and Rule 3745-35-07, approved effective December 27, 1994. *See* 59 *Fed. Reg.* 53586 (Oct. 25, 1994).

[85] *See, e.g.*, 59 *Fed. Reg.* 10349 (Mar. 4, 1994), 61 *Fed. Reg.* 17669 (Apr. 22, 1996)(NSR rules); 59 *Fed. Reg.* 23796 (May 9, 1994) (VOC rules); 59 *Fed. Reg.* 27464 (May 27, 1994) (PM rules).

modify, or operate an air contaminant source without first obtaining a permit"; and "Do not emit more than the amount allowed by any applicable rule, permit, or order."[86]

Section 3704.05(G) provides that no person shall violate any order, rule, or determination issued by the Director under Chapter 3704. Rule 3745-31-02 of the Administrative Code establishes, with exception, that no person shall allow the installation of a new air source or the modification of an existing source without first obtaining a permit from the Director. Rule 3745-35-02(A) similarly provides, with exception, that no person may allow the operation or other use of any air contaminant source without obtaining a permit to operate from the Director.[87]

Section 3704.05 of the Revised Code further prohibits the violation of any applicable requirement contained in a Title V permit or any terms or conditions of a permit or variance.[88] Failure to install and maintain monitoring devices or to submit reports required by the Director,[89] to allow entry of an authorized representative of the Director to a permitted facility,[90] or to pay noncompliance penalties or Title V emission fees[91] also are prohibited by Section 3704.05. In addition, the statute sets out broad prohibitions against the falsification of information required to be kept or submitted pursuant to the Ohio Air Pollution Control Act.[92]

Violation of the prohibitions contained in Section 3704.05 may result in civil and criminal liability. Enforcement can be initiated only by the Director. Section 3704.06 of the Revised Code requires the Attorney General, upon the request of the Director, to prosecute any person who violates any of the prohibitions of Section 3704.05. Under Section 3704.06(C), violations of the prohibitions of Section 3704.05 can lead to injunctive relief and

---

86 It should be noted that there are important nuances and exceptions to these simplified generalizations.

87 The exceptions to the PTO requirement include: (1) sources covered by a variance issued pursuant to Rule 3745-35-03; (2) sources subject to PTO exemptions listed in Rule 3745-35-05; (3) sources exempted from the PTI requirement under Rule 3745-31-03; (4) sources covered by the Title V permit program under Rule 3745-77-02; (5) *de minimis* sources exempted by Section 3704.011 of the Revised Code and Rule 3745-15-05; and (6) sources operating pursuant to a PTI for up to one year after startup (or lesser period specified by the Director) pursuant to Section 3704.03(F) of the Revised Code.

88 ORC § 3704.05(A) - (C), (J)(2).

89 ORC § 3704.05(D).

90 ORC § 3704.05(E), (J)(2).

91 ORC § 3704.05(J)(1).

92 ORC § 3704.05(H), (J).

civil penalties of not more than $25,000 for each day of each violation. Section 3704.99 prescribes criminal penalties for knowing or reckless violation of air pollution laws, including fines of up to $25,000 and imprisonment of up to one year.[93]

8.0 PROVISIONS RELATED TO OZONE NONATTAINMENT

The Clean Air Act Amendments of 1990 added extensive new requirements for ozone nonattainment areas. Twenty-four counties in Ohio were designated attainment for ozone in 1991. As of this writing, only the four-county Cincinnati-Hamilton Area (Hamilton, Butler, Clermont, and Warren counties) remains nonattainment for ozone.[94] The various regulatory initiatives related to ozone nonattainment areas are described below.[95]

8.1 VOC Reasonably Available Control Technology Rule Corrections

Section 182(a)(2)(A) of the Act requires the "fixup" of VOC RACT rules considered inadequate under U.S. EPA's guidance in effect prior to November 15, 1990.[96] Section 182(b)(2) of the Act requires the adoption of VOC RACT rules for sources covered by Control Techniques Guidelines issued by U.S. EPA after November 15, 1990, and for major VOC sources not yet covered by RACT rules.[97] A number of VOC RACT rule changes submitted for SIP approval in 1988 and 1990 were approved by U.S. EPA in 1994.[98]

8.2 NO_x As An Ozone Precursor

The 1990 Amendments to the federal Clean Air Act added Section 182(f) to require that NO_x emissions, in addition to VOC emissions, be regulated as ozone precursors

---

93 For further discussion of air enforcement cases, see Chapter XIII of this Handbook.

94 *See* 62 *Fed. Reg.* 7194 (Feb. 18,1997) (Cincinnati-Hamilton area); 62 *Fed. Reg.* 7194 (Feb. 18, 1997); 61 *Fed.* Reg. 11560 (Mar. 21, 1996) (Clinton County); 61 *Fed. Reg.* 3591 (Feb. 1, 1996) (Columbus area); 61 *Fed. Reg.* 3319 (Jan. 31, 1996) (Canton-Youngstown area); 60 *Fed. Reg.* 39115 (Aug. 1, 1995) (Toledo); 60 *Fed. Reg.* 22289 (May 5, 1995) (Dayton-Springfield area); 60 *Fed. Reg.* 7453 (Feb, 8, 1995) (Preble, Columbiana, and Jefferson counties).

95 For further discussion of these requirements, *see* U.S. EPA's proposed "General Preamble for the Implementation of Title I of the Clean Air Act Amendments of 1990," 57 *Fed. Reg.* 13498 (Apr. 16, 1992), and U.S. EPA's proposed "Nitrogen Oxides Supplement to the General Preamble," 57 *Fed. Reg.* 55620 (Nov. 25, 1992). *See also* discussion of new NAAQS for ozone in Part 2.0 of this chapter.

96 RACT "fixup" is the term U.S. EPA uses to describe RACT measures needed to fully satisfy requirements in effect under Section 172(b)(3) of the Act and related guidance prior to the 1990 Amendments. *See* 42 USC § 7511a(a)(2)(A).

97 42 USC § 7511a(b)(2).

98 59 *Fed. Reg.* 23796 (May 9, 1994).

unless U.S. EPA grants an exemption.[99] (Prior to the 1990 Amendments, *only* VOCs were regulated as ozone precursors.) This means that major sources of NO_x emissions in ozone nonattainment areas are subject to RACT and nonattainment NSR provisions in the absence of an exemption pursuant to Section 182(f).

Ohio EPA sought to defer action on NO_x RACT emission regulation in the Cincinnati moderate ozone nonattainment area (Hamilton, Butler, Clermont, and Warren counties) until the completion of a SIP attainment demonstration,[100] but U.S. EPA's authority to approve such deferral was rejected in *Natural Resources Defense Council v. Browner.*[101] U.S. EPA approved a Section 182(f) NO_x RACT waiver for the Toledo and Dayton moderate ozone nonattainment areas due to the fact that monitoring data show both areas to be attaining the ozone NAAQS.[102] U.S. EPA also conditionally approved a Section 182(f) NO_x RACT waiver for the Cincinnati-Hamilton area in 1995.[103]

8.3 NO_x RACT Rules

In response to the requirements of Section 182(f) of the Act, Ohio EPA promulgated NO_x RACT rules that became effective June 21, 1994, for all the moderate ozone nonattainment counties except for the four in the Cincinnati area (for which a NO_x RACT waiver was conditionally approved in July 1995).[104] The NO_x RACT rules are contained in Chapter 3745-14 of the Administrative Code. However, they no longer apply to those counties that have been redesignated to attainment for ozone.

---

[99] 42 USC § 7511a(f). For areas not within an ozone transport region (Ohio is not), NO_x emission sources are not regulated as ozone precursors if U.S. EPA finds that net air quality benefits are greater in the absence of NO_x reductions from the sources concerned, or that additional NO_x reductions would not contribute to attainment of the ozone NAAQS.

[100] Ohio EPA's so-called "committal SIP" was based upon U.S. EPA's interpretation of Section 110(k)(4) of the Act. The request was made for only the Cincinnati area because it is the only *multi-state* moderate ozone nonattainment area in Ohio, and therefore required by Section 182 of the Act to use the complex and data-intensive Urban Airshed Model to demonstrate attainment. The Urban Airshed Model is the only methodology currently acceptable to U.S. EPA for determining whether NO_x emission reductions hurt or help attainment of the ozone NAAQS.

[101] 22 F.3d 1125 (D.C. Cir. 1994).

[102] 60 *Fed. Reg.* 3760 (Jan. 19, 1995).

[103] 60 *Fed. Reg.* 36051 (July 13, 1995).

[104] The NO_x RACT rules initially applied to major sources of NO_x emissions located in Ashtabula, Clark, Cuyahoga, Geauga, Greene, Lake, Lorain, Lucas, Medina, Miami, Montgomery, Portage, Summit, and Wood counties. OAC 3745-14-02(A).

8.4 Emission Statements

Section 182(a)(3)(B) of the Act requires SIP revisions that call for annual reporting by source owners or operators of actual emissions of VOCs and NO_x in ozone nonattainment areas.[105] In response, Ohio EPA has adopted "Emission Statement" rules in Chapter 3745-24 of the Administrative Code, which became effective March 1, 1994. The obligation to file an emission statement applies to the owners or operators of facilities located in an ozone nonattainment area with actual emissions of twenty-five tons per year or more of *either* VOCs or NO_x during the year covered by the report.

8.5 Motor Vehicle Inspection And Maintenance

Chapter 3745-26 of the Administrative Code sets forth rules to implement Ohio's motor vehicle inspection and maintenance ("I/M") statute, Section 3704.14 of the Revised Code. Under the basic I/M program, motor vehicles in any Ohio county classified as moderate, serious, severe, or extreme nonattainment for carbon monoxide or ozone must have annual anti-tampering and tailpipe emission inspections to ensure compliance with pollution standards.

The 1990 Amendments to the Act provided that areas designated as moderate nonattainment may choose to implement an enhanced I/M program if there is sufficient support at the local level. Enhanced I/M has three elements: a tailpipe test measuring vehicle emissions during various driving cycles; a purge flow test of the evaporative canister; and a pressure test of the evaporative system. In 1993, the General Assembly passed legislation that authorized Ohio EPA, acting in response to locally elected officials, to implement an enhanced I/M program in the three moderate nonattainment areas.[106] Ohio EPA began an enhanced I/M program in the Cincinnati, Dayton, and Cleveland-Akron areas in January 1996. Although the General Assembly passed HB 172 in 1997 that would require basic rather than enhanced I/M in the Dayton and Cleveland-Akron areas, and legislative approval prior to any new or expanded I/M requirements, the Governor vetoed the measure.

---

[105] 42 USC § 7511a(a)(3)(B).

[106] SB 18, 120th General Assembly (Eff. Sept. 27, 1993).

9.0 OHIO'S BASIC AIR POLLUTION REGULATIONS

Pursuant to the rulemaking authority granted under various subsections of Section 3704.03 of the Revised Code, the Director of Ohio EPA has adopted extensive rules to regulate air pollution in the State. The rules governing allowable emissions are set forth in Chapters 3745-15 through 3745-26 of the Administrative Code. In addition, certain permitting and procedural requirements codified elsewhere in the Administrative Code have applicability to the regulation of air pollution in Ohio.[107]

9.1 General Provisions On Air Pollution Control

Chapter 3745-15 of the Administrative Code provides certain generally applicable definitions that are "used in all air pollution rules, except as may otherwise be specifically provided."[108] Chapter 3745-15 also provides for the measurement of emissions and the submission of emission information, addresses the malfunction of air pollution control equipment, prohibits air pollution nuisances, and specifies recordkeeping and other criteria for *de minimis* source exemptions.

9.2 Particulate Matter Standards

Chapter 3745-17 of the Administrative Code, which sets out standards for particulate matter, has been amended from time to time since it was adopted initially in the early 1970s. It includes emission limitations for point sources in two general categories – fuel burning equipment (Rule 3745-17-10) and industrial processes (Rule 3745-17-11) – as well as a variety of requirements for the control of fugitive dust emissions sources (Rules 3745-17-07 and 3745-17-08). Following U.S. EPA's adoption of a new NAAQS for fine (respirable) particulates, known as the "PM_{10} NAAQS," in July 1987, Ohio EPA adopted significant amendments to its particulate matter standards in 1991, including PM_{10} emission

[107] The relevant permitting rules are contained in Chapters 3745-31 (PTIs), 3745-35 (PTOs and variances), and 3745-77 (Title V permits) of the Administrative Code. For a discussion of Ohio EPA rulemaking, see Chapter II, Part 4.0, of this Handbook.

[108] OAC 3745-15-01.

limitations for the Cleveland and Steubenville areas.[109] It is still too early to predict the impact of U.S. EPA's new $PM_{2.5}$ NAAQS discussed in Part 2.0 above.

9.3 SO_2 Standards

Chapter 3745-18 of the Administrative Code sets out Ohio's SO_2 regulations that replace a federally promulgated SO_2 plan adopted by U.S. EPA in 1976 and 1977. Like U.S. EPA's SO_2 rules, Ohio EPA's SO_2 rules have both generally applicable limits and source-specific limits arranged on a county-by-county basis. Most of the provisions of Ohio's SO_2 rules have been federally approved.

9.4 Open Burning Prohibition

Chapter 3745-19 of the Administrative Code prohibits open burning in Ohio, with certain narrow exceptions. The exceptions are more limited in areas defined as "restricted" (in and near municipal corporations).

9.5 VOC Standards

Chapter 3745-21 of the Administrative Code regulates emissions of organic compounds and carbon monoxide. Only one short, simple rule (3745-21-08), which requires afterburners for certain iron and steel making and petroleum refining processes, is devoted to limiting carbon monoxide emissions. The regulations for control of organic compounds, however, are many. Rules 3745-21-07 and 3745-21-09 through 3745-21-11, limiting emissions of organic compounds – in some cases the subset defined as "photochemically reactive materials" and in some cases the subset defined as "volatile organic compounds" ("VOCs") – and the related definitions set forth in Rule 3745-21-01, are by far the most complicated and perplexing of all Ohio EPA's air pollution rules. These rules regulate many different uses of organic compounds, some by source category and some on an individual facility basis. Rule 3745-21-11, added in 1990, requires facilities located in any of eighteen counties to submit studies for the development of source-specific emission requirements if potential emissions of VOCs from sources not already regulated under Section 3745-21-09

---

[109] Ohio's particulate matter regulations for the entire State and PM_{10} emission limits for the Cleveland and Steubenville areas have been given limited approval and limited disapproval by U.S. EPA. *See* 59 *Fed. Reg.* 27464 (May 27, 1994).

exceed 100 tons per year. Ohio EPA developed new RACT emission limits for a number of facilities that submitted studies under this requirement.[110]

The manner in which the emission standard rules and compliance provisions are phrased is often confusing and complicated. For example, Rule 3745-21-01 sets out definitions for nearly 200 different terms necessary to apply Ohio's organic compound rules. In contrast to particulate matter and SO_2 rules, the VOC rules often address much smaller sources. In recent years, a much greater proportion of Ohio's regulatory and enforcement resources has been directed at VOC emission sources.

9.6 NO_x Standards

Chapter 3745-23 sets out ambient standards for nitrogen oxide (NO_x). Ohio has never had any area classified nonattainment for NO_x and there are no existing source NO_x emission control requirements. Existing major sources of NO_x emissions located in certain areas classified as moderate nonattainment for ozone, however, had been subject to NO_x RACT requirements set out in Chapter 3745-14, but all the counties to which those rules were applicable have been redesignated to attainment and thus, as noted in Section 8.3 above, the rules no longer apply.

9.7 Air Pollution Emergencies

Chapter 3745-25 of the Administrative Code sets out rules for air pollution emergencies and calls for emission control action programs to be put into effect during an air pollution "Alert," "Warning," or "Emergency." Consequently, Ohio EPA has determined that the Emergency Action Plan ("EAP") required by Rule 3745-25-03 need not be submitted at this time. In the future, should an EAP be deemed necessary (due to new or revised air quality standards or a degradation in air quality) Ohio EPA will notify facilities, which will have up to sixty days to develop and submit a plan.[111]

---

[110] U.S. EPA has given final approval to various VOC RACT rules submitted by Ohio EPA. *See, e.g.*, 59 *Fed. Reg*. 22973 (May 5, 1994); 59 *Fed. Reg*. 23796 (May 9, 1994); 59 *Fed. Reg*. 52911 (Oct, 20, 1994); 60 *Fed. Reg*. 15235 (Mar. 23, 1995); 61 *Fed. Reg*. 18255 (Apr. 25, 1996).

[111] *See* Ohio EPA Engineering Guide #64 (Oct. 1995), http://www.epa.state.oh.us/dapc/engineer/eguides.html.

9.8 Other Provisions

Provisions of Chapters 3745-31 (PTIs), 3745-35 (PTOs), and 3745-77 (Title V permits) of the Administrative Code apply to sources of air pollution and are addressed under separate headings below. In addition, Ohio EPA's general procedural rules, set out at Chapter 3745-47, apply to actions of the Director of Ohio EPA with respect to air pollution and air pollution sources. Ohio EPA added emission rules to the Administrative Code for several classes of sources in 1991.[112]

10.0 PERMITS FOR NEW AND MODIFIED SOURCES

As noted in Part 2.0 above, Ohio EPA has fully approved authority to issue PSD and nonattainment NSR permits and to enforce NSPSs and NESHAPs in Ohio. In addition to these federal law requirements, Ohio law requires a PTI, issued pursuant to Chapter 3745-31 of the Administrative Code, prior to the commencement of construction of any new or modified air contaminant source not specifically exempt. The PTI exemptions are set out in Rule 3745-31-03. *De minimis* exemptions are provided in Section 3704.011 of the Revised Code and in Rule 3745-15-05.

10.1 Relationship Of Federal And State Laws To New, Modified, And Reconstructed Sources

The boundary between federal and State law applicability to new and modified source permitting is an important one for the Ohio air program. On the federal side, NSPSs and NESHAPs apply only to affected facilities within the source categories for which they have been promulgated. Existing sources within these categories must comply with NSPSs if they are "modified" or "reconstructed" as defined at 40 CFR 60.14, 60.15, and 61.07. NESHAPs ordinarily apply in the same manner to both new and existing sources, although existing sources may qualify for temporary waivers.[113] Any "facility" that can emit more than 100 tons per year of a regulated pollutant is "major" for purposes of nonattainment

[112] *See* OAC Chapters 3745-73 (Kraft Pulp Mills), 3745-74 (Acrylonitrile, ABS, and Polymer Plants), and 3745-75 (Infectious Waste Incinerators).

[113] *See* 40 CFR 61.11. In 1996, EPA issued a final regulation requiring owners and operators of major HAP sources that are constructed or reconstructed to install MACT. *See* 61 *Fed. Reg.* 68384 (Dec. 27, 1996). The rule does not apply to modifications of existing pollution sources. For further discussion, see Part 2.0 of this chapter.

NSR review,[114] and also for PSD review if it is in any of twenty-eight source categories listed in Section 169(l) of the Act.[115] If the source is not in the listed categories, it is considered "major" for PSD purposes only if it has the *potential* to emit 250 tons per year or more of a regulated pollutant.[116] If a physical change or change in the method of operation[117] of an existing "major" source would result in increased emissions exceeding certain significance levels, PSD review is required.[118] If such a change occurs at a source that is "major" for a pollutant for which the area is classified nonattainment, then nonattainment NSR is required.

Ohio EPA administers the federal PSD and nonattainment NSR programs through its PTI rules, set forth in Chapter 3745-31 of the Administrative Code. In addition, the PTI rules govern certain permitting requirements that apply as a matter of Ohio law only. The PTI rules require a permit for the installation of a new source, or the modification of an existing source, of air contaminants.

Ohio EPA has interpreted the term "installation" in the PTI rules broadly, so as to apply to virtually any work on a new or modified air contaminant source, other than site grading and clearing, before a permit is issued.[119] The term "air contaminant source" is defined as "each separate operation or activity that results or may result in the emission of any air contaminant."[120] The term "modification" is defined to include "[a]ny physical change in, or change in the method of operation of ... [a]ny air contaminant source that ...

---

[114] The nonattainment NSR major source threshold is lower for nonattainment areas classified "serious" or above and for VOC sources in ozone transport regions, but as of this writing no such areas exist in Ohio.

[115] 42 USC § 7479(l). For a more comprehensive discussion of PSD and nonattainment NSR, see *Draft New Source Review Workshop Manual*, U.S. EPA (Oct. 1990).

[116] 42 USC § 7479(l). A point of frequent confusion in the "major" source annual emissions threshold is the concept of "potential emissions." For PSD and nonattainment NSR purposes, "potential emissions" means "the maximum capacity of a stationary source to emit a pollutant under its physical and operational design." Until relatively recently, the effects of control equipment or restrictions on the hours of operation or rate of production of a source could be excluded from the potential to emit if, and only if, they were "federally enforceable." *See* 40 CFR 52.21(b)(4). In two different cases, the D.C. Circuit Court of Appeals held that "federal enforceability" is not a requirement. *See* National Mining Assoc. v. EPA, 59 F.3d 1351 (D.C. Cir. 1995) (vacating "federal enforceability requirement in Section 112 definition of "major source"); Chemical Mfrs. Assoc. v. EPA, Nos. 89-1514 to 89-1516 (D.C. Cir. 1995) (vacating the "federal enforceability" requirement as applied to NSR definition of potential to emit).

[117] There are important exclusions from the term "physical change or change in the method of operation" set forth in 40 CFR 52.21 (b)(2)(iii).

[118] Significance levels are expressed in tons per year (tpy) and include: carbon monoxide – 100 tpy; nitrogen oxide – 40 tpy; sulfur dioxide – 40 tpy; particulate matter – 25 tpy of total suspended particulate matter, and 15 tpy of PM_{10},; ozone – 40 tpy of volatile organic compounds; and lead – 0.6 tpy. *See* 40 CFR 52.21(b)(23).

[119] OAC 3745-31-02(A).

[120] OAC 3745-31-01(D).

[r]esults in the increase in emission of greater than the *de minimis* levels in [R]ule 3745-15-05."[121] Modification also includes the relocation of an existing source to a new location, as well as any action that would constitute a modification under applicable federal laws.[122] Absent a *de minimis* exemption or an explicit exemption in the PTI rules, a PTI is required for any new or modified air contamination source.

In February 1996, Ohio EPA adopted significant amendments to the PTI rules. The amendments were submitted to U.S. EPA to revise the Ohio SIP for minor NSR, and to enable full approval of Ohio's PSD and nonattainment NSR programs. Among other things, the amendments change the definition of "modification" in Rule 3745-31-01 for minor NSR purposes to exclude routine maintenance, repair, and replacement; use of an alternative fuel or raw material that the source is capable of accommodating; and certain pollution control projects. U.S. EPA conditionally approved the nonattainment NSR rules later that year.[123]

Ohio EPA's 1996 NSR SIP revisions inadvertently omitted provisions known as the "WEPCO fix" (resulting from the case of *Wisconsin Electric Power Co. v. Reilly*[124]) from its definitions. Ohio EPA initiated additional rulemaking to incorporate the WEPCO fix provisions into the rules and to revise the "potential to emit" definition to conform with U.S. EPA guidance issued in January 1996 pursuant to the D.C. Circuit Court of Appeals decisions in *National Mining Assoc. v. EPA*[125] and *Chemical Mfrs. Assoc. v. EPA.*[126] Under that guidance, "potential to emit" can be limited by restrictions on operations or emissions that are "legally and practically enforceable by the state" even if they are not "federally enforceable." U.S. EPA fully approved Ohio's nonattainment NSR rules in January of 2003.[127]

---

[121] OAC 3745-31-01(KK). *See* State ex rel. Celebrezze v. National Lime & Stone Co., 68 Ohio St.3d 377, 627 N.E.2d 538 (1994).

[122] *See* OAC 3745-31-01(KK).

[123] *See* 61 *Fed. Reg.* 17669 (Apr. 22, 1996).

[124] 893 F.2d 901 (7th Cir. 1990).

[125] 59 F.3d 1351 (D.C. Cir. 1995).

[126] Nos. 89-1514 to 89-1516 (D.C. Cir. 1995).

[127] 68 *Fed. Reg.* 1366 (Jan. 10, 2003). As indicated in Part 2.0, above, U.S. EPA recently revised the federal NSR regulations.

PTI applicants may request Registration Status[128] for sources that will have maximum uncontrolled emissions of not more than five tpy of particulate matter, sulfur dioxide, nitrogen oxides, and organic compounds, if the source will employ BAT and not be subject to NSPSs, NESHAPs, or MACT standards under the federal Clean Air Act.[129] If the Director has not acted on the application within sixty days, installation or construction of the source may commence.[130]

Section 3704.03(W) of the Revised Code gives the Director discretion to authorize installation or modification of a source prior to the issuance of a PTI in hardship cases that would not result in a conflict with federal law or other applicable requirements.

Proposed PTIs that involve PSD, NSR, netting,[131] or synthetic minors[132] are submitted to and closely reviewed by U.S. EPA.

10.2 PTI Application

Applications for a PTI must be submitted on forms provided by Ohio EPA.[133] The PTI rule sets forth criteria that the Director is to apply in acting on applications. These include: (1) that the new or modified source will not interfere with attainment of the NAAQS; (2) that the source will not violate applicable laws (including various federal new source requirements, if applicable); and (3) that the source will employ BAT, which is distinct from BACT required under the federal PSD program.[134] BAT ordinarily will be deemed to be the same as BACT for major sources, but it also applies to smaller sources that

---

[128] For further discussion, see Section 11.2.2 of this chapter.

[129] OAC 3745-31-05(E).

[130] *Id.*

[131] "Netting" is a technique to avoid PSD or nonattainment NSR jurisdiction by reducing actual annual emissions from one or more existing units to compensate for new emissions from expansion at the same plant site.

[132] "Synthetic minors" are sources that would be "major," and thus subject to PSD and/or nonattainment NSR (or the Title V permit program), except for the fact that a federally enforceable restriction on hours of operation, rates of production, or emission rates shrinks the annual potential emissions of the source.

[133] OAC 3745-31-04. *See* http://www.epa.state.oh.us/dapc/files/files.html.

[134] *See* ORC § 3704.01(F); OAC 3745-31-05(A). The BAT requirement does not apply to PTI applications submitted pursuant to Rule 3745-31-02(A)(2) for a voluntary cap on allowable emissions.

are not subject to BACT under the federal law. Proposed action on a PTI application is required within six months after a complete application is filed.[135]

10.3 Enforcement

Ohio EPA's Division of Air Pollution Control requires strict adherence to the PTI program and has been aggressive in enforcing violations of the PTI rule. Cases where unpermitted sources have emissions greater than would be allowed under either applicable emission limits or BAT requirements that would have been imposed had a permit been secured are considered more serious than "paper" violations where no excess emissions are involved. Ohio EPA generally follows U.S. EPA's civil penalty policy for air matters.[136]

11.0 AIR PERMITS TO OPERATE AND VARIANCES

The Ohio EPA Director has adopted rules requiring either a PTO or a variance for air contaminant sources.[137] For sources subject to the Title V federal operating permit program, no other operating permit is required.[138]

11.1 PTO Application

With the advent of the Title V operating permit program, the term "PTO" is used to refer to State-only permits applicable to nonmajor sources not covered by the requirement to obtain a Title V permit. As in the case of PTIs, the application for a PTO must be made on forms provided by Ohio EPA.[139] The principal requirement for securing a PTO is that the source operate in compliance with applicable air pollution control laws.[140] In addition, the source must include required monitoring equipment and conduct required emission testing.[141] A PTO is also a vehicle for the Director of Ohio EPA to impose certain

[135] OAC 3745-31-05(E). A completeness determination on a PTI application is required within sixty days after receipt by Ohio EPA. ORC § 3704.034. The applicant may bring a mandamus action to compel final action by the Director on a PTI application that has been complete and pending for more than six months. *Id.*

[136] *See* http://www.epa.gov/compliance/resources/policies/civil/caa/stationary/penpol/pdf.

[137] OAC 3745-35-02; *see* http://www.epa.state.oh.us/dapc/files/files.html.

[138] OAC 3745-35-02(A)(3), -77-02(A).

[139] OAC 3745-35-02(B).

[140] OAC 3745-35-02(C).

[141] *Id.*

conditions necessary to ensure compliance with applicable law. A PTO can be issued for up to five years, after which a renewal application must be submitted and acted upon. However, if a renewal application is timely submitted, a source is permitted to continue in operation pending Ohio EPA action on the renewal application.[142] A single PTO application may be filed to cover all air contaminant sources located at the same facility.[143] An application for an initial PTO must be acted upon within six months after Ohio EPA determines the application to be complete.[144]

11.2 PTO Exemptions

There are several exemptions to the requirement that air contaminant sources possess a PTO, including sources covered by a variance, sources covered by registration status, small sources subject to an exemption because of *de minimis* or insignificant emissions, and sources covered by the Title V permit program.

11.2.1 Variances

An exemption from the PTO requirement applies to sources that have secured a variance under Rule 3745-35-03. A variance can authorize, under certain conditions, a source to operate without complying with applicable emission control requirements. A variance may be issued for sources that will achieve eventual compliance with emission limits as well as sources that will not. To secure a variance, a source owner or operator must demonstrate that operation in accordance with the requested variance will not interfere with ambient air quality standard attainment and maintenance, and that compliance with applicable emission standards is technically infeasible, economically unreasonable, or impossible.[145] Provision is specifically made for "bubble concept" variances, under which emissions at a particular source in excess of requirements may be allowed where there are offsetting decreases beyond legal requirements provided elsewhere.[146] Variances to emission

[142] ORC § 119.06; OAC 3745-35-02(D).

[143] OAC 3745-35-02(B)(7).

[144] The completeness determination must be made within sixty days after receipt by Ohio EPA. ORC § 3704.034.

[145] OAC 3745-35-03(E)(2).

[146] OAC 3745-35-03(E)(2)(d).

limitations or other requirements that have been federally approved must be submitted to U.S. EPA for approval as a revision to the Ohio SIP.[147] Variances are not available for new sources.[148]

11.2.2 Registration Status

Another exemption from the PTO requirement is known as "Registration Status." Under Rule 3745-35-05(B) of the Administrative Code, the Director of Ohio EPA has discretion to place certain permit applications on Registration Status if the permit application demonstrates that either the source is not subject to an emission requirement or its emissions are sufficiently small not to warrant formal permitting. If a permit application is placed on Registration Status, the owner or operator is notified and no further action is needed unless and until the Director requires submission of an updated permit application.[149]

11.2.3 Small Sources

Small source exemptions from the PTO requirement are provided as follows. First, a *de minimis* exemption for qualifying sources that emit no more than ten pounds per day of any one pollutant and no more than one tpy of hazardous air pollutants is provided in Section 3704.011 of the Revised Code.[150] Second, Rule 3745-35-05(A) contains a longstanding list of very small PTO-exempt sources, including: comfort ventilating systems; incinerators located in dwellings containing six or fewer units; gasoline dispensing facilities that are not located in various urban counties; and gasoline storage tanks, certain grain dryers, and storage silos used in connection with farming activities. Third, all sources exempted from PTI requirements under Rule 3745-31-03 also are exempted from PTO requirements.[151]

---

[147] OAC 3745-35-03(E)(2)(f).

[148] OAC 3745-35-03(C).

[149] OAC 3745-35-05(B)(4).

[150] *See* OAC 3745-15-05.

[151] OAC 3745-35-02(A)(2).

12.0 TITLE V PERMITS

Ohio's Title V permit program was approved by U.S. EPA effective October 1, 1995.[152] Normally a single Title V permit will cover an entire plant or facility subject to the program, but an applicant has the option of applying for and obtaining more than one Title V permit for a given facility.[153] The rules governing Title V permit applications and Ohio EPA's action on those applications, which are set out in Chapter 3745-77 of the Administrative Code, closely parallel U.S. EPA's rules in 40 CFR Part 70.

Title V permits are intended to collect all existing "applicable requirements" for a facility into one comprehensive document.[154] In addition, Title V permits include greater monitoring, recordkeeping, and reporting requirements than may have existed previously. The Title V permit is also the vehicle through which Ohio EPA will include Compliance Assurance Monitoring ("CAM") Rule requirements for those sources subject to the rule.[155] As indicated above, the 1990 Clean Air Act Amendments require the establishment of case-by-case MACT standards for source categories in which no applicable MACT standard has been promulgated by the relevant deadline. Those case-by-case MACT determinations will be administered through Title V permits.

13.0 ENGINEERING GUIDES

Ohio EPA's Division of Air Pollution Control over the years has developed a series of policy determinations on the manner in which various provisions of the air pollution regulatory program should be applied. Known as "Engineering Guides,"[156] these determinations ordinarily are issued in response to questions from local air agencies or Ohio

---

[152] *See* 60 *Fed. Reg.* 42045 (Aug. 15, 1995).

[153] OAC 3745-77-03(B).

[154] OAC 3745-77-07.

[155] *See* 40 CFR Part 64. CAM requirements will apply to stationary sources that (1) are equipped with post-process pollutant control devices, (2) have pre-control device emissions equal to or greater than 100 percent of the major source threshold for a pollutant, and (3) are subject to the Title V permit program. The rule requires that a CAM Plan be developed for each affected pollutant emitted from each affected source, in order to identify parameters to be monitored to ensure and document proper operation of the control device, thereby assuring compliance with the applicable emission limit.

[156] *See* http://www.epa.state.oh.us/dapc/engineer/eguides.html. The guides are available in both zip and pdf formats; the web site also includes a keyword index and a cross reference index.

EPA field offices, and deal with precise questions of how Ohio's rules should be applied in a given situation.

Beyond setting forth Ohio EPA's response to specific questions, the Engineering Guides often are used by the Agency as presumptive requirements in similar situations. To the extent that the Guides are applied generally throughout the State, a question exists as to whether they are in reality rules that have not been adopted through the rulemaking procedures required by law.[157] This question has not yet been decided, and for now Ohio EPA's day-to-day approach to air pollution regulation is shaped by the policies contained in the Guides.

14.0 OHIO'S APPROACH TO AIR TOXICS

One area of air pollution regulation that saw considerable regulatory activity in the 1980s, particularly at the State and local levels, was the regulation of "air toxics."[158] Air toxics generally are those pollutants that pose hazards to the public but that are not regulated under the more traditional air pollution programs (criteria pollutants, NSPSs, NESHAPs). Like many other states, Ohio has developed an approach for regulating emissions of air toxics that addresses new sources differently than it addresses existing sources.[159]

14.1 New Air Toxics Sources

For new sources of emissions considered to be toxic, Ohio EPA has chosen to proceed by way of policy rather than by rule. The policy, which has been in place since 1985, is known as a "fraction of TLV" approach. It is applied to only new or modified sources required to obtain a PTI. Under the policy, a determination is made whether the proposed new or modified source will emit air contaminants for which the American Conference of Governmental Industrial Hygienists has devised a "threshold limit value," or TLV, for workplace safety.[160] Eight-hour TLVs are divided by "42" to account for greater

[157] For further discussion, see Chapter II of this Handbook.

[158] For further discussion, see Chapter X of this Handbook.

[159] Ohio EPA from time to time has considered proposals to tighten its toxics policy to include a risk assessment feature for carcinogens and to reduce the acceptable ambient impacts for all air toxics. Although drafts of new policies have been circulated, the Agency has not issued a revised policy and it is uncertain whether or when changes will be made.

[160] *See* http://www.acgih.org/TLV.

sensitivity in the population at large than in the workforce, continuous potential exposure, and an arbitrary safety factor, to produce a plant-property-line standard that should not be exceeded.[161] Computer modeling is used for air toxics ambient air quality impact assessments. If emissions from the new or modified facility would be expected to exceed 1/42 of an eight-hour TLV at the plant property line (known as the maximum acceptable ground level concentration, or "MAGLC"), Ohio EPA will require additional controls as a condition to issuing a PTI.

14.2 Existing Air Toxics Sources

For existing sources of emissions considered to be toxic, Ohio EPA has chosen to proceed on a contaminant-by-contaminant basis, and to adopt rules where circumstances warrant. The first compound Ohio addressed was acrylonitrile; final regulations became effective January 30, 1991.[162] For other pollutants, the Agency commissioned a study by Battelle Memorial Institute to prioritize air toxics deserving attention within Ohio.[163] Based on the Battelle study, Ohio EPA has identified twenty-eight contaminants, the first six of which are under current consideration: chromium, formaldehyde, lead, benzene, coke oven emissions, and beryllium. Ohio EPA's approach is to evaluate the compounds on the basis of risk, exposure, and the extent to which other State or federal regulations already provide protection, and decide if additional requirements are warranted.

Ohio EPA relies upon its air pollution nuisance regulation, Rule 3745-15-07, to provide it with the necessary interim authority to deal with any serious air toxics situations that have not been addressed through a PTI or an existing source rule.

15.0 OHIO'S CLEAN AIR ACT SECTION 105 GRANT

Each year Ohio EPA applies to U.S. EPA for air pollution control program grant funding pursuant to Section 105 of the Clean Air Act. The Section 105 grant application process has become increasingly detailed and time consuming, and significantly influences

---

[161] If a TLV is expressed for a period other than eight hours, the fraction would be different for air toxics purposes.

[162] *See* OAC Chapter 3745-74.

[163] *The Identification and Prioritization of Toxic Air Pollutants in Ohio*, Battelle Memorial Institute (June 1987).

Ohio EPA's policies, priorities, and resource allocations. The grant is conditioned upon the State's commitment to a number of separate "projected project accomplishments" ("PPAs"). These PPAs describe with considerable particularity a range of rulemaking, surveillance, and enforcement activities that Ohio EPA will undertake in the following year. Although the grant documents are public information that provide useful insights into the current and near-term future direction of Ohio's air program, the grant conditions also have the potential for becoming "law through the back door," shielded from public scrutiny and opportunity for comment.

16.0 ASBESTOS DEMOLITION / REMOVAL PROGRAM

Ohio EPA has been delegated authority to implement and enforce U.S. EPA's NESHAP for asbestos.[164] In order to enhance its ability to enforce the asbestos NESHAP with respect to demolition, renovation, and waste disposal activities, Ohio EPA promulgated certain portions of the federal NESHAP as Ohio rules in May 1990. Codified in Chapter 3745-20 of the Administrative Code, these rules include specific standards for demolition and renovation at operations exceeding certain thresholds, for handling of asbestos wastes, and for both active and inactive waste disposal sites.

In addition, the Ohio Department of Health[165] has adopted asbestos hazard abatement rules that provide for the licensing of "asbestos hazard abatement contractors" and "asbestos hazard evaluation specialists."[166] Any evaluation, abatement, or removal of asbestos-containing materials must be performed by a contractor licensed by the Department of Health.[167] Contractors providing asbestos evaluation, abatement, or removal services, and persons contracting for such services, are provided with a limited immunity for asbestos-related injuries or property damage when such work is conducted in accordance with applicable State and federal laws.[168]

---

[164] 40 CFR Part 61, Subpart M.

[165] *See* http://www.odh.state.oh.us.

[166] *See* OAC Chapter 3701-34.

[167] ORC § 3710.03, .05.

[168] ORC § 3710.17.

17.0 PERTINENT CASE LAW

Courts have played an important role in shaping Ohio's air pollution control program. Some of the more significant decisions are discussed below.[169]

New Boston Coke Corp. v. Tyler[170] involved a challenge to Ohio EPA's promulgation of a rule limiting visible emissions from coke battery doors. In a split decision, the Ohio Supreme Court ruled that since the company had failed to participate in the rulemaking proceeding before the Director of Ohio EPA, the company lacked standing to challenge the rules on appeal. In dissent, however, three justices agreed on the merits that the regulation was unlawful because the Director had failed to consider evidence relating to the criteria set forth in Section 3704.03(E) of the Revised Code.[171]

In *Dayton-Walther Corp. v. Williams*,[172] the Franklin County Court of Appeals held that, where other reliable data are available to show compliance with emission standards, Ohio opacity standards may not be used as the primary test for determining compliance. Rather, "Ohio opacity standards may be used only as a means of determining, in the first instance, whether a pollution source appears to be violating a mass emission standard."[173]

In *Swan Super Cleaners, Inc. v. Tyler*,[174] the Director appealed from a decision of the Ohio Environmental Board of Review, now the Environmental Review Appeals Commission ("ERAC"), ordering the Director to vacate the adoption of an Ohio EPA regulation relating to perchloroethylene emissions from drycleaning facilities. The Franklin County Court of Appeals ruled that the regulation was unreasonable and unlawful because it lacked a factual foundation. U.S. EPA, the court said, had "repudiated its earlier regulation of [perchloroethylene]" after it concluded that "the photochemical reactivity of perc in controlling ozone is negligible."[175]

---

[169] For additional air enforcement cases, see Chapter XIII of this Handbook.

[170] 32 Ohio St.3d 216, 513 N.E.2d 302 (1987).

[171] *See id.* at 221-223, 513 N.E.2d at 307-309.

[172] No. 79AP-356 (Franklin Cty. App. Mar. 20, 1980).

[173] *Id.*, slip op. at 12.

[174] 48 Ohio App.3d 215, 549 N.E.2d 526 (Franklin Cty. 1988).

[175] *Id.* at 220, 549 N.E.2d at 530.

In *United States Steel Corp. v. Williams*,[176] the Franklin County Court of Appeals considered a rule of the Director prohibiting the issuance of variances after a certain date. Recognizing that the statute authorizing variances, Section 3704.03(H) of the Revised Code, provides for no such limitation, the court held that the Director may not adopt a regulation flatly refusing to consider variances where the variance will not affect the timely attainment of NAAQS and will not violate federal law.

In *State ex rel. Celebrezze v. National Lime & Stone Co.*,[177] the Ohio Supreme Court held that the like-kind replacement of a Raymond mill used to grind processed limestone (hydrate) with a virtually identical mill, deemed by the court to be "a piece of equipment that is a component of a complex manufacturing operation," did not constitute the "installation" of a new source of air contaminants within the meaning of Rule 3745-31-02(A) of the Administrative Code, and therefore did not require a PTI.[178]

In *Williams v. Schregardus*,[179] the Franklin County Court of Appeals issued a ruling which may expand Ohio EPA's permitting focus. In two cases involving a challenge by local residents to air PTIs issued by Ohio EPA to two facilities in Lebanon, the court held that, in issuing PTIs for air contaminant sources in the state, the Ohio EPA must consider not only whether the PTI applicant meets all requirements that apply to air emissions, but also whether the source to be permitted complies with all other applicable regulations, including those governing water pollution.

In *Stone Container Corp. v. U.S. EPA*,[180] the U.S. Sixth Circuit upheld a U.S. EPA-Region V order prescribing particulate emission test conditions for a wood waste and natural gas boiler at Stone Container's mill. The company took exception to Region V's mandate to test the boiler at its maximum design capacity rather than at its historical average steam rate. The court deferred to the region's interpretation that operation of the boiler at maximum design capacity constituted "representative performance" within the meaning of

---

[176] 65 Ohio App.2d 178, 417 N.E.2d 576 (Franklin Cty. 1979).

[177] 68 Ohio St.3d 377, 627 N.E.2d 538 (1994).

[178] *Id.* at 385, 627 N.E.2d at 544.

[179] 96 Ohio App.3d 664, 645 N.E.2d 840 (Franklin Cty. 1994).

[180] 1996 U.S. App. LEXIS 33268 (6th Cir. 1996) (opinion "not for publication").

U.S. EPA's NSPS regulations, even though the boiler was operated at or above its design capacity less than one percent of the time over the last three years.

In *Ashland Chem. Co. v. Jones,*[181] the Ohio Supreme Court unanimously upheld a decision by the ERAC that Rule 3745-21-07(G)(2), which regulates operations "employing, applying, evaporating or drying" photochemically reactive materials, was never intended to serve as a catchall regulation. As the court noted, "the language used in the regulation does not justify this conclusion." Specifically at issue in Ashland was the term "employing," and whether "employing" could reasonably be interpreted to mean "using" in the broadest sense, such that anyone who uses any photochemically reactive materials is subject to Rule 3745-21-07(G)(2). The court found that there was not support for such a broad interpretation.

In *Dayton Power & Light Co. v. Jones,*[182] the Director of Ohio EPA appealed from an ERAC decision ordering the Director to recalculate the 1997 Title V fees for The Dayton Power and Light Company's Killen and Stuart Generating Station facilities. In its decision, ERAC ordered the Director to calculate Title V fees based upon the emission of the air contaminant known as PM_{10}, which is particulate matter that is less than ten microns in diameter, rather than upon the emission of total particulate matter. On appeal, the court reversed ERAC and found that Ohio EPA's imposition of fees based on particulate matter was supported by the law and the regulations.

In numerous decisions, the U.S. Court of Appeals for the Sixth Circuit has addressed the procedural and substantive requirements for the promulgation and revision of Ohio's SIP.[183] The Sixth Circuit also has looked at the propriety of U.S. EPA's attainment designations in Ohio, addressing the validity of both the procedures used and the modeling techniques followed in making such designations.[184]

---

[181] 92 Ohio St.3d 234, 749 N.E.2d 744 (2001).

[182] 140 Ohio App.3d 675, 748 N.E.2d 1171 (Franklin Cty. 2000).

[183] *See, e.g.*, State of Ohio v. EPA, 784 F.2d 224, *aff'd upon rehearing*, 798 F.2d 880 (6th Cir. 1986); Ohio Power Co. v. EPA, 729 F.2d 1096 (6th Cir. 1984), *cert. denied*, 469 U.S. 1034 (1984); Cincinnati Gas & Elec. Co. v. EPA, 578 F.2d 660 (6th Cir. 1978), *cert. denied*, 439 U.S. 114 (1979); Cleveland Elec. Illuminating Co. v. EPA, 572 F.2d 1150 (6th Cir. 1978), *cert. denied*, 439 U.S. 910 (1978); Buckeye Power, Inc. v. EPA, 525 F.2d 80 (6th Cir. 1975).

[184] *See, e.g.*, State of Ohio v. Ruckelshaus, 776 F.2d 1333 (6th Cir. 1985), *cert. denied*, 476 U.S. 1169 (1986); Gen'l Motors Corp. v, Costle, 631 F.2d 466 (6th Cir. 1980); PPG Indus., Inc. v. Costle, 630 F.2d 462 (6th Cir. 1980); Republic Steel Corp. v. Costle, 621 F.2d 797 (6th Cir. 1980).

Chapter IV

WATER POLLUTION CONTROL

1.0 OHIO'S WATER POLLUTION REGULATORY SCHEME

The prevention, control, and abatement of water pollution in Ohio is prescribed under a broad programmatic and regulatory scheme developed pursuant to both federal and State authorities.

The requirements of the Federal Water Pollution Control Act ("Clean Water Act" or "Act")[1] are echoed and supplemented in Chapter 6111 of the Ohio Revised Code, which gives the Director of Ohio EPA authority to develop programs to regulate new or existing sources of pollution of the waters of the State,[2] and in Chapters 3745-1 and 3745-33 of the Ohio Administrative Code, which set out the applicable regulations.

This chapter discusses Ohio's water pollution regulatory scheme. The State's programs include federally authorized water quality standards, the National Pollutant Discharge Elimination System ("NPDES") permitting program, the wastewater pretreatment program, storm water management, and the biosolids program. The Director also is responsible for State-specific programs including the permitting program for new facility installations or modifications. Finally, this chapter also covers programs for state certification of federal permits, including permits for filling of wetlands, isolated wetlands, and nonpoint source control.

---

1 33 USC §§ 1251 - 1387 ("CWA"). The Federal Water Pollution Control Act was redesignated the Clean Water Act in the 1977 amendments to the Act.

2 ORC § 6111.03(A).

2.0 OVERVIEW OF THE FEDERAL CLEAN WATER ACT AND OHIO REVISED CODE CHAPTER 6111

The Clean Water Act provides a comprehensive regulatory framework for controlling discharges of pollutants into the navigable waters of the United States. Under provisions of the Act, the discharge of pollutants from a point source to the waters of the United States without a permit is strictly prohibited.[3] National technology-based effluent limitations establish the quantities or concentrations of pollutants that can be discharged from new and existing point source discharges to surface waters through the application of technology-based standards. These standards include best conventional technology ("BCT"), more stringent best practicable technology ("BPT") for conventional pollutants, and best available technology ("BAT") for toxic and nonconventional pollutants.[4]

Limitations are imposed upon individual sources through the NPDES permit system established in Section 402 of the Clean Water Act.[5] States are required to participate in a goal-setting process for improving the quality of waters within their jurisdictions.[6] They may assume the authority to issue NPDES permits requiring dischargers to meet not only technology-based limitations but also any more stringent limitation necessary to meet water quality standards.[7] States are authorized to develop, administer, and enforce their own programs and to issue state NPDES permits, subject to federal oversight.

Indirect discharges of pollutants to a publicly owned treatment works ("POTW") are subject to pretreatment limitations designed to protect the POTW from pollutants that would pass through or interfere with its operations.[8] These standards generally are imposed and enforced by the authority responsible for the POTW's operation.

The Clean Water Act also establishes programs for regional wastewater treatment planning, storm water management, nonpoint source pollution abatement, and biosolids

---

[3] 33 USC § 1311(a).

[4] 33 USC §§ 1311, 1314. National standards of performance are established for new and modified sources, and incorporate standards at least as stringent as BAT. 33 USC § 1316. Variances from the federal standards are available for individual sources under certain circumstances, and generally only within a limited period of time after promulgation of the otherwise applicable effluent limitation. 33 USC § 1311(j).

[5] 33 USC § 1342.

[6] 33 USC § 1342(b).

[7] 33 USC § 1313.

[8] 33 USC § 1317.

management.[9] Each of these programs supplements the NPDES permit program and involves significant State involvement.

In Ohio, the Director of Ohio EPA is responsible for implementing the provisions of the federal Clean Water Act. In addition to the requirements imposed by the Act, however, Ohio EPA implements two unique State requirements under Chapter 6111 of the Revised Code. First, unlike the federal program, Ohio law requires a permit from Ohio EPA prior to construction of any new treatment facility. Thus, Ohio EPA is responsible for issuing a permit to install ("PTI") prior to construction of a treatment facility. There is no equivalent requirement under the Act.

Second, Ohio EPA is responsible for issuing State dredge-and-fill permits for activities in isolated wetlands that are outside the authority of the U.S. Army Corps of Engineers under the Act. This permit program is discussed in more detail in Part 8.0 below.

3.0 WATER QUALITY STANDARDS

Water quality standards are an integral part of the Clean Water Act. The standards themselves, however, are written and enforced by individual states, based in part on water quality criteria established by U.S. EPA, and in part on biological and chemical data collected from individual stream segments within the states. Water quality standards form the basis of a state's review of applications for discharge permits and allow the state to predict the impact of discharges on ecological systems and the continued suitability of the receiving waters for drinking and recreation.

Ohio's water quality standards establish the minimum water quality requirements for all surface waters of the State. The standards are designed to maintain the quality of State waters to protect public health and welfare and to enable the use of such waters for public water supplies; industrial and agricultural needs; propagation of fish, aquatic life and wildlife; and recreational purposes.[10] Water quality standards also are used as the benchmarks for determining what steps are necessary to improve the quality of impaired waters of the State.

---

[9] 33 USC §§ 1281, 1288, 1329, 1342, 1345.

[10] ORC § 6111.041.

3.1 Use Designations

Water quality standards consist of one or more use designations, and numerical or narrative criteria designed to protect those uses.[11] Use designations fall into three major categories: (a) aquatic life habitat, (b) water supply, and (c) recreational.[12] Each water body in the State is assigned one or more aquatic life habitat use designations, one or more water supply use designations, and one recreational use designation.[13] Once use designations are established, specific numerical or narrative criteria for pollutants can be determined for the specific water body. The specific numerical or narrative criteria are established to protect and maintain the designated uses taking into consideration the location and current condition of the water body and the potential of an impaired water body to achieve its use designation. In cases where multiple specific numerical and narrative criteria for a pollutant are applicable, the most stringent criteria associated with any one of the use designations assigned to a water body will apply to that water body, and will be met outside the mixing zone.[14]

3.2 Criteria Applicable To All Surface Waters / Exceptions

Certain water quality criteria apply to all surface waters of the State, including mixing zones. These narrative water quality standards generally require that the waters be free from the following contaminants resulting from human activity: suspended solids or other substances that settle to form objectionable sludge deposits, or that will adversely affect aquatic life;[15] floating debris, oil, scum, and other materials in amounts that are unsightly or cause degradation;[16] materials that produce color, odor, or other substances to such a degree

---

[11] OAC 3745-1-07.

[12] *Id.* Aquatic life habitat designations can include warmwater habitat, limited warmwater habitat, modified warmwater habitat, exceptional warmwater habitat, seasonal salmonid, coldwater habitat, or limited resource waters. Water supply use designations include public (drinking), agricultural, and industrial water supplies. Recreational uses include bathing waters, primary contact recreation, and secondary contact recreation.

[13] OAC 3745-1-07(A)(1).

[14] OAC 3745-1-07(A)(2), (4).

[15] OAC 3745-1-04(A).

[16] OAC 3745-1-04(B).

as to create a nuisance;[17] substances in concentrations that are toxic or harmful to human, animal, or aquatic life and/or are rapidly lethal in the mixing zone;[18] and nutrients in concentrations that create nuisance growths of aquatic weeds and algae.[19]

These general narrative water quality criteria do not apply where they are exceeded due to natural conditions alone, or when the stream flow is less than the seven-day, ten-year low-flow value or other critical low-flow values dependent on low-flow or point source augmentation.[20] In limited circumstances for specific reasons or activities, exceptions from specific chemical water quality criteria exist. These exceptions include: (1) the application of chemicals to control aquatic plants or animals if upon prior notice the Ohio EPA Director finds the application poses no unreasonable danger to human or aquatic life; (2) dredging or construction activities that were authorized by the Corps of Engineers and/or Ohio EPA; and (3) coal remining activities subject to a permit if there is no potential for degradation of existing instream conditions and a demonstrated potential for improved water quality from the remaining operation.[21]

3.3 Specific Chemical And Physical Water Quality Criteria

Ohio EPA has established specific numeric criteria for more than 130 chemical parameters, in addition to temperature criteria for all waters of the State.[22] Numeric criteria for specific chemicals are used to establish specific discharge limitations, which are incorporated into individual NPDES permits, in order to protect the designated uses of individual stream segments.

If specific chemicals present in a discharge, either alone or in combination, are not governed by the numeric criteria listed in the water quality standards, Ohio EPA can derive numeric limits based on acute or chronic toxicity for aquatic life in the receiving stream. An acute aquatic criterion ("AAC") applies outside the mixing zone in all aquatic

---

[17] OAC 3745-1-04(C).

[18] OAC 3745-1-04(D).

[19] OAC 3745-1-04(E).

[20] OAC 3745-1-01(D).

[21] OAC 3745-1-01(E).

[22] OAC 3745-1-07, Tables 7-1 to 7-16.

life habitat use designations. The AAC is based on toxicity data for at least one species of water flea and one of either the fathead minnows, bluegill, or rainbow trout.[23] A chronic aquatic criterion ("CAC") also can be calculated for either a specific chemical or combination of chemicals, in any use designation except limited resource waters.[24] If a combination of chemicals is suspected of causing adverse chronic or acute conditions, Ohio EPA's "whole-effluent" toxicity approach may be used to provide a measure of the concentration of effluent that exhibits toxic effects on representative species.[25]

Ohio EPA also has provided a mechanism to directly measure attainment of various aquatic life habitat use designations, known as the "biological criteria," which can be used to establish limitations that are either more or less stringent than the specific numeric criteria associated with a particular chemical, or that vary from the AAC, CAC, or whole-effluent toxicity units calculated for a specific chemical or combination of chemicals.[26]

3.4 Variances

Variances from water quality standards are available based on site-specific information concerning designated uses, water quality criteria, naturally occurring or non-induced conditions in the stream segment where the discharge occurs, and the impact of compliance.[27] Variances are not available to facilitate the installation of any new source; they are temporary and can be issued for a period of not more than three years, but may be renewed at the end of the three-year period.[28] A variance will not be renewed if the discharger has not substantially complied with all the terms and conditions associated with the variance. Variances are part of the water quality standards revision process and are subject to State and federal rulemaking requirements.[29]

---

23 OAC 3745-1-07(C)(1).

24 OAC 3745-1-07(C)(2).

25 OAC 3745-1-07(D).

26 OAC 3745-1-07(A)(6).

27 OAC 3745-1-01(G).

28 *Id.*

3.5 Analytical Methods

Analytical methods used in the measurement of water quality – including those for sample collection and preservation, mixing zones for thermal discharges, whole-effluent toxicity testing, and application of biological criteria – must comply with procedures set out in 40 CFR Part 136, as amended, and/or various other manuals and guidelines specified by Ohio EPA.[30]

3.6 Antidegradation Policy

Legislation enacted in 1993[31] required the Director of Ohio EPA to revise the Agency's antidegradation policy to ensure that the surface waters in the state are maintained at "levels of water quality that are currently better than prescribed by applicable standards except in situations when a need to allow a lower level of water quality is demonstrated based on technical, social, and economic criteria."[32]

Accordingly, in 1996 Ohio EPA significantly modified its policy to prescribe the quantity of pollutants that may be discharged into a river.[33] The quantities themselves are based on the designated use of the water, together with the ecological, social, and economic impacts of the discharge.

In order to implement the antidegradation policy, Ohio EPA has developed additional categories for the waters of the state. Generally these antidegradation categories relate to water quality use designations; however, they are separate and distinct categories. Surface waters of the State initially are designated as either High Quality Waters or Limited Quality Waters.[34] High Quality Waters are further subdivided into five categories: General High Quality Waters, Superior High Quality Waters, State Resource Waters, Outstanding National Resource Waters, and Outstanding High Quality Waters.[35] The designation of a particular water body within a category of High Quality Waters will determine the nature of

---

29 *Id.*

30 *See* OAC 3745-1-03.

31 HB 152, 120th General Assembly (Eff. July 1, 1993).

32 ORC § 6111.12(A).

33 *See* OAC 3745-1-05.

34 OAC 3745-1-05(A)(9).

the review process and decision-making criteria applicable to the Director's authorization of new discharges into the water body.[36]

For purposes of the antidegradation rule, Limited Quality Waters include the following water quality use designations: Limited Resource Water, Nuisance Prevention, Limited Warmwater Habitat, and Modified Warmwater Habitat.[37] The requirements under the antidegradation rule for discharges to Limited Quality Waters are reduced significantly.

In cases involving waters other than Outstanding National Resource Waters, Outstanding High Quality Waters, and Limited Quality Waters, the Director, after an extensive investigation, may permit activities that lower the water quality.[38] Specifically, the Director must determine that important social or economic justifications exist to support the lowering of water quality. The Director accomplishes this by examining nondegradation, minimal degradation, mitigative technique alternatives, relevant social and economic issues, public participation, and intergovernmental participation.[39]

For purposes of the antidegradation rule, both Outstanding National Resource Waters and Outstanding High Quality Waters receive the maximum protections. Generally, new discharges are not allowed to either category of waters and no existing sources can undergo modifications that increase either the mass load or concentration of any pollutant.[40] Waters designated as Limited Quality Waters are excluded from many of the rule requirements.[41]

In conducting the antidegradation review, the Director, upon determining that an alternative is technically feasible and economically justifiable, may require the applicant to implement a nondegradation, minimal degradation, or mitigative technique alternative to offset all or part of the proposed lower water quality.[42] To help the Director decide which

---

[35] OAC 3745-1-05(A)(9)(a) - (d).

[36] OAC 3745-1-05(C).

[37] OAC 3745-1-05(A)(11).

[38] OAC 3745-1-05(C)(6).

[39] *Id.*

[40] OAC 3745-1-05(C)(4), (5). There is an exception for increased concentrations only if the increase is the result of water conservation. OAC 3745-1-05(C)(5)(a).

[41] OAC 3745-1-05(D)(1)(a).

[42] OAC 3745-1-05(C)(6).

course of action to follow, the antidegradation rule mandates consideration of technical, social, and economic criteria, including the anticipated effects of lower water quality on human health, aquatic life, and wildlife.[43]

3.6.1 Regulatory Categories

The acceptable level of pollutants that a facility may discharge into an Ohio river or stream is dictated by the classification of that particular body of water. Ohio EPA has classified all Ohio rivers and streams as General High Quality Waters except for those specifically designated under the rule.[44] The Agency must review each of the High Quality Water category designations every three years.[45] Any person "adversely affected" by a water designation has the right to petition Ohio EPA to change the designation.[46]

3.6.2 Scope Of Rule

The antidegradation policy applies to facility activities, permits, certifications, and other circumstances as follows:[47]

(1) renewal or modification of an NPDES permit because of physical changes or modifications to the operation of the facility's wastewater treatment processes, if the changes would cause a net increase in the discharge of a regulated pollutant;

(2) a PTI or an NPDES permit that would cause a net increase in the discharge of a regulated pollutant;

(3) an unpermitted source causing a net increase in the discharge of a regulated pollutant above certain levels and flows;

(4) a Clean Water Act Section 401 water quality certification application;

(5) a nonpoint source of pollution that results in a net increase in the release of a regulated pollutant;

---

[43] OAC 3745-1-05(C)(6)(a) - (m).

[44] OAC 3745-1-05(A)(9)(a).

[45] OAC 3745-1-05(E)(2).

[46] OAC 3745-1-05(E)(3).

[47] *See* OAC 3745-1-05(B)(1)(a) - (h).

(6) a PTI application that involves the deposit of fill or any portion of a sewerage system near a stream bed, provided that the Director of Ohio EPA determines that stream habitat alterations caused by the activity would lower the water quality;

(7) transfer of all or a portion of a discharge by a POTW to a different receiving water body or different POTW discharging to a different water body, unless certain conditions are met; or

(8) a dredge and fill permit authorizing discharge of dredged or fill material into isolated waters of the state.

3.6.3 Submittal Requirements For Facilities

Facilities that are subject to the antidegradation rule are required to perform numerous activities – *e.g.*, identifying the type and quantity of the substances to be discharged or providing a description of construction work to be performed and the fill to be used in or near a stream bed.[48] In addition, the applicant must provide to Ohio EPA descriptions and analyses of nondegradation and mitigative alternatives for the design and operation of an activity that has been considered,[49] and an estimate of the "important social, economic and environmental benefits" to be gained or lost if the water quality is to be lowered, including the number and types of jobs created and the tax revenues generated by the activities.[50] Finally, the Agency requires a listing and description of all governmental or privately sponsored conservation projects targeting improved water quality and/or enhanced recreational opportunities on the affected water body.[51]

3.6.4 Antidegradation Review Requirements

An antidegradation review is required to obtain permits, permit modifications, and certifications that result in a net increase in the discharge of any regulated pollutant.[52] One provision of the antidegradation statute has been struck down by the Franklin County

[48] OAC 3745-1-05(B)(2)(a) - (b).

[49] OAC 3745-1-05(B)(2)(c) - (d).

[50] OAC 3745-1-05(B)(2)(e) - (f).

[51] OAC 3745-1-05(B)(2)(g).

[52] OAC 3745-1-05(C).

Court of Common Pleas.[53] Section 6111.12(A)(3) of the Revised Code had allowed an existing facility to be allocated up to eighty percent of a stream's pollutant assimilative capacity without going through a further antidegradation review, provided that its previous permit limits were based on existing effluent quality, and that the river or stream in question lacked "exceptional recreational or ecological value." The court held that the law violated the Clean Water Act because it failed to provide mandatory public notice allowing public participation. The remaining provisions of the law, although challenged as violating the Supremacy and Commerce clauses of the United States Constitution, were left intact.[54]

The "public involvement" provisions of the antidegradation rules require the Ohio EPA Director to provide for intergovernmental coordination and extensive public participation before acting on matters within the scope of the rule.[55] Among the governmental agencies that must receive notice of any proposed action are the Ohio Department of Natural Resources, U.S. Fish and Wildlife Service, U.S. EPA, and any affected local agencies.[56] It also may be necessary to notify the Ohio Department of Development and other local government departments. Further intergovernmental coordination is discretionary and may be initiated by either the Ohio EPA Director or another agency.[57]

3.6.5 Exclusions And Waivers

Any source discharging to Limited Quality Waters and any *de minimis* net increase, as determined by criteria established in the rule, are excluded from the antidegradation submittal and review requirements. Other circumstances where an exclusion may apply include, but are not limited to, combined sewer overflow elimination or reduction projects, and a disposal system dedicated exclusively to the treatment of volatile organic compounds at response action cleanup sites.[58] Ohio EPA also may waive various submittal

---

[53] *See* Rivers Unlimited, Inc. v. Schregardus, Case No. 95-CVH12-8797 (Franklin Cty. Comm. Pl., Mar. 3, 1997).

[54] *Id.*

[55] OAC 3745-1-05(C)(3).

[56] OAC 3745-1-05(C)(3)(f).

[57] *Id.*

[58] *See* OAC 3745-1-05(D)(1)(a) - (k).

review requirements if certain criteria are met.[59] The Director may lower water quality on a temporary basis whenever he determines the existence of an emergency that requires immediate action to protect public health and welfare.[60]

3.7 Mixing Zones

The methodology for establishing mixing zones (both thermal and nonthermal) is set out in the Ohio Administrative Code. Under the regulations, both types of mixing zones must preserve the vitality of the established aquatic community of the receiving waters. Mixing zones of either type are not allowed to include State Resource Waters in lakes or reservoirs (except Lake Erie). In addition, thermal zones are prohibited in cold water habitat and exceptional warmwater habitat water courses.[61]

3.8 Review Of Standards

Under the Clean Water Act, a state's water quality standards must be reviewed every three years. During the review process, additional or more stringent standards (in the form of either new standards or a change in the use designation) may be developed.[62]

Major provisions in Ohio's water quality standards deal with specific numeric chemical criteria; biological criteria; aquatic life, water supply, and recreational use designations; aquatic life criteria calculation procedures for parameters not subject to specific numeric criteria; aquatic life whole-effluent toxicity standards; antidegradation; mixing zone criteria; analytical methods; and variances.

3.9 Section 304(*l*) Toxics Control Program

Section 304(*l*) of the Clean Water Act,[63] requires states to develop lists of waters within their jurisdictions that cannot reasonably be expected to attain or maintain

---

[59] *See* OAC 3745-1-05(D)(3) - (4), (6).

[60] OAC 3745-1-05(D)(5).

[61] OAC 3745-1-06.

[62] 33 USC § 1313(c)(1), (2); *see* ORC § 6111.041.

[63] 33 USC § 1314(*l*).

water quality standards, to identify specific point sources and amounts of toxic pollutants, and to develop individual control strategies ("ICSs") to reduce the discharges from these point sources through establishing effluent limitations and water quality standards to achieve compliance with applicable standards. If a state fails to submit, or U.S. EPA does not approve, a list or an ICS, U.S. EPA is required to develop such a list or implement an ICS, in cooperation with the state and after opportunity for public comment.[64]

Accordingly, early in 1989 Ohio EPA submitted, and U.S. EPA has since approved, the State's lists of waters unable to attain or maintain water quality standards due to both point or nonpoint sources, including both those waters that could not meet standards for any conventional, nonconventional, or toxic pollutant, as well as those that have failed to attain state numeric water quality standards under Section 303(c)(2)(B) of the Clean Water Act[65] for the toxic pollutants listed under Section 307(a)(1) of the Act.[66]

3.10 Great Lakes Initiative

Amendments to the Clean Water Act in 1990[67] required U.S. EPA to promulgate water quality guidance for the Great Lakes System, which includes the five Great Lakes and their connecting channels, along with streams, rivers, and other bodies of water within the drainage basin of the lakes.[68]

In 1995, U.S. EPA published the "Final Water Quality Guidance for the Great Lakes System" – commonly known as the Great Lakes Initiative ("GLI")[69] – setting out elements that each of the eight states bordering the lakes must incorporate into its water pollution control programs. Although the GLI directed the states to adopt uniform water quality standards that form the basis for controlling discharges of pollutants from industrial and municipal facilities, it gave the states flexibility in determining how to meet the standards.

---

[64] *Id.*

[65] 33 USC § 1313(c)(2)(B).

[66] 33 USC § 1317(a)(1).

[67] Pub. L. 101-596, 104 STAT. 3000-3004 (1990).

[68] 33 USC § 1268(c)(2).

[69] *See* 60 *Fed. Reg.* 14366 (Mar. 23, 1995), codified at 40 CFR Part 132.

A major innovation in the GLI is the use of bioaccumulation factors ("BAFs") in calculating wildlife and human health criteria. The BAFs are used to account for the property of certain chemicals to concentrate at higher levels in the food chain than may be found in the water itself. Historically, most states, as well as U.S. EPA, have considered only bioconcentration factors ("BCFs") in the uptake from the water, not the food chain. In addition to establishing numerical limits on toxic pollutants, the GLI sets out minimum requirements for antidegradation and implementation procedures.[70]

Pursuant to U.S. EPA's GLI guidance, Ohio EPA adopted water quality standards for the Lake Erie basin (involving parts or all of thirty-five northern Ohio counties), and other water quality rules that impact rivers and streams statewide. The rules are set out in Chapters 3745-1, 3745-2, and 3745-33 of the Ohio Administrative Code.

Chapter 3745-1 includes definitions, the antidegradation rule for the Lake Erie basin, bioaccumulative chemicals of concern, limitations on mixing zones, and specific water quality criteria for the drainage basin. The chapter also incorporates GLI methodologies for developing aquatic life criteria, deriving BAFs, and developing human health criteria and wildlife criteria.

Rules in Chapter 3745-2 outline implementation procedures for Ohio's water pollution control program. These critical rules govern the development of water quality-based effluent limitations, the calculation of wasteload allocations, the determination of reasonable potential to exceed water quality standards, and the calculation of total maximum daily loads. While those rules were initially associated with GLI, many of these procedures apply statewide, and not just to the Lake Erie basin.

NPDES permit provisions are contained in Chapter 3745-33, which includes a rule on pollutant minimization programs and adds provisions on establishing final limitations for whole effluent toxicity, variances from water quality standards, and how to deal with water quality-based effluent limitations below quantification levels.

---

[70] *Id.*

4.0 NPDES PERMITS

Ohio's federally approved NPDES program has been in place since 1974. Under the provisions of Chapter 3745-33 of the Ohio Administrative Code and pursuant to Chapter 6111 of the Ohio Revised Code, the Director of Ohio EPA issues permits for point source discharges that are in compliance with authorized discharge levels or that may include a schedule that will bring the point source into compliance with new or lower levels.[71] "Point source" is defined as "any discernible, confined and discrete conveyance, including but not limited to any pipe, ditch, channel, tunnel, conduit, well, discrete fissure, container, rolling stock, concentrated animal feeding operation, or vessel or other floating craft, from which pollutants are or may be discharged."[72]

No person – including a publicly owned treatment works ("POTW") – may discharge any pollutant from a point source in Ohio to surface waters of the State without obtaining an NPDES permit.[73] "Waters of the state" means all streams, lakes, ponds, marshes, watercourses, waterways, wells, springs, irrigation systems, drainage systems, and all other bodies or accumulations of water, surface and underground, natural or artificial, that are situated wholly or partly within, or border upon, Ohio, or are within its jurisdiction, except those private waters that do not combine or effect a junction with natural surface or underground waters.[74] Certain types of discharges do not require an NPDES permit and are based on the exemptions provided in the federal regulations.[75]

Ohio EPA reviews and reissues NPDES permits on a "watershed" basis. That is, all major NPDES permits within a single watershed or drainage basin are reissued in a single year, to facilitate the collection and evaluation of adequate monitoring data within the receiving streams. Minor permits are reissued at time of expiration. Under the watershed permitting system, Ohio EPA reissues approximately one-fifth of all existing permits each year, consolidates field survey activities, and evaluates the interaction of multiple discharges within a single watershed.

---

[71] OAC 3745-33-01(Y).

[72] OAC 3745-33-01(AA).

[73] OAC 3745-33-02(A).

[74] ORC § 6111.01(H); OAC 3745-33-01(UU).

[75] OAC Chapter 3745-33-02; *compare* 40 CFR 122.3.

4.1 Application

Initial NPDES applications must be filed on Ohio EPA approved forms at least 180 days prior to commencement of the discharge.[76] Applications for renewal of a permit must be filed 180 days prior to the expiration date of the existing permit.[77] Action by Ohio EPA on either type of application is required within 180 days of receipt of the complete application package, including plans, specifications, and construction schedules.[78] Final permits are subject to review and approval by U.S. EPA, and may be challenged in accordance with the rules of procedure set out in Chapter 3745-47 of the Administrative Code.[79] While Ohio EPA is required to act on an application within 180 days, this requirement applies only to complete applications. Ohio EPA typically requests additional information from an applicant prior to determining that an application is complete. In the case of permit renewals, the failure of Ohio EPA to act does not require the discharge to stop. The applicant only must continue to meet the effluent limits in the expired permit to remain in compliance.

4.2 Criteria For Issuance

Issuance of an Ohio NPDES permit is contingent on a finding by the Ohio EPA Director that the authorized discharge levels for all pollutants in the permit are not being exceeded, the discharge is in compliance with the authorized levels, and there are adequate provisions for monitoring to collect any additional information required by Ohio EPA.[80] If an applicant cannot meet these requirements, the Director still may grant a permit, incorporating a satisfactory schedule of compliance as a condition of the permit.[81] Each

[76] OAC 3745-33-03(A) - (B). *See* http://www.epa.state.oh.us/dsw/permits/permits.html.

[77] OAC 3745-33-04(C).

[78] OAC 3745-33-04(B).

[79] OAC 3745-33-04(A)(2)(c).

[80] OAC 3745-33-04(A)(1).

[81] OAC 3745-33-05(F)(2)(c).

permit expires on a date indicated in the permit, and no permit is issued for more than five years.[82]

4.2.1 General Permit Conditions

Each NPDES permit issued by Ohio EPA contains certain general conditions in addition to the authorized discharge levels, either as concentration limits or mass limits. These conditions establish reporting and notification requirements; data monitoring and recording requirements; provisions for Ohio EPA entry and inspection; maintenance and operation requirements; personnel requirements; and provisions for permit modification, suspension, or revocation.[83] There are additional reporting and compliance requirements for a POTW permittee.[84]

4.2.2 Final Or Interim Limitations

When issuing a permit, the Ohio EPA Director may establish interim effluent limitations for purposes of allowing an applicant a sufficient period of time to meet final limitations. Interim effluent limitations are set at levels representing the current maximum level of discharge.[85] Final limitations are those specified in the permit as the maximum levels of pollutants that may be discharged to ensure compliance with applicable water quality standards, effluent limitations,[86] antidegradation standards, and any more stringent requirements necessary to comply with either an area-wide waste treatment management plan or any other State or federal law or regulation.[87] Interim limitations are discharge levels authorized only for the period of a compliance program.[88]

---

[82] OAC 3745-33-04(F).

[83] OAC 3745-33-08(A)(1) - (9), (11) - (12).

[84] OAC 3745-33-08(A)(10).

[85] OAC 3745-33-05(B)

[86] Applicable effluent limitations are the national technology-based effluent limitations and guidelines adopted by U.S. EPA pursuant to Sections 301 and 302 of the Act, 33 USC §§ 1311, 1312; national standards of performance for new sources pursuant to Section 306 of the Act, 33 USC § 1316; and national toxic and pretreatment effluent limitations pursuant to Section 307 of the Act, 33 USC § 1317. OAC 3745-33-05(A)(1)(b).

[87] OAC 3745-33-05(A)(1).

[88] OAC 3745-33-05(B).

Dischargers whose effluent is suspected to produce toxic effects will be required to perform bioassay studies on effluent and to initiate toxicity reduction programs where toxicity problems are confirmed.[89] Whole Effluent Technology ("WET") testing is frequently included in the permit to establish the frequency of toxicity testing.

4.3 Modification / Transfer / Revocation

4.3.1 Modification

Modification of a permit may be requested by the permittee and will be approved if the Ohio EPA Director finds that the permit as modified will comply with all applicable State and federal laws, and that (1) it would have been issued as modified if current information had been available at the time of issuance; (2) valid cause for the revision exists over which the permittee had little or no control; or (3) a good faith modification in the nature of the operation was made. The U.S. EPA Regional Administrator may object to a proposed modification within thirty days of being notified by the Director.[90]

4.3.2 Transfer

Ohio NPDES permits are transferable, provided that a sixty-day advance written notice is given to Ohio EPA. The Director may deny the transfer on a finding that it would jeopardize compliance with terms and conditions of the permit. The decision by the Director must include written notice to the original permittee and the proposed transferee.[91]

4.3.3 Revocation

The Director may revoke a permit at any time upon finding a violation of any applicable laws, rules, regulations, or permit terms or conditions. The Director must provide notification of the proposed revocation to the permittee and provide an opportunity for a hearing in accordance with Ohio's Administrative Procedure Act.[92]

---

[89] OAC 3745-33-07(B).

[90] OAC 3745-33-04(D)(2).

[91] OAC 3745-33-04(E).

[92] OAC 3745-33-04(G).

4.4 Storm Water Regulation

Storm water discharges are regulated by U.S. EPA as a component of the NPDES program. With the enactment of the Water Quality Act of 1987,[93] the Administrator of U.S. EPA was required to promulgate regulations governing storm water discharges associated with industrial activity and separate municipal storm sewers serving populations of 100,000 or more ("Phase I"). The Phase I regulations were promulgated on November 16, 1990, and became effective one month later.[94] On December 8, 1999, U.S. EPA expanded its coverage of sources of storm water discharges from additional sources to include small municipalities and small construction sites ("Phase II").[95]

4.4.1 General Provisions Of Phase I For Industrial Activities

Generally, the regulations require that certain facilities submit either group or individual applications for storm water discharge permits by established deadlines. A facility must satisfy two criteria to be subject to the regulations: it must have a storm water discharge "associated with industrial activity"; and the discharge must flow to either surface waters or a separate storm sewer system. Discharges to a combined system (those sewer systems receiving combined sanitary and storm water flows) were specifically exempted from permitting under Phase I.[96]

4.4.2 Discharges Associated With Industrial Activity

A storm water discharge associated with industrial activity is a discharge from any type of conveyance used for collecting and conveying storm water that is directly related to manufacturing, processing, or raw material storage areas at an industrial plant.[97] The federal regulations provide a detailed description of such discharges in addition to articulating eleven specific categories of facilities subject to regulation:[98]

---

93 Pub. L. 100-4, 100 STAT. 7 (1987).

94 55 *Fed. Reg.* 48062 (Nov. 16, 1990), codified at 40 CFR 122.26.

95 64 *Fed. Reg.* 68721 (Dec. 8, 1999), codified at 40 CFR 122.30 - .37.

96 40 CFR 122.26(a)(7).

97 40 CFR 122.26(b)(14).

98 *See* 40 CFR 122.26(b)(14)(i) - (xi).

(1) facilities subject to national effluent limitation guidelines;

(2) heavy industrial facilities classified in SIC codes 24 (except 2434), 26 (except 265 and 267), 28 (except 283), 29, 311, 32 (except 323), 33, 3441, and 373; these codes include lumber, paper mills, chemical manufacturing, petroleum products, rubber, leather tanning and finishing, stone, clay and concrete, enameled iron and metal sanitary ware, and ship and boat manufacturing facilities;

(3) facilities in SIC codes 10-14, active and inactive mining and oil and gas operations with contaminated storm water discharges;

(4) vehicle maintenance, equipment cleaning, and airport de-icing operations at certain transportation related facilities;

(5) treatment works with a design flow of 1.0 mgd or more or those required to have a pretreatment program;

(6) hazardous waste treatment, storage, or disposal facilities;

(7) landfills, land application sites, and open dumps that receive industrial wastes;

(8) recycling facilities in SIC codes 5015 and 5093, which include metal scrap yards, battery reclaimers, salvage yards, and automobile junkyards;

(9) steam electric power generating facilities (including coal handling sites);

(10) construction activities except for disturbances of less than five acres which are not part of a larger common plan of development or sale;

(11) facilities where materials or industrial activities are exposed to storm water, and which are classified in SIC codes 20, 21, 22, 23, 2434, 25, 265, 267, 27, 283, 285, 30, 31 (except 311), 323, 34 (except 3441), 35, 36, 37 (except 373), 38, 39, and 4221-4225.

Facilities in these categories must apply for a storm water permit in one of three ways: submit an individual permit application; submit a group application; or file a

Notice of Intent ("NOI") to be covered by an appropriate general permit.[99] Ohio EPA was delegated the general permit program on August 17, 1992 with the original general permits being issued in October 1992. The Agency adopted administrative regulations for a general permit program for discharges associated with industrial activity,[100] and also elected to utilize a general permit to regulate discharges associated with construction activities involving disturbances greater than five acres.

Facilities that either do not qualify for coverage under a general permit or are voluntarily seeking a permit through the individual application process are required to submit a detailed application with analytical data from samples of storm water discharged from the facility. The application must include, but is not limited to: a site map showing topography/drainage areas; an estimate of impervious surfaces and total area drained by each outfall; a description of materials exposed to storm water and current management practices; a certification of evaluation or testing of outfalls for non-storm water discharges; the incidence of significant leaks or spills in the last three years; and certain designated quantitative testing data.[101]

4.4.3 Development And Construction Projects Under Phase I

New land development or construction projects that disturb more than five acres are subject to Phase I regulations. The requirements are more lenient under the Ohio general permit. Owners or operators of these projects must submit a NOI to obtain coverage under the general storm water discharge permit. The notice must provide certain information including: the location and nature of the construction activity; the total area to be excavated; the proposed measures to control pollution; an estimate of runoff coefficient and increase in impervious surface after construction is completed; and the name of the receiving water. The application must be submitted at least forty-five days before the date on which construction is to commence.[102]

---

[99] 40 CFR 122.26(b)(14), (a)(6).

[100] OAC Chapter 3745-38.

[101] OAC 3745-33-03-04.

[102] *See* NPDES Permit No. OHR10000, Ohio General Permit for Storm Water Discharges Associated With Construction Activities, http://www.state.oh.us/dsw/documents.const.pdf.

To obtain coverage under the Ohio general permit for storm water discharges at construction sites, the owner or operator of the site must develop a storm water pollution prevention plan ("SWP3") and submit a NOI to Ohio EPA. Once Ohio EPA has acknowledged receipt of the NOI, it is important for the construction activities to be conducted in accordance with the SWP3, particularly the Best Management Practices ("BMPs") designed to reduce and/or prevent the discharge of contaminated storm water from the construction site.[103]

4.4.4 Notification To Separate Municipal Systems

There are special reporting requirements for facilities discharging storm water associated with industrial activity to large and medium separate municipal storm sewer systems. These facilities must notify the operator of the system of the intended discharge 180 days before commencing the discharge. The notification must contain the following information: the name of the facility; a contact person and phone number; the location of the discharge; a description (and SIC code) of the principal products or services; and the number of any existing NPDES permit.[104] Ohio communities that have been preliminarily identified as having large or medium municipal separate storm sewer systems are: Akron, Cincinnati, Cleveland, Columbus, Dayton, Toledo, and Youngstown.[105]

4.4.5 Permit Application Requirements For Municipal Systems

Large and medium municipal separate storm sewer systems ("MS4s") also are required to apply for storm water discharge permits. These systems must submit a two-part application, similar to the group application for individual dischargers.[106] Cincinnati, Cleveland, Columbus, and Toledo are considered large municipal storm water systems. Akron, Dayton, and Youngstown have been identified as medium storm water systems.[107]

---

[103] *Id.*

[104] 40 CFR 122.26(a)(4).

[105] 40 CFR Part 122, Appendices F and G.

[106] 40 CFR 122.26(d).

[107] 40 CFR Part 122, Appendices F and G.

Part 1 of the storm water permit application for a municipal separate system must include general information such as the facility location, contact person, and a description of existing legal authority to control discharges to the storm water system.[108] Municipal systems also will be required to submit information concerning each discharge source including: existing use ordinances for controlling non-storm water discharges to POTWs covering the same service area; topographic maps showing all system outfalls; and existing land uses and runoff coefficients, population densities, and major structural controls.[109] Each large and medium separate storm sewer system must characterize discharges and include qualitative and quantitative data for storm water discharges in the permit application.[110] The application also must include the results of a field screening for illicit connections to the system.[111] Finally, in the Part 1 application, the municipal system must provide a description of the fiscal resources necessary to complete Part 2 of the application process.[112]

Part 2 of the process for municipal systems includes the submission of detailed quantitative data taken from five to ten representative outfalls during three storm events.[113] The municipal systems must sample for a broad range of pollutants including toxic metals, cyanides, phenols, organics, and conventional pollutants.[114] For the duration of the permit, the system must propose a management plan that addresses structural controls to minimize discharges from residential and commercial areas, a detection system to eliminate illicit discharges and illegal dumping, monitoring and control requirements for discharges from landfills, hazardous waste management areas and facilities reporting under Section 313 of the Superfund Amendment and Reauthorization Act ("SARA"),[115] and a system of best

---

[108] 40 CFR 122.26(d)(1)(i) - (ii).

[109] 40 CFR 122.26(d)(1)(iii).

[110] 40 CFR 122.26(d)(1)(iv).

[111] 40 CFR 122.26(d)(1)(iv)(D).

[112] 40 CFR 122.26(d)(1)(vi).

[113] 40 CFR 122.26(d)(2)(iii)(A).

[114] 40 CFR 122.26(d)(2)(iii)(A)(3).

[115] 42 USC § 11023.

management control practices for construction sites.[116] The Part 2 application also must contain a fiscal analysis for each year of the permit term.[117]

4.4.6 Requirements Under Phase II of the Storm Water Program

On December 8, 1999, U.S. EPA promulgated rules for Phase II of the storm water program. The rules expanded coverage under the storm water program to include small municipalities, small construction sites, and municipally owned industrial facilities.[118] In addition, Phase II rules include a program for industrial sources to certify that their operations do not impact storm water quality. This "no exposure certification" will exempt the industrial source from coverage under either Phase I or Phase II regulation.[119] All entities covered by the Phase II program must obtain coverage by March 10, 2003.[120]

4.4.6.1 Regulation of Small Municipalities Under Phase II Rules

There are about 280 municipalities in Ohio that operate MS4s that will be regulated under the Phase II program, including the large and medium systems first regulated under Phase I. It is important to note that the definition of a municipal separate storm sewer does not include combined sewer systems that transport both sewage and storm water flows.[121] Consequently, the Phase II rules do not address combined sewer overflows ("CSOs") created by wet weather events.

Under the Phase II program, MS4s will need to show measurable and cost-effective improvements in storm water quality through the implementation of BMPs in a storm water management plan. Minimum control measures include:[122]

- public education and outreach;
- public involvement and participation;
- elimination of illicit discharges;

---

[116] 40 CFR 122.26(d)(2)(iv).

[117] 40 CFR 122.26(d)(2)(vi).

[118] 40 CFR 122.26, .30 - .36.

[119] 40 CFR 122.26(8).

[120] 40 CFR 122.26(e)(9).

[121] 40 CFR 122.26(b)(8).

[122] 40 CFR 122.34(b)

- construction site storm water runoff control;
- post-construction storm water management; and
- pollution prevention and good housekeeping.

Ohio EPA may waive these requirements for small MS4s serving less than 1,000 people if storm water controls are not needed, based upon a TMDL wasteload allocation analysis, or less than 10,000 people if the Agency has evaluated all receiving streams and determined that storm water controls are not necessary. Both waivers depend on MS4 discharges that do not impact water quality as determined under the TMDL program.[123]

4.4.6.2 Small Construction Sites

With the arrival of the Phase II rules, construction sites larger than one acre will require a permit. The program provides exemptions for construction sites that either will not lead to significant sediment erosion or will not impact water quality as demonstrated by compliance with an appropriate TMDL allocation. Ohio EPA is expected to issue a general permit covering construction activities.

4.4.6.3 Municipally Owned Industrial Facilities

Under the Phase II rules, municipally owned industrial facilities such as waste water treatment facilities that discharge more than one million gallons a day are required to obtain a permit by March 10, 2003.[124]

4.4.7 No Exposure Certification

Facilities covered under the Phase I program may be able to forego permit coverage if they are able to satisfactorily certify that storm water run-off at the facility is not exposed to any sources of pollutants. The "no exposure" certification requires that all industrial activities and materials are protected to prevent exposure to rain, snow, snowmelt, and runoff. Certain items – drums, tanks, vehicles – do not require a protective structure provided they are in good repair and do not leak. Final products, with the exception of those

[123] 40 CFR 122.32(c) - (e).

[124] 40 CFR 122.26(b)(14)(ix).

that can be mobilized by precipitation such as rock salt, also are exempt.[125] Ohio EPA currently uses U.S. EPA's "no exposure" certification form and checklist for this program.

5.0 PRETREATMENT PROGRAM

Releases of industrial wastewater into a POTW, referred to as "indirect discharges," are regulated under the Ohio's pretreatment program, established by the authority of Sections 6111.03 and 6111.042 of the Revised Code, and published in Chapters 3745-3 and 3745-36 of the Administrative Code. Approved by U.S. EPA in 1983, Ohio's pretreatment program closely follows the federal model set out in 40 CFR Part 403.

A local pretreatment program must be approved by Ohio EPA before it can be enforced by the local POTW. In the absence of an approved local program, Ohio EPA will administer the general State pretreatment standards set out in Chapter 3745-3.[126]

Any POTW having a daily design flow of five million gallons or more that receives, from industrial users, pollutants that pass through or interfere with its operations, or that are otherwise subject to the national categorical pretreatment standards, is required to have a pretreatment program that meets both federal requirements published at 40 CFR Part 403 and Ohio's pretreatment rules in Chapter 3745-3.[127] Ohio EPA may require a POTW with a daily design flow of less than five million gallons to establish a pretreatment program if the Agency finds that such a program is necessary to prevent interference or pass through.[128] "Interference" means a discharge that alone or in conjunction with another discharge inhibits or disrupts a POTW's operations and violates the POTW's NPDES permit or other applicable regulation.[129] "Pass through" is defined as a discharge that exits the POTW in quantities or concentrations that alone or in conjunction with another discharge violates the POTW's NPDES permit.[130]

---

[125] 40 CFR 122.26(g)(2).

[126] OAC 3745-3-02, -03.

[127] OAC 3745-3-03(A)(1).

[128] OAC 3745-3-03(A)(2).

[129] OAC 3745-3-01(I).

[130] OAC 3745-3-01(O).

5.1 Pretreatment Standards

Industrial wastewater discharges to a POTW with a pretreatment program are subject to both general and industry-specific (or "categorical") pretreatment requirements. These standards are designed to prevent releases into a POTW of any pollutant that will interfere with, pass through, or otherwise be incompatible with the operation of a POTW, and to improve wastewater and sludge recycling and reclamation opportunities.[131]

5.1.1 General Pretreatment Standards

General pretreatment standards prohibit the release of any pollutant that creates a fire or explosion; causes corrosive structural damage; has a pH lower than 5.0; obstructs sewer flow; discharges at a problematic flow rate or concentration level; creates excessive heat; causes interference or pass through; results in toxic gases, vapors, or fumes; or is trucked or hauled, except at designated discharge points.[132]

5.1.2 Categorical Pretreatment Standards

Ohio has incorporated by reference the national categorical pretreatment standards established by U.S. EPA.[133] The standards apply unless an enforceable alternative limit to the national categorical standard applies under provisions set out in 40 CFR Part 403 for removal credits, combined wastestream formulas, a fundamentally different factors variance, net/gross calculations, or equivalent limitations.[134] Such an alternative limit is enforceable only if compliance is required by local ordinance or contract administered under an approved pretreatment program, or if ordered by Ohio EPA.[135]

5.1.3 Reporting And Testing Requirements

Ohio's pretreatment program sets out extensive notification, reporting, and recordkeeping requirements for both existing industrial users and new sources. Included are

---

[131] OAC 3745-3-02(B).

[132] OAC 3745-3-04.

[133] OAC Chapter 3745-3; *see* 40 CFR 403.6, 405 - 424. Ohio EPA repealed the State categorical standards, OAC 3745-3-10 through -30, effective May 2001.

[134] OAC 3745-3-09(I)(1).

[135] OAC 3745-3-09(I)(2).

a baseline report that must be submitted within 180 days of a national categorical pretreatment standard's effective date or within 180 days of the final administrative decision on the applicability of a pretreatment standard, whichever is later; an initial compliance report due within ninety days after final compliance with applicable categorical standards, or for a new source, following commencement of releases into a POTW; and periodic compliance monitoring reports.[136] Sampling and analysis performed in preparation of any report are to be conducted in accordance with techniques prescribed in 40 CFR Part 136, as amended, and other procedures specified in Ohio's rule.[137]

Upon discovery of any slug loading, an industrial user must immediately notify the POTW and follow up with a written report within five business days to the POTW and the appropriate Ohio EPA District Office.[138] "Slug loading" refers to any pollutant, including oxygen demanding pollutants, released in a discharge at a flow rate and/or pollutant concentration that may cause interference in the POTW.[139]

The regulations provide for confidentiality of certain information obtained under the reporting and recordkeeping requirements, including information that would divulge methods or processes entitled to protection as trade secrets.[140]

5.2 Indirect Discharge Permits

OAC Chapter 3745-36 establishes, as a part of Ohio's pretreatment program, permitting requirements for the indirect discharges of nondomestic wastewater into a POTW.[141] To assure compliance with pretreatment standards, Ohio EPA will issue an indirect discharge permit to any industrial user not under the regulatory jurisdiction of a POTW with an approved pretreatment program.[142]

---

136 OAC 3745-3-06(B) - (E).

137 OAC 3745-3-06(H).

138 OAC 3745-3-05.

139 *See* OAC 3745-3-04(B)(4).

140 OAC 3745-3-07.

141 OAC 3745-36-01.

142 OAC 3745-36-03(A), (B). If a POTW's pretreatment program has been withdrawn or revoked, all industrial users of the POTW are required to apply for a permit within ninety days of the withdrawal or revocation. OAC 3745-36-03(C).

5.2.1 Application

Policies and procedures for the indirect discharge permit program are similar to those for the NPDES permit program discussed in Part 4.0 of this chapter. Both initial and renewal applications must be filed on Ohio EPA forms 180 days prior to commencement of a discharge or expiration of the permit, respectively.[143] Permits are effective for fixed terms not to exceed five years.[144]

Applications for indirect discharge permits and requests for modifications are acted upon and may be challenged in accordance with the provisions of Chapter 3745-47 of the Administrative Code.[145]

5.2.2 Criteria For Issuance

Criteria for issuing an indirect discharge permit include compliance of discharge levels with the pretreatment effluent limitations, adequate monitoring, and performance tests as required.[146] In addition, the applicant must submit a written authorization from the POTW.[147] A permit application will be denied if the discharge would violate any of the general pretreatment standards discussed above or if it will interfere with, pass through, or be incompatible with the POTW's treatment processes.[148]

5.2.3 Permit-By-Rule

If an industrial user is not under the jurisdiction of a POTW with an approved pretreatment program, is not a significant industrial user, and is in compliance with pretreatment regulations, the user is deemed to have an indirect discharge permit-by-rule.[149] "Significant industrial user" means: all industrial users subject to categorical pretreatment standards; and any other user that has an average daily discharge of 25,000 gallons or more of process wastewater (exclusive of sanitary wastewater, noncontact cooling water, and

---

143 OAC 3745-36-03(D), (G). *See* http://www.epa.state.oh.us/dsw/permits/permits.html.

144 OAC 3745-36-03(H).

145 OAC 3745-36-03(L).

146 OAC 3745-36-03(F).

147 OAC 3745-36-03(E).

148 OAC 3745-36-03(F)(2).

boiler blowdown wastewater), contributes a process wastestream making up five percent or more of the average dry weather hydraulic or organic capacity of the treatment plant, or is designated as such by the Director on the basis that the user has a reasonable potential for adversely affecting the POTW's operation or violating any pretreatment standard or requirement.[150]

5.2.4 Modification / Transfer / Revocation

5.2.4.1 Modification

Indirect discharge permits may be modified; however, only the conditions subject to modification are reopened.[151] Causes for modification include facility or activity alterations, new information, new regulations, issuance of a variance, incorporation of an applicable toxic effluent standard or prohibition, correction of technical errors, and when required by reopener conditions in a permit.[152] Modifications to require more frequent monitoring and reporting or to allow for a change in ownership are considered minor and may be made without following the rules of procedure under Chapter 3745-47 of the Administrative Code.[153] Requests for modification must be filed on appropriate Ohio EPA forms.[154]

5.2.4.2 Transfer

Indirect discharge permits are transferable to a new owner/operator only through a minor permit modification to identify the new permittee and incorporate any other requirements deemed necessary by the Ohio EPA Director to effect the transfer.[155] The notice must include a written agreement between the old and new permittees containing a specific date for the transfer.[156]

---

149 OAC 3745-36-06(A).

150 OAC 3745-36-02(U).

151 OAC 3745-36-03(I)(1).

152 OAC 3745-36-03(I)(2).

153 OAC 3745-36-03(I)(3).

154 OAC 3745-36-03(I)(4). *See* http://www.epa.state.oh.us/dsw/permits/permits.html.

155 OAC 3745-36-03(J).

156 OAC 3745-36-03(J); *see* OAC 3745-36-03(I)(3)(b)(iii).

5.2.4.3 Revocation

Indirect discharge permits are revocable for reasons of noncompliance; failure to disclose information or misrepresentation of facts; loss of classification as a significant industrial user; upon a finding that the permitted activity endangers human health, POTW worker safety, or the environment, and can be regulated to acceptable levels only by permit revocation; upon revocation of the written authorization issued by the POTW; when the POTW is damaged or disabled; or the authorized discharge has been permanently discontinued.[157]

6.0 PERMITS TO INSTALL

Ohio requires a permit to install ("PTI") or plan approval for any new project that involves the "installation" of any new "disposal system" or facilities for the collection, treatment, or disposal of sewage or industrial wastes.[158] In the rules promulgated by Ohio EPA pursuant to these statutory provisions,[159] no new disposal system or modification of an existing system is allowed without prior approval of the Director.[160] "Disposal system" is defined in the regulations to include a treatment works for disposing of industrial waste.[161] "Installation" means the construction of a treatment works.[162] "Modification" is defined to include any physical change or change in method of operation for a treatment works to allow processing of water pollutants in increased quantities or higher concentrations, or of a materially different character. The addition of a new connection to a public sewerage system is not considered a modification.[163]

---

[157] OAC 3745-36-03(K).

[158] ORC § 6111.44 - .45.

[159] OAC Chapter 3745-31.

[160] OAC 3745-31-02(A).

[161] OAC 3745-31-01(X).

[162] OAC 3745-31-01(LL).

[163] OAC 3745-31-01(VV)(1)(c).

6.1 Application

An application for a PTI or plan approval is made on Ohio EPA forms and must provide adequate information for the Director to determine whether the criteria for issuance or approval are met.[164] Action on the application is required within 180 days of the filing of a complete application, and is governed by rules of procedure set out in Chapter 3745-47 of the Administrative Code.[165]

6.2 Criteria For Issuance

Issuance of a PTI or a plan approval is based on a finding that the proposed activity will not violate any applicable laws, including ambient water quality standards or effluent standards established by State or federal authorities.[166] In addition, the installation or modification is required to use BAT, if appropriate, and to meet other conditions necessary to ensure protection of the environment.[167] The social, economic, and environmental impact of the permit may be considered in the Director's decision.[168]

If the application involves more than one disposal system controlled by the same owner/operator and located in the same county, or several pollutants in a single system, the Director may issue a single permit in either case.[169]

6.3 Termination / Revocation

A PTI or plan approval terminates eighteen months after issuance if installation or modification has not begun, or if the permittee has not contracted to undertake either activity, unless the Ohio EPA Director approves an extension of up to twelve months.[170] Both may be revoked at any time for violations of any applicable law.[171]

---

[164] OAC 3745-31-04(A). *See* http://www.epa.state.oh.us/dsw/permits/permits.html.

[165] OAC 3745-31-05(H).

[166] OAC 3745-31-05(A)(1), (2).

[167] OAC 3745-31-05(A)(3), (D).

[168] OAC 3745-31-05(C).

[169] OAC 3745-31-02(D).

[170] OAC 3745-31-06. A plan approval also may be terminated within six months of approval of detail plans, whichever is later.

[171] OAC 3745-31-07.

7.0 SECTION 401 CERTIFICATION / WETLANDS

Section 401 of the Clean Water Act requires any applicant for a federal permit or license to conduct any activities, including construction, that may result in any discharge to the navigable waters, to obtain from an appropriate state agency a certification that the proposed activity will comply with all applicable effluent limitations, new source performance standards, water quality standards, and toxic pollutant standards.[172] A Section 401 certification typically is sought simultaneously with the federal permit or license. The state procedure for granting or denying certification must include public notice of the application, and provide an opportunity for public hearings, if appropriate. Certification must be granted or denied within one year, or the right to issue the certification is deemed to be waived. If certification is denied, no federal license or permit for the proposed activity may be issued.[173]

7.1 Activities Requiring Federal Permits And State Certification

The most common activity governed by a federal permit or license for which state certification must be obtained is the dredging or filling of navigable waters. Pursuant to Section 404 of the Clean Water Act, the Secretary of the Army, through the Chief of the U.S. Army Corps of Engineers ("Corps"), is authorized to issue permits for the discharge of "dredged or fill material" into navigable waters at specified disposal locations.[174] The Corps also issues permits under Section 10 of the Rivers and Harbors Act to allow excavation, construction, and maintenance within navigable waterways.[175] Construction of boat ramps, docks, dams, dikes, or stream diversion or channelization structures, and the placement of riprap or fill for erosion control or in wetlands, require a federal permit, and, accordingly, also must receive a Section 401 certification from Ohio EPA.[176] Although states may receive

---

[172] 33 USC § 1341(a).

[173] *Id.*

[174] 33 USC § 1344.

[175] 33 USC § 403.

[176] OAC 3745-32-02.

approval and delegated authority to administer the Section 404 program,[177] Ohio has not been delegated this authority.

7.2 Exempt Activities

Section 404 contains several legislative exemptions from the requirement to obtain a Corps permit for the discharge of dredged and fill material, including (1) discharges from normal farming, ranching, or silvicultural activities such as plowing, seeding, cultivating, minor drainage, harvesting, and soil and water conservation practices; (2) maintenance and emergency repairs of existing structures such as dams, dikes, bridges, riprap, and transportation structures; (3) construction or maintenance of farm ponds or irrigation ditches, and the maintenance of drainage ditches; (4) construction of sedimentation basins on a construction site that does not include placement of fill into navigable waters; (5) construction of farm roads, or forest or temporary mining roads in accordance with best management practices; and (6) activities regulated under an approved state program.[178] These activities likewise would be exempt from the requirement to obtain a Section 401 certification.

7.3 Section 404 / Section 10 Permits

7.3.1 Individual Permits

A permit application for authorization under Section 404 or Section 10 must be filed with the appropriate District Office of the Corps for review. Prior contact with the District Engineer can help resolve issues such as whether the proposed activity qualifies for an exemption or is covered by a general permit. For Section 404 permits, the District Office must issue a public notice within fifteen days of receipt of a completed application, and provide an opportunity for a public hearing.[179] U.S. EPA has the authority to veto the specification of a disposal site in a Section 404 permit, after notice and an opportunity for public hearings, if the discharge would have unacceptable adverse effects on municipal water

---

177 33 USC § 1344(g) - (*l*).

178 33 USC § 1344(f).

179 33 USC § 1344(a).

supplies, fish and shellfish, wildlife, or recreation areas.[180] The issuance of either a Section 404 or Section 10 permit triggers the requirements of the National Environmental Policy Act,[181] and may require the preparation of an environmental impact statement for significant projects.

U.S. EPA and the Corps have developed guidelines to specify acceptable disposal sites for purposes of Section 404.[182] Generally, discharges are not permitted "if there is a practicable alternative to the proposed discharge which would have less adverse impact on the aquatic ecosystem, so long as the alternative does not have other significant adverse environmental consequences."[183] An alternative is "practicable" if it is available and the purposes of the project are achievable after taking into consideration the relative costs of the alternative, existing technology, and logistics in light of the overall purposes of the project.[184] Properties not currently owned by an applicant which could reasonably be obtained, utilized, expanded, or managed in order to fulfill the basic purpose of the proposed activity may be considered.[185] Practicable alternatives are presumed to be available if the proposed activity does not require proximity to or siting within a special aquatic site in order to fulfill its basic purpose, unless clearly demonstrated otherwise.[186] In addition, any alternative that does not involve a discharge to a special aquatic site is presumed to have less adverse impact on an aquatic ecosystem unless clearly demonstrated otherwise.[187] In essence, an individual application for a Section 404 permit must demonstrate that there is no practicable alternative that would result in less adverse impact to the environment.[188]

---

180 33 USC § 1344(c).

181 42 USC §§ 4321 - 4370f.

182 33 USC § 1344(b)(1); 40 CFR Part 230.

183 40 CFR 230.10(a).

184 40 CFR 230.10(a)(2).

185 *Id.*

186 40 CFR 230.10(a)(3).

187 *Id.*

188 40 CFR 230.10.

7.3.2 General Nationwide Permits

Section 404 of the Clean Water Act also authorizes the Corps to issue general permits, on a regional or nationwide basis, for certain activities.[189] The Corps has issued a number of general Nationwide Permits by regulation that authorize routine projects which, separately or cumulatively, will have a minimal adverse impact on water quality.[190] Nationwide Permits have a maximum term of five years.[191]

Certain general Nationwide Permits authorize a particular type of activity without prior notice to the Corps. It is the responsibility of the person undertaking any particular activity to ascertain whether the activity satisfies the terms and conditions of a Nationwide Permit, and whether prior notice to the Corps is required. Informal consultation with the Corps District Office is encouraged.

When prior notification is required by the terms of a Nationwide Permit, the notice must be made in writing, and must supply all the information required by the particular Nationwide Permit.[192] Within thirty days after the notice is received, the District Engineer must either notify the applicant that the notice is incomplete, add specific terms and conditions to the Nationwide Permit in order to minimize any potential adverse effects, or notify the applicant that an individual permit application must be submitted.[193] The Corps retains the discretionary authority to require an individual application for any activity authorized by a Nationwide Permit. If the District Engineer takes no action within thirty days after the notice is received, the applicant can proceed with the proposed activity.[194]

The following activities are currently authorized pursuant to a Nationwide Permit:[195]

(1) the placement of navigation aids and/or regulatory markers approved by the U.S. Coast Guard;

(2) structures in artificial canals in residential developments;

---

[189] 33 USC § 1344(e)(1).

[190] *See generally* 33 CFR Part 330.

[191] 33 USC § 1344(e)(2).

[192] 33 CFR 330.1(e)(1).

[193] 33 CFR 330.1(d) - (e).

[194] 33 CFR 330.1(e)(1).

[195] 67 *Fed. Reg.* 2019 (Jan. 15, 2002).

(3) maintenance of previously authorized structures or fill that will not change their use;

(4) placement of fish and wildlife harvesting, enhancement, or attraction devices or activities, not including impoundments or reefs;

(5) placement of scientific measurement devices, including small weirs or flumes;

(6) core sampling, seismic explorations, and other survey activities;

(7) construction of intake and outfall structures associated with discharges authorized by or exempted from the NPDES permit requirements;

(8) certain structures for the exploration, production, and transportation of oil, gas, and minerals within certain federal leased lands;

(9) structures, buoys, and floats to facilitate moorage of vessels in anchorage or fleeting areas established by the U.S. Coast Guard;

(10) placement of noncommercial single boat mooring buoys;

(11) temporary buoys, markers, and floating docks for special events;

(12) backfill or bedding for utility lines, provided there is no change in preconstruction contours;

(13) certain bank stabilization activities less than 500 feet in length without prior notification, and more than 500 feet in length with prior notification;[196]

(14) fills for road crossings;

(15) construction of bridges approved by the U.S. Coast Guard;

(16) return water from upland dredged material disposal sites;

---

196 Ohio limits bank stabilization activities to less than 1,000 feet under this general permit.

(17) certain hydropower projects;

(18) discharges of less than twenty-five cubic yards or causing the loss of less than 0.10 acre of a special aquatic site, including wetlands;

(19) dredging of less than twenty-five cubic yards except in certain defined areas;

(20) oil spill containment or cleanup procedures subject to the National Contingency Plan;

(21) surface mining activities authorized by a federal or state agency;

(22) discharges or dredging associated with the removal of abandoned vessels or manmade obstructions to navigation;

(23) activities which are categorically exempted from the National Environmental Policy Act because they have no individual or cumulative significant effect on the human environment;

(24) activities permitted under an authorized state administered Section 404 permit program;

(25) discharges necessary to construct structural members for standard pile supported structures, such as piers and docks;

(26) [Reserved];

(27) wetland and riparian restoration and creation activities;

(28) reconfiguration, but not expansion, of existing marinas;

(29) single family housing;

(30) moist soil management for wildlife;

(31) maintenance of existing flood control facilities;

(32) structures or fill undertaken in connection with a settlement or final decree in any completed enforcement action;

(33) temporary construction, access, or dewatering structures in connection with other authorized activities;

(34) cranberry production activities;

(35) maintenance dredging of existing basins;

(36) construction of boat ramps satisfying certain specific criteria;

(37) emergency watershed protection activities and rehabilitation work performed or funded by the Soil Conservation Service or the Forest Service;

(38) work required by a governmental agency in order to contain, stabilize, or remove a release of hazardous or toxic waste materials;

(39) residential, commercial, and institutional developments;

(40) discharges of up to one acre into certain jurisdictional wetlands for foundations or supports for farm buildings on land in crop production prior to December 23, 1985;

(41) reshaping existing drainage ditches;

(42) recreational facilities;

(43) storm water management facilities; and

(44) mining activities.

In addition to prior notification to the District Engineer, some or all of the general conditions prescribed in the regulations may apply to the Nationwide Permits listed above. The general conditions require state certification pursuant to Section 401 of the Clean Water Act, unless prior certification has been granted or waived by the state in which the discharge will occur. They also proscribe activities that would adversely affect aquatic life movement, wild or scenic rivers, endangered species, historic properties, shellfish production or spawning areas, or waterfowl breeding areas. A wetlands delineation is required if any of the proposed activities will be conducted in or affect wetlands.[197]

[197] 67 *Fed. Reg.* 2019 (Jan. 15, 2002).

7.3.3 Special Considerations For Wetlands

Where proposed activities or projects involve areas identified as wetlands, special considerations apply. Wetlands are defined as:[198]

> those areas that are inundated or saturated by surface or ground water at a frequency and duration sufficient to support, and that under normal circumstances do support, a prevalence of vegetation typically adapted for life in saturated soil conditions. Wetlands generally include swamps, marshes, bogs, and similar areas.

Considerable controversy currently surrounds the practical application of this definition. U.S. EPA and the Corps jointly developed a manual to be used to identify and delineate wetlands.[199] The manual relies on three basic criteria: hydrophytic vegetation; hydric soils; and wetland hydrology.

In January 2001, the U.S. Supreme Court restricted the jurisdiction of the Army Corps of Engineers under the Clean Water Act to wetlands adjacent to navigable waters.[200] Following this decision, the Corps was deprived of jurisdiction over "isolated" wetlands – wetlands that do not affect a juncture with navigable waters. Under the Supreme Court decision, regulation of these isolated waters is left to the individual states. The Ohio isolated wetland program is described in Part 8.0 below.

For projects that impact wetlands subject to the jurisdiction of the Army Corps, an applicant must first make the demonstration that no "practicable alternative" exists for the proposed wetland fill.[201] In addition, U.S. EPA and Corps guidelines require the applicant to take "all appropriate and practicable measures to minimize potential harm to the aquatic ecosystem."[202] This "mitigation" requirement includes measures to avoid, minimize, and rectify adverse impacts, measures designed to reduce adverse impacts over time, and compensatory measures to replace unavoidable losses of wetlands.[203] Compensatory measures generally must be undertaken in areas adjacent or contiguous to the discharge site;

---

198 33 CFR 328.3(b); 40 CFR 230.3(t).

199 *Federal Manual for Identifying and Delineating Jurisdictional Wetlands* (1989).

200 Solid Waste Agency of Northern Cook County v. United States Army Corps of Engineers, 531 U.S. 159 (2001).

201 40 CFR 230.10(a).

202 40 CFR 230.12(a)(3)(iii).

203 40 CFR 1508.20; *see also* 40 CFR 230.70 - .77.

however, off-site mitigation also is allowed when on-site mitigation is not practicable. To encourage avoidance rather than compensation, the Corps often requests mitigation to include more acreage than is lost due to the project, with replacement exceeding loss by ratios of up to 2:1. The ratio often varies in accordance with the functional value of the replacement acreage versus the functional value of the filled wetlands.

7.4 State Certification Procedures

A Section 401 certification is required from the state in which a proposed discharge will occur, before a Section 404/Section 10 permit can be issued.[204] The permit application to the Corps constitutes a Section 401 certification request to Ohio EPA.[205] Ohio EPA will not issue a Section 401 certification if the proposed activity will result in the violation of any effluent limitation or water quality standard, or if it will result in short-term or long-term adverse impacts on water quality.[206] The Agency also may impose conditions upon the issuance of a certification, in order to assure adequate protection of water quality.[207]

On January 15, 2002, the Army Corps reissued Nationwide Permits covering the addition of dredge and fill material to waters of the United States.[208] These Nationwide Permits are applicable to wetlands falling within the jurisdiction of the Army Corps. Ohio EPA is currently in the process of reviewing a general 401 Certification for the Nationwide Permits. If Ohio EPA follows its historical approach to certification of Nationwide Permits, the Agency will impose additional limits on impacts to wetlands and streams. Ohio EPA hopes to public notice its draft 401 certification of the Nationwide Permits in April, 2002.

Ohio EPA previously has granted certification to earlier Nationwide Permits with additional conditions. In addition, the Agency has required all applicants for coverage under a Nationwide Permit to submit to Ohio EPA and the Ohio Department of Natural Resources a copy of the pre-activity notification submitted to the Army Corps. This allows

---

204 33 USC § 1341(a).

205 OAC 3745-32-04(A).

206 OAC 3745-32-05(A) - (B).

207 OAC 3745-32-05(C).

208 67 *Fed. Reg.* 2019 (Jan. 15, 2002).

these agencies to request that the District Engineer exercise his discretionary authority to require an individual permit application for the project.

State certifications for projects involving wetlands are particularly scrutinized by Ohio EPA. As part of the development of the antidegradation rule, wetlands are subject to additional requirements and compensatory mitigation.[209] Generally, an applicant for a 401 certification will be required to comply with the general alternatives analysis of the antidegradation rule,[210] and provide mitigation for any impacts. The mitigation requirements are dictated by the quality of wetlands impacted, as the quality is measured in accordance with the Ohio Rapid Assessment Method for wetlands ("ORAM") version 5.0. Mitigation may include the restoration, creation, enhancement, or preservation of wetlands with varying requirements for the acreage and location of the compensatory wetlands.[211] Pursuant to the requirements of Section 401 of the Clean Water Act, the Army Corps cannot issue a permit for the filling of wetlands until Ohio EPA issues or waives the certification requirement. Ohio EPA rules prevent the issuance of a 401 Certification unless the applicant has demonstrated to the satisfaction of the Director that the discharge will not prevent or interfere with attainment of water quality standard or other applicable rules.[212]

8.0 ISOLATED WETLANDS

On January 9, 2001, the U.S. Supreme Court issued a decision striking down the authority of the Army Corps of Engineers to regulate isolated wetlands.[213] As a result, states had to assume responsibility for regulating the dredging and filling of isolated wetlands within their boundaries. Accordingly, Ohio adopted new legislation to create a regulatory program for the oversight of activities that result in the introduction of dredge or fill material to isolated wetlands.[214] This new regulatory program builds upon the current Section 404

---

209 OAC 3745-1-54.

210 OAC 3745-1-05.

211 OAC 3745-1-54(D).

212 OAC 3745-32-05.

213 Solid Waste Agency of Northern Cook County v. United States Army Corps of Engineers, 531 US 159 (2001).

214 HB 231, 124th General Assembly (Eff. July 17, 2001).

permitting program and the Section 401 certification process. In particular, it uses the ORAM for wetlands to conduct a tiered review based upon wetlands quality.

The tiered review requires Ohio EPA to authorize smaller fills of lesser quality wetlands by a general isolated wetland permit. In February 2002, Ohio EPA issued a general permit for the filling of Category 1 and Category 2 isolated wetlands of less than one-half acre. The general permit requires a pre-activity notice to be filed with Ohio EPA prior to the filling of the isolated wetland as well as a mitigation proposal to address any impacts.

The new regulatory program for isolated wetlands also includes a more stringent review for larger fills of Category 1 and Category 2 wetlands. The level two review requires an alternatives analysis and a finding by the Director that no practical on-site alternative exists to the proposed fill and that reasonable buffers are provided for isolated wetlands.[215] The requirements for the filling of Category 3 wetlands and larger Category 2 wetlands are more stringent than those for Category 1 and Category 2 wetlands; they also require that the Director find that the proposed filling of the isolated wetland will not prevent or interfere with attainment or maintenance of applicable water quality standards.[216]

Mitigation requirements under the new isolated wetlands regulatory program are the same under the Section 401 Certification program except for projects covered by the general isolated wetland permit.[217] The statute provides that the mitigation ratio for Category 1 and Category 2 nonforested wetlands shall be two acres of mitigation for every acre affected.[218] For forested Category 2 isolated wetlands, the mitigation at an off-site approved wetland mitigation bank shall be two and one-half times the size of the isolated wetlands that was impacted.[219] All other mitigation shall be conducted in accordance with the requirements established pursuant to the Section 401 Certification requirements set out in the Ohio Administrative Code.[220]

---

215 ORC § 6111.023.

216 ORC § 6111.024.

217 ORC § 6111.027.

218 ORC § 6111.027(A)(1).

219 ORC § 6111.027(A)(2).

220 *See* ORC § 6111.027(A)(3).

9.0 TMDL PROGRAM

Ohio is pursuing the development of total maximum daily loads ("TMDLs") for impaired water bodies in the state. Established under Section 303(d) of the Clean Water Act, the TMDL program focuses on identifying and restoring polluted rivers, streams, lakes, and other surface water bodies.[221] A TMDL is a quantitative assessment of the sources of water quality impairment affecting a particular water body. It establishes the amount of individual pollutants within a water body and the levels of reduction necessary to obtain water quality standards. A TMDL also attempts to reach water quality standards by allocating the pollutant load among all sources of pollution affecting a particular water body. Conceptually, the allocation of a pollutant load to particular sources is designed to allow Ohio EPA and other state and local authorities to take actions to restore a water body to water quality standards. As a practical matter, the development of a TMDL provides the basis for Ohio EPA to limit or reduce the levels of discharges from point sources, which may result in the detriment of existing point source discharges.

The TMDL program is triggered by what is referred to as the "303(d)" list and schedule. Under Section 303(d) of the Clean Water Act, each state is required to submit to U.S. EPA a list of impaired waters requiring the development of a TMDL.[222] In 1988, Ohio provided to U.S. EPA for approval a list of impaired waters, showing that 881 of 5,000 water body segments in Ohio are impaired or threatened and that 276 watersheds within the State contain at least one water body segment on the 303(d) list. Originally, Ohio had proposed to U.S. EPA to develop TMDLs for all impaired waters within the state by 2013. In a letter dated August 1, 2001, Ohio EPA informed U.S. EPA that its schedule for completing the TMDLs within the State would have to be extended by about ten years due too reductions in resource availability.

As a result of Ohio's delay in developing TMDLs, several environmental groups filed suit against U.S. EPA in U.S. District Court, seeking to have U.S. EPA develop and implement the TMDL program within Ohio.[223] The status and outcome of this citizen suit could affect the future issuance of NPDES permits in Ohio.

---

[221] 33 USC § 1313(d).

[222] *Id.*

[223] *See* National Wildlife, et al. v. EPA, et al., No. 2:01CV-01052-GLF-TPK (S.D. Ohio).

10.0 SLUDGE MANAGEMENT

In March 2000, the Ohio General Assembly modified language in Chapter 6111 of the Revised Code to provide the Director of Ohio EPA with exclusive authority to manage sewage sludge in the State.[224] Pursuant to this statutory enactment, the Director has adopted rules addressing the disposal of sewage sludge from treatment works. The rules, which are found in Chapter 3745-40 of the Administrative Code, establish requirements for the agronomic management of sewage sludge land application to assure that the amount of sewage sludge applied to land application locations does not lead to the over-application of nutrients resulting in discharges to the waters of the state through storm water run-off or migration of nutrient contaminates to ground water.[225] The rules also require monitoring of land application sites and reporting to Ohio EPA by each POTW in the State.[226]

The statutory amendments coupled with the establishment of new rules regarding the management and land application of sewage sludge should position Ohio EPA to apply for delegation under the provisions of Section 503 of the Clean Water Act related to sludge management. While Ohio EPA has yet to obtain delegation from U.S. EPA, such delegation should reduce the need for additional permits and approvals for sludge management within the State. Currently, under Chapter 3745-31 of the Administrative Code, sludge management plans must be approved by Ohio EPA prior to the land application of sludge. The land application of sludge currently requires compliance with both Ohio EPA's sludge management rules as well as the federal biosolids program. Generally speaking, the management of sludge from a POTW is managed in accordance with the terms and conditions of the NPDES permit issued by Ohio EPA.

---

224 HB 197, 123rd General Assembly (Eff. Mar. 17, 2000); *see* ORC § 6111.03(S).

225 OAC 3745-40-04.

226 *See* OAC 3745-40-05 (requires monitoring for pathogen reduction requirements, vector attraction/reduction requirements, and nutrients); *see also* OAC 3745-40-06 (establishes monitoring frequency for nutrient and other requirements related to sludge management).

11.0 NONPOINT SOURCE CONTROL

Nonpoint source pollution refers to water pollution resulting from a variety of human land use practices – *e.g.*, farming that includes application of pesticides and herbicides. It is controllable by implementing land management practices that protect and/or restore water quality, while taking into consideration economic, social, and political interests.

Ohio's Nonpoint Source Management Program was approved by U.S. EPA in 1989. Submitted pursuant to the requirements of Section 319 of the Clean Water Act,[227] the Program identifies best management practices ("BMPs") and measures to reduce pollution, taking into account the impact of the practices on ground water quality. It also includes initiatives for education and training, technical assistance, financial incentives, and voluntary actions as opposed to regulatory mandates or permits. Essentially, it is a geographically focused program based on innovation and voluntary compliance.

Although Ohio has had a number of programs in place to monitor and control certain nonpoint sources – *e.g.*, an agricultural pollution abatement program and an abandoned mine reclamation program – the Nonpoint Source Management Program represents the State's attempt to analyze comprehensively the extent and severity of nonpoint pollution and to develop a coordinated approach to reducing its impact on Ohio's streams, rivers, lakes, and ground water.

Each year, Ohio EPA's Division of Surface Water receives CWA Section 319 funding from U.S. EPA to implement, on a watershed-by-watershed basis, the initiatives set out in the Nonpoint Source Management Program. Ohio's program relies heavily on watershed management plans to address water quality concerns, emphasizing identification of the nature, extent, and cause of the problems; development of an implementation plan; implementation of BMPs; education; and evaluation. The plans are developed locally with input and support from Ohio EPA, the Ohio Department of Natural Resources, and other governmental agencies.

---

[227] 33 USC § 1329.

Chapter V

DRINKING WATER AND GROUND WATER

1.0 DRINKING WATER

The federal Safe Drinking Water Act ("SDWA" or "Act")[1] establishes a national safe drinking water program to be developed by U.S. EPA, through the promulgation of national primary and secondary drinking water standards for specific contaminants (set out in 40 CFR Parts 141 and 143, respectively), and enforced concurrently by federal and state regulatory authorities.

Chapter 6109 of the Revised Code enables Ohio to assume and retain primary enforcement responsibility for the safe drinking water program in the State. Under regulations established pursuant to the SDWA requirements, and set out in Chapters 3745-81 and 3745-82 of the Administrative Code, Ohio EPA is responsible for overseeing the safety and quality of drinking water supplied by public water systems.[2] Any plans for the construction or installation of a public water system must meet the approval of the Director.[3]

---

1 42 USC §§ 300f - 300j-26.

2 "Public water systems" supply drinking water for human consumption to at least fifteen service connections or twenty-five people. Private water systems and individual residential wells are not subject to the standards in Chapters 3745-81 and 3745-82, but are governed under rules developed by the Ohio Department of Health. *See generally* ORC §§ 3701.344 - .352; OAC Chapters 3701-28 to -36.

3 *See* OAC Chapter 3745-91. Additional regulations for the public water supply are set out in the Administrative Code as follows: operational requirements, Chapter 3745-83; contingency plans, Chapter 3745-85; laboratory approval, Chapter 3745-89; escrow requirements, Chapter 3745-92; backflow prevention and cross-connection control, Chapter 3745-95; and miscellaneous, Chapter 3745-99.

In August 1996, President Clinton signed into law S. 1316, the Safe Drinking Water Act Amendments of 1996.[4] Highlights of the 1996 Amendments include the following:

(1) All community water systems must prepare and distribute annual reports about the water they provide, including information on detected contaminants, possible health effects, and the water's source.

(2) U.S. EPA must conduct a cost-benefit analysis for every new standard to determine whether the benefits of a drinking water standard justify the costs.

(3) State Revolving Fund is available to help water systems make infrastructure or management improvements or to help systems assess and protect their source water.

(4) U.S. EPA must strengthen protection for microbial contaminants, while strengthening control over the byproducts of chemical disinfection.

(5) Water system operators must be certified to ensure that systems are operated safely.

(6) Consumers should have information about what is in their drinking water, where it comes from, how it is treated, and how to help protect it.

(7) Small water systems should receive special consideration and resources.

(8) Every state must conduct an assessment of its sources of drinking water to identify significant potential sources of contamination and to determine how susceptible the sources are to these threats.

1.1 Primary Drinking Water Regulations

The primary drinking water regulations established by the SDWA, and adopted by Ohio, are health-based standards that establish maximum contaminant levels ("MCLs") or treatment techniques for microbiological, radiological, organic, and inorganic contaminants that may adversely affect human health.[5] They apply to each public water system in the State that is considered a "community water system" unless the system consists of only distribution and storage facilities, obtains its water from (but is not owned or operated

---

[4] Pub. L. 104-182, 110 STAT. 1613 (1996).

[5] MCLs are established for nitrate (applicable to all public water systems) and nine other inorganic chemicals (applicable to only community water systems); three groups of organic chemicals (applicable to only community water systems); turbidity (applicable to all public water systems); microbiological contaminants or coliform bacteria (applicable to all public water systems); radium-226, radium-228, and gross alpha particle radioactivity (applicable to only community water systems); and beta particle and photon radioactivity from manmade radio nuclides (applicable to only community water systems). OAC 3745-81-11 to -16.

by) another public water system, does not sell water, and is not an interstate carrier of passengers.[6] "Public water system" means a system which provides water for human consumption through pipes or other constructed conveyances, if such system has at least fifteen service connections or regularly serves at least twenty-five individuals daily at least sixty days out of the year. The term is defined to include either a community water system or a non-community water system.[7] A "community water system" serves at least fifteen service connections used by year-round residents or at least twenty-five year-round residents.[8] A "non-community water system" is any public water system that is not a community water system; it includes resorts, restaurants, and other public accommodations serving fewer than twenty-five persons or primarily serving transient users.[9] Non-community water systems are subject to some, but not all, of the primary MCLs.

The State primary drinking water regulations contain specific monitoring, sampling, analytical, and laboratory requirements for the contaminants to be regulated.[10]

1.1.1 Variances

The Ohio EPA Director may grant variances to a public water system that cannot meet an MCL requirement despite application of best available technology ("BAT") or other treatment. If a public water system demonstrates that the use of a specified treatment technique is not necessary to protect the public health, it may be granted a variance, but only if the variance will not cause an unreasonable health risk to the system's users.[11] Within one year of granting a variance from any MCL requirement, the Director must propose a schedule for compliance and for implementation of any control measures required.[12] A request for a variance must be in writing and include detailed justification for

---

[6] OAC 3745-81-02.

[7] OAC 3745-81-01(AAA).

[8] OAC 3745-81-01(AAA)(1).

[9] OAC 3745-81-01(AAA)(2).

[10] OAC 3745-81-21 to -29.

[11] OAC 3745-81-40. The Director also may grant a variance upon a showing that reduction of contamination can be achieved through use of an alternative treatment technique. OAC 3745-81-46.

[12] OAC 3745-81-43(C), (G).

the variance.[13] The Director must act on the request within ninety days, taking into account the availability of treatment methods, cost of treatment, quality of the water source, and source protection measures employed by the system.[14] A proposed variance or schedule is subject to public notice and hearing requirements.[15] Because Ohio MCLs are based on federal standards promulgated under the SDWA, it is difficult to obtain such variances.

1.1.2 Exemptions

Exemptions from MCL or treatment technique requirements may be granted by the Ohio EPA Director upon a finding that a public water system: is unable to comply with either set of requirements due to economic or other compelling factors; was in operation when the MCL or treatment technique became effective; and will operate under the exemption so as not to create an unreasonable risk to health.[16] Within one year of granting an exemption, the Director must propose schedules for compliance with MCLs and treatment techniques covered by the exemption, and for implementation of any control measures required.[17] An exemption request is required to be in writing and must contain detailed information as to reasons for an exemption.[18] The Director must act on an exemption request within ninety days, considering such factors as what is needed for the system to come into compliance, the time involved, and the economic feasibility of compliance.[19] Proposed exemptions and schedules are subject to public notice and hearing requirements.[20]

1.1.3 Reporting And Public Notification

The public water supplier is required to report the results of a test, measurement, or analysis to the Ohio EPA Director within the first ten days following the month in which the result is received or within the first ten days following the end of the

---

[13] OAC 3745-81-41.

[14] OAC 3745-81-42.

[15] OAC 3745-81-44.

[16] OAC 3745-81-50.

[17] OAC 3745-81-53(C) - (D).

[18] OAC 3745-81-51.

[19] OAC 3745-81-52.

[20] OAC 3745-81-54.

required monitoring period as specified by the Director, whichever occurs first.[21] Failure to comply with any applicable requirement of the primary drinking water regulations must be reported to the Director within forty-eight hours.[22]

If a community water system fails to comply with an applicable MCL or testing procedure, is granted a variance or exemption from an MCL, fails to comply with the requirements of any schedule prescribed pursuant to a variance or exemption, or fails to perform certain required monitoring or testing procedures, the supplier must notify its customers of such failure. Notice may be provided by newspaper publication, mail delivery, or, if the violation poses an acute health risk, by radio and television announcements.[23] Specific advisories regarding the potential adverse health effects associated with violations of the MCLs for specific contaminants also are prescribed.[24] Non-community water systems and areas not served by a daily or weekly newspaper may give notice by posting in lieu of publication.[25]

1.2 Secondary Drinking Water Regulations

The secondary regulations or MCLs established in the federal drinking water statute are not health-based. Adopted by Ohio and set out in Chapter 3745-82 of the Administrative Code, the rules apply only to contaminants that affect aesthetic qualities relating to public acceptance of drinking water. These regulations are not federally enforceable, but are intended to be used as guidelines by the State.[26]

"Secondary MCLs" are defined in the Ohio regulations as the advisable maximum levels of contaminants in water delivered to the free-flowing outlet of the user of a public water system.[27] Levels set by the State are identical to those published in 40 CFR 143.3, except for the pH MCL, which is set at 7.0 to 10.5 rather than at 6.5 to 8.5 as in the

---

[21] OAC 3745-81-31(A).

[22] OAC 3745-81-31(B).

[23] OAC 3745-81-32(A)(1) - (2).

[24] OAC 3745-81-32(A)(6).

[25] OAC 3745-81-32(A)(1)(b) - (c).

[26] *See* 40 CFR 143.1.

[27] OAC 3745-82-01(B).

federal rule.[28] Monitoring requirements for secondary regulations closely follow those established in the federal regulations.[29]

Community water systems exceeding the secondary MCL for fluoride must send a prescribed notice to customers, appropriate local public health officials, the Department of Health, and Ohio EPA at least every twelve months as long as the exceedance continues.[30]

2.0 GROUND WATER

Almost ninety percent of Ohio's 1,500 community water systems utilize ground water exclusively. This is in addition to the nearly one and one-half million rural ground water users in the State. In total, about five million residents of Ohio depend on ground water as a primary source of drinking water.[31] Ground water is also important in meeting the demands of industry and agriculture. Total ground water pumpage in Ohio – from both private wells and public water systems – is estimated at approximately one billion gallons per day.[32]

With the enactment of the SDWA Amendments of 1986, Congress required each state to adopt and submit to U.S. EPA, by June 19, 1989, a plan to protect designated wellhead areas from contaminants that may have an adverse effect on human health.[33] Accordingly, Ohio EPA submitted the State's draft Wellhead Protection Plan to U.S. EPA in June 1989. After a series of public hearings and federal review, Ohio's final Plan was approved in May 1992.

All state wellhead protection programs, including Ohio's, must follow the guidelines established by Congress and must address certain minimum requirements including:[34]

(1) the specification of duties of affected state agencies, local governmental entities, and public water supply systems;

(2) the determination of wellhead protection areas;

---

[28] OAC 3745-82-02.

[29] OAC 3745-82-03.

[30] OAC 3745-82-05.

[31] *See* Ohio Water Resource Inventory: Volume IV - Ohio's Groundwater (Ohio EPA, 1996).

[32] *Id.*

[33] *See* 42 USC § 300h-7(a).

[34] *See* 42 USC § 300h-7.

(3) the identification of all potential anthropogenic sources of contaminants within each wellhead protection area that may have an adverse effect on human health;

(4) the description of a program containing technical and financial assistance and education, training, and demonstration projects to protect the water supply within wellhead protection areas;

(5) the development of contingency plans for the location and provision of alternate drinking water supplies for public water systems; and

(6) the consideration of each potential source of contaminants within the wellhead area of any new water well serving the public water system.

Ohio's water well standards are set forth at OAC Chapter 3745-9. Ohio EPA's Division of Drinking and Ground Waters ("DDAGW")[35] has promulgated ten new rules governing construction and sealing of public water system ("PWS") wells, non-PWS wells, and monitoring wells.[36] The new rules, effective in May 2003, provide a greater level of detail and specificity for the construction of wells in Ohio as recommended by the State Coordinating Committee on Ground Water. Rules pertaining to PWS wells are based upon the protection of the ground water and compliance with the Safe Drinking Water Act and industry performance standards. The rules pertaining to non-PWS wells and monitoring wells are based solely on protection of the ground water in accordance with Section 6111.42(E) of the Revised Code. Private water system wells, which are regulated by the Ohio Department of Health, are exempted from these rules.

Although the DDAGW has taken the lead in implementing the wellhead protection program developed under the Plan, several other State agencies are involved in ground water protection: the Departments of Agriculture, Health, Natural Resources, and Transportation; the State Fire Marshal; and the Public Utilities Commission of Ohio.

---

[35] *See* http://www.epa.state.oh.us/ddagw.

[36] OAC 3745-9-01 to -10.

Chapter VI

HAZARDOUS WASTE MANAGEMENT

1.0 OVERVIEW OF FEDERAL AND STATE REGULATION

The Resource Conservation and Recovery Act ("RCRA")[1] and Chapter 3734 of the Ohio Revised Code together create a comprehensive scheme of federal and State regulation of hazardous waste in Ohio. Subtitle C of RCRA creates a management control system that requires "cradle-to-grave" responsibility for solid wastes defined by U.S. EPA as hazardous. Chapter 3734 of the Revised Code gives Ohio EPA broad authority to regulate the generation, transportation, storage, treatment, and disposal of hazardous waste in the State.

2.0 HAZARDOUS WASTE MANAGEMENT

Ohio law authorizes the Director of Ohio EPA to adopt hazardous waste rules "which shall be consistent with and equivalent to the regulations promulgated under [RCRA]," except for rules relating to: (1) performance standards for owners and operators of solid and hazardous waste facilities necessary to protect human health or safety or the environment; and (2) information requirements for solid and hazardous waste permit applications.[2] Although the Director has authority to regulate beyond the bounds of RCRA in these two areas, he has not done so. Ohio's rules for hazardous waste management and its list of regulated wastes are equivalent to RCRA standards.

---

[1] 42 USC §§ 6901 - 6992k.

[2] ORC § 3734.12.

2.1 Regulation Of Generators And Transporters

Ohio law grants the Ohio EPA Director specific authority to adopt standards for generators and transporters of hazardous waste.[3] Pursuant to this authority, Ohio EPA has set out such standards in the Administrative Code, Chapter 3745-52, "Generators of Hazardous Wastes." These rules are consistent with RCRA standards and provide evaluation, identification, manifest, packaging, labeling, recordkeeping, and reporting standards and guidelines.[4]

Any generator who violates these rules will be liable for any damage or injury caused by the violation and for the costs of rectifying the resulting conditions. The generator also may be subject to civil penalties or criminal fines.[5] The statute prohibits anyone from accepting for transportation, treatment, storage, or disposal, any hazardous waste whose generator has violated any of the rules; any such person may be liable for damages and costs of rectifying the resulting conditions, and may be subject to civil penalties or criminal fines.[6]

Ohio also has adopted standards and regulations for the transportation of hazardous waste.[7] Only persons who have registered with and obtained a uniform permit from the Public Utilities Commission of Ohio ("PUCO") may transport hazardous waste within the State.[8] Ohio transportation rules are consistent with RCRA and set forth requirements for registration, transfer facility, acceptance and handling, manifest, recordkeeping, immediate action, and discharge cleanup.[9]

Any transporter who violates these rules will be liable for any resulting damage or injury and for the costs of rectifying the resulting conditions.[10] The PUCO, after conducting a hearing, also may suspend, revoke, or deny a transporter's uniform permit for

---

3 ORC § 3734.12(B) - (C).

4 *See* OAC 3745-52-10 to -70.

5 ORC § 3734.16.

6 ORC § 3734.17.

7 *See* OAC Chapter 3745-53.

8 ORC § 3734.15(A).

9 *See* OAC 3745-53-10 to -31.

10 ORC § 3734.15(B).

violations of transporter requirements.[11] If a generator causes an unregistered transporter to transport hazardous waste, the generator, the transporter, and anyone who accepts the waste for treatment, storage, or disposal will be jointly and severally liable for any damage or injury caused by the handling of the waste and for the costs of rectifying the violation and the resulting conditions.[12]

2.2 Hazardous Waste Facilities Permit System

2.2.1 Application

Anyone who proposes to establish or operate a hazardous waste facility in Ohio must submit to Ohio EPA an application for a hazardous waste facility installation and operation permit, accompanying detail plans, specifications, and any other required information.[13] The applicant also must notify the legislative authority of each municipal corporation, township, and county in which the facility is proposed to be located, of the submission of the application.[14] Ohio EPA must make a preliminary determination that the application appears to comply with Agency rules and standards and then transmit the application to the Hazardous Waste Facility Board ("HWFB"), the body with primary responsibility for the approval or disapproval of hazardous waste facility applications.[15]

Once the HWFB has received an application for a hazardous waste facility permit, it will hold a public hearing, at which time any person may submit written or oral comments or objections to the approval or disapproval of the application.[16]

The HWFB also will hold an adjudicatory hearing at which it will hear and decide all disputed issues between the parties regarding the approval or disapproval of the application.[17] For purposes of this hearing, the parties are: the applicant; the staff of Ohio EPA; the Board of County Commissioners of the county, the Board of Township Trustees of

---

[11] ORC § 4905.80(G).

[12] ORC § 3734.15(C).

[13] ORC § 3734.05(C).

[14] *Id.*

[15] ORC § 3734.05(D).

[16] ORC § 3734.05(D)(3)(a).

[17] ORC § 3734.05(D)(3)(c); *see* OAC Chapter 3734-1.

the township, and the chief executive officer of the municipal corporation in which the facility is proposed to be located; and "[a]ny other person who would be aggrieved or adversely affected by the proposed facility and who files a petition to intervene" in the proceeding.[18]

2.2.2 Criteria For Issuance

The HWFB may not approve an application for a hazardous waste facility installation and operation permit unless it finds and determines that the facility will meet specified criteria, including *inter alia*, that the facility represents the minimum adverse environmental impact; that the facility represents the minimum risk of (1) contamination of ground and surface waters, (2) fires or explosions, (3) accident during transportation of hazardous waste to or from the facility, (4) impact on the public health and safety, (5) air pollution, and (6) soil contamination; and that if the owner or operator of the facility, or any other person in a position to influence the installation and operation of the facility, has been involved in any prior hazardous waste-related activity, that person has a history of compliance with environmental rules and regulations under applicable Ohio and federal law, as well as the laws of other states in which those specified persons have engaged in such activities.[19]

In rendering a decision upon an application, the HWFB must issue a written order and opinion that includes specific findings of fact and conclusions of law supporting its approval or disapproval of the application. If the HWFB approves an application for a permit, as part of its written order it must issue the permit upon such terms and conditions as it finds necessary to ensure the construction and operation of the facility in accordance with State standards.[20]

Any party adversely affected by an order of the HWFB may appeal the order and decision to the Franklin County Court of Appeals. In hearing the appeal, the court is confined to the record as certified to it by the HWFB. The court must affirm the Board's

---

[18] ORC § 3734.05(D)(4).

[19] ORC § 3734.05(D)(6).

[20] ORC § 3734.05(D)(6)(h).

order if it finds that the order is supported by "reliable, probative, and substantial evidence and is in accordance with law."[21]

2.2.3 Modifications

Any change or alteration to a hazardous waste facility or its operations that is inconsistent with or not authorized by its existing permit or authorization to operate is called a "modification." There are several reasons a permit may be modified:[22]

(1) the permittee desires to accomplish alterations, additions, or deletions to the permitted facility, or to undertake alterations, additions, deletions, or activities that are inconsistent with or not authorized by the existing permit; or

(2) new data or information justify permit conditions in addition to or different from those in the existing permit; or

(3) the standards, criteria, or rules upon which the existing permit is based have been changed by new, amended, or rescinded standards, criteria, or rules, or by judicial decision after the existing permit was issued, and the change justifies permit conditions in addition to or different from those in the existing permit; or

(4) the permittee proposes to transfer the permit to another person.

Except when in actual conflict with Ohio's statute regarding modifications, rules governing the classification of and procedures for the modification of hazardous waste permits must be substantively and procedurally identical to the regulations governing hazardous waste facility permitting and permit modifications adopted under RCRA.[23]

Modifications must be classified as Class 1, 2, or 3 modifications. The Director is required to approve or disapprove Class 1 and 2 modifications as well as Class 3 modifications that are not under the jurisdiction of the HWFB. Any modification that

[21] ORC § 3734.05(D)(7).

[22] OAC 3745-50-51(A)(1) - (4).

[23] ORC § 3734.05 (K).

involves the transfer of a hazardous waste facility installation and operation permit to a new owner or operator must be classified as a Class 3 modification.[24]

The HWFB has jurisdiction to approve or disapprove applications for any of the following Class 3 modifications:[25]

(1) authority to conduct treatment, storage, or disposal at a site, location, or tract of land that has not been authorized for the proposed category of treatment, storage, or disposal activity by the facility's permit;

(2) modification or addition of a hazardous waste management unit that results in an increase in a facility's storage capacity of more than twenty-five per cent over the capacity authorized by the facility's permit, an increase in a facility's treatment rate of more than twenty-five per cent over the rate so authorized, or an increase in a facility's disposal capacity over the capacity so authorized.

(3) authority to add any of the following categories of regulated activities not previously authorized at a facility by the facility's permit: storage at a facility not previously authorized to store hazardous waste, treatment at a facility not previously authorized to treat hazardous waste, or disposal at a facility not previously authorized to dispose of hazardous waste; or authority to add a category of hazardous waste management unit not previously authorized at the facility by the facility's permit. A request for authority to add or to modify an activity or a hazardous waste management unit for the purposes of performing a corrective action shall be classified and approved or disapproved by the Director.

(4) authority to treat, store, or dispose of waste types listed or characterized as reactive or explosive or any acute hazardous waste listed in federal regulations, at a facility not previously authorized to treat, store, or dispose of those types of wastes by the facility's permit unless the requested authority is limited to wastes that no longer exhibit characteristics meeting the criteria for listing or characterization as reactive or explosive wastes, or for listing as acute hazardous waste, but still are required to carry those waste codes because of the requirements in the

[24] ORC § 3734.05(I)(1).

[25] ORC § 3734.05(I)(3).

federal "mixture," "derived-from," or "contained-in" regulations.

A permittee seeking a modification must submit a written request to the Director and include information necessary to support the request. The Director must transmit to the HWFB requests for Class 3 modifications described in items (1) to (4) above.[26]

For those modification applications involving a transfer of a permit to a new owner or operator of a facility, the Director must determine that, if the transferee owner or operator has been involved in any prior activity involving the transportation, treatment, storage, or disposal of hazardous waste, the transferee has a history of compliance with State laws governing solid, infectious, and hazardous waste, air pollution control, and water pollution control, and all rules and standards adopted under them; RCRA and all regulations adopted under it; and similar laws and rules of another state if the transferee owns or operates in that state a facility that demonstrates sufficient reliability, expertise, and competency to operate a hazardous waste facility. A permit may be transferred to a new owner or operator pursuant only to a Class 3 modification.[27] "Owner" means the person who owns a majority or controlling interest in a facility and "operator" means the person who is responsible for the overall operation of a facility.[28]

The Director must approve or disapprove an application for modification that requires such action within a certain number of days after receiving the request: sixty days for a Class 1 modification, 300 days for a Class 2 modification, and 365 days for a Class 3 modification that is not under the jurisdiction of the HWFB.[29]

The Director's approval or disapproval of a Class 1 modification application is not a final action that is appealable to the Environmental Review Appeals Commission ("ERAC"); however, the Director's approval or disapproval of a Class 2 modification, or a Class 3 modification that is not within the jurisdiction of the HWFB, is a final action that is

---

[26] ORC § 3734.05(I)(4).

[27] ORC § 3734.05(I)(5).

[28] *Id.*

[29] *Id.*

appealable to the ERAC. In approving or disapproving a request for a modification, the Director must consider all comments pertaining to the request that are received during the public comment period and the public meetings.[30]

The HWFB must approve or disapprove an application for a Class 3 modification transmitted to it by the Director in accordance with continuing statutory provisions governing the approval or disapproval of initial permits. No other request for a modification is subject to the criteria established in those provisions governing approval or disapproval of initial permits by the HWFB.[31]

A permit renewal application that also contains, or would constitute an application for, a modification must be acted upon in accordance with the above requirements in the same manner as an application for a modification.[32] The HWFB must approve or disapprove applications for hazardous waste facility installation and operation permits for new facilities and applications for modifications to existing permits for which it has jurisdiction.[33]

3.0 QUALIFICATIONS OF LICENSEES AND RELATED PERSONS

Off-site treatment, storage, and disposal of hazardous waste is considered to be "critical" to Ohio's economic structure and, when properly controlled, makes "substantial contributions to the general welfare, health, and prosperity" of the State and its inhabitants.[34] Pursuant to its goal of fostering and justifying the "public confidence and trust in the credibility and integrity" of these activities, the Ohio General Assembly has adopted a scheme that prevents "persons who are not competent and reliable or who have pursued economic gains in an occupational manner or context violative of the criminal code or civil public policies" of Ohio from operating off-site facilities.[35] The scheme provides for the submission of a disclosure statement, grants the Ohio Attorney General authority to conduct

---

[30] ORC § 3734.05(I)(6).

[31] ORC § 3734.05(I)(7).

[32] ORC § 3734.05(H)(3).

[33] ORC § 3734.05(D)(2)(b).

[34] ORC § 3734.40(A).

[35] ORC § 3734.40(B), (E).

background investigations, and sets out the criteria for disqualification from receipt of a permit or license.[36]

3.1 Disclosure Statement

Every application for an off-site facility permit must include a "disclosure statement" submitted on forms provided by Ohio EPA.[37] This statement must disclose extensive specified information regarding the applicant and, if a business, its officers, directors, partners, and key employees, as well as holders of equity in the business.[38] The statement must include a description of the credentials and experience of these persons (excluding equity holders). The applicant must list and explain the following: any civil or criminal prosecution by government agencies, administrative enforcement actions resulting in the imposition of sanctions, or license revocations or denials issued in the ten years immediately preceding the filing of the application, that are pending or have resulted in a finding of violation of any environmental protection statute; and any judgment, liability, or conviction under any federal, state, or local law, that resulted in a sanction against the applicant, or, if a business, against the business or any of its officers, directors, partners, or key employees. The applicant also must list all agencies outside Ohio that have or have had regulatory responsibility over the applicant in connection with hazardous waste-related activities. In addition, the Ohio Attorney General or the Ohio EPA Director may require the applicant to disclose other information "that relates to the competency, reliability, or good character of the applicant."[39]

Anyone who already holds a permit or license for an off-site facility and otherwise is not required to file a disclosure statement, must file a disclosure statement according to a schedule established by the Attorney General.[40] Whenever there is a change of ownership of any off-site facility, the prospective owner must file a disclosure statement

---

[36] ORC §§ 3734.42(A) - (B), 3734.44.

[37] ORC § 3734.42(A)(1).

[38] ORC § 3734.42(D).

[39] ORC § 3734.41(D).

[40] ORC § 3734.42(E).

with the Attorney General and the Director of Ohio EPA at least 180 days prior to the proposed change.[41]

3.2 Background Investigation

Within a specified time after receipt of the disclosure statement, the Ohio Attorney General will prepare and submit to Ohio EPA an investigative report. The Attorney General will base this report on information revealed on the disclosure statement, but also may receive criminal history information from the Federal Bureau of Investigation or any other law enforcement agency.[42]

With regard to this investigation, the Attorney General has several important information-gathering and enforcement powers. First, all applicants and permittees must provide any assistance or information requested by the Attorney General or the Ohio EPA Director. Refusal to cooperate in an investigation or inquiry may result in denial or revocation of a permit or license.[43] Second, the Attorney General may issue an "investigative demand" upon persons or businesses believed to possess documentary materials relevant to an investigation. This demand may require: production of documents, answers to interrogatories, or appearance and testimony.[44] Finally, the court of common pleas has authority to modify, set aside, and enforce investigative demands; unless the information is confidential, privileged, or otherwise subject to immunity, the Attorney General may use the disclosed information as evidence in any other proceeding.[45]

3.3 Disqualification

The Revised Code also sets out the possible grounds for disqualification from receipt of a license or permit. No permit or license may be issued or renewed unless Ohio EPA, the HWFB, or the Board of Health finds that the applicant's prior performance record in the handling of hazardous waste demonstrates "sufficient reliability, expertise, and

[41] ORC § 3734.42(F)(1).

[42] ORC § 3734.42(A)(3).

[43] ORC § 3734.42(B).

[44] ORC § 3734.43(B) - (C).

[45] ORC § 3734.43(H) - (R).

competency" to operate a waste facility. If no prior record exists, it must be found that the applicant is "likely to exhibit" that reliability, expertise, and competence.[46]

No permit or license may be issued or renewed if any individual or business listed in the disclosure statement or shown to have a beneficial interest in the business, other than an equity interest or debt liability, has been convicted of any of twenty-one enumerated crimes. These crimes vary from murder and kidnapping to crimes relating to firearms and controlled substances.[47] Notwithstanding this list of crimes, no one may be denied the issuance or renewal of a permit or license on the basis of a conviction, if the applicant "has affirmatively demonstrated rehabilitation" of the individual or business by a preponderance of the evidence.[48] If the offense disclosed is a felony, a permit "shall be denied" unless five years have elapsed since discharge from imprisonment, probation, or parole.[49] Revised Code Section 3734.44(C) sets out the criteria by which the Director, the HWFB, or the Board of Health may determine that an applicant has affirmatively demonstrated rehabilitation.[50]

Finally, no one may receive a permit or license unless the Director, the HWFB, or the Board of Health finds that the applicant has a history of compliance with environmental laws and is currently in substantial compliance with, or on a schedule that will ensure compliance with, environmental laws.[51]

3.4 Revocation / Denial

If the Director of Ohio EPA determines that the disclosure statement of a permittee and the related investigative report contain information that would require the denial of a permit application, the Director may revoke any previously issued permits or may deny any application for a renewal.[52] With regard to prospective owners, if the Director determines that the disclosure statement and investigative report contain information that

46 ORC § 3734.44(A).

47 ORC § 3734.44(B).

48 ORC § 3734.44(C).

49 *Id.*

50 *See* ORC § 3734.44(C)(1) - (9).

51 ORC § 3734.44(D).

52 ORC § 3734.42(E)(4).

would require the denial of a permit application, he may disapprove the change in ownership.[53] If the parties proceed with the change prior to the Director's approval, the parties must include in the contract language expressly making the change in ownership subject to the approval of the Director and expressly negating the change if approval is not given.[54]

The Director of Ohio EPA or the Board of Health may revoke a permit or license for any of the following causes: (1) any cause that would disqualify an applicant from receiving a permit; (2) fraud, deceit, or misrepresentation in securing a permit or in conducting permitted activities; (3) inducement of another individual to violate any law relating to the handling of hazardous waste; (4) coercion of any customer to utilize the services of the permittee; or (5) prevention of the transfer or disposal of hazardous waste at a facility not owned or operated by the applicant or licensee.[55]

4.0 CORRECTIVE ACTION

Sections 3004(u), 3004(v) and 3008(h) of RCRA provide U.S. EPA with authority to require remediation or corrective action measures at certain hazardous waste facilities. These corrective action authorities are implemented on a case-by-case basis in facility permits or orders. The corrective action process is defined by various policy and guidance documents, rather than through a regulatory program. The program allows RCRA facilities to address investigation and cleanup of contaminant releases which pose a threat to human health or the environment.

4.1 Corrective Action In Ohio

U.S. EPA authorized Ohio's RCRA Corrective Action Program effective December 23, 1996. Ohio's authorization directly impacts the 48 permitted facilities in Ohio and any facilities to whom Ohio issues a post closure permit. Many of these facilities already have been required to conduct corrective action work by either a federal permit or

---

[53] ORC § 3734.42(F)(1).

[54] ORC § 3734.42(F)(2).

[55] ORC § 3734.45.

enforcement order. There also are some permitted facilities whose permits do not require them to conduct corrective action work because there has been no release, or potential for a release, of hazardous waste or hazardous waste constituents from waste management units at the facilities.

In addition to the 48 permitted hazardous waste facilities subject to RCRA corrective action, U.S. EPA lists approximately 430 unpermitted facilities in Ohio that are subject to RCRA corrective action. Facilities that have engaged in permitted hazardous waste management activities at any time must comply with RCRA corrective action requirements. These facilities do not have permits and are not seeking permits. Corrective action requirements can be imposed on them by a federal or state enforcement order. U.S. EPA has developed a prioritization system, called the National Corrective Action Prioritization System ("NCAPS"), for these facilities. NCAPS, which also includes the permitted facilities, acts as a guide in determining which facilities warrant the allocation of state or federal resources for development and oversight of such an enforcement order. These facilities are not directly affected by Ohio's authorization to implement the RCRA Corrective Action Program.

Ohio will include RCRA corrective action requirements in Ohio hazardous waste permits upon initial issuance or renewal of the permits, unless circumstances warrant that requirements are added through a permit modification. If the facility has been conducting corrective action work pursuant to a federal permit or enforcement order, the Ohio permit will recognize work completed at the time of permit issuance and require additional work only if the results of the work completed warrant it. Ohio generally will follow the federal RCRA corrective action process set forth in U.S. EPA's Corrective Action Plan ("CAP"), as necessary, and will utilize federal guidance and applicable Ohio guidance to review facility work products. Ohio's approach is set forth in the state version of the CAP, available from Ohio EPA's Division of Hazardous Waste Management.[56]

---

[56] *See* www.epa.state.oh.us/dhwm.

4.2 The Corrective Action Process

Implementation of RCRA corrective action at a permitted facility in Ohio necessitates that Ohio EPA and the facility owner/operator go through several steps to complete the process. The degree to which each step is necessary, if it is in fact necessary, depends on the available quantity and quality of environmental data and information for a particular facility, the analysis of that data and information, and the collective decisions made by both Ohio EPA and the facility, with public input, on how to respond to that data and information. A general description of the steps is as follows:

- Facility Assessment – Updated or conducted by Ohio EPA. It answers two questions: Is there a current release and/or imminent threat? Is there a potential release and/or imminent threat?

- Interim Measure(s) – Undertaken by the facility. It addresses in the near term a release or potential release and/or an imminent threat or potential imminent threat. An Interim Measure may be required to be implemented at any step in the process.

- Investigation – Conducted by the facility. It answers the question: How significant is the release or potential release and/or imminent threat or potential imminent threat? It also provides further definition of the release or potential release and/or imminent threat or potential imminent threat.

- Corrective Measure(s) Study and Decisions – Undertaken by both the facility and Ohio EPA. It determines how to best address the release or potential release and/or imminent threat or potential imminent threat.

- Corrective Measure(s) Implementation – Performed by the facility. It designs the solution and addresses the release or potential release and/or imminent threat or potential imminent threat.

- Operation and Maintenance – Performed by the facility (if necessary). It ensures continuation of the corrective measure that addresses the release or potential release and/or imminent threat or potential imminent threat.

Chapter VII

SITE REMEDIATION AND CLEANUP

1.0 OHIO'S "SUPERFUND" STATUTE

Chapter 3734 of the Revised Code governs remediation and cleanup of contaminated sites in Ohio. The statute authorizes the Director of Ohio EPA to conduct certain hazardous waste cleanup activities and, where necessary, to pay for these activities out of a hazardous waste cleanup fund.[1] The law thus creates a program similar in principle to the federal "Superfund" program for the cleanup of hazardous waste.[2] The Director's authority includes the power to conduct investigations and make inquiries to determine the necessity for abatement activities; the power to pay the costs of closing, constructing, or restoring facilities; and the power to acquire, transfer, and sell specified facilities.[3] The law also provides for certain moneys, including penalties and fines, to be credited to the cleanup fund.[4]

2.0 INVESTIGATION AND REMEDIATION

Ohio EPA's Division of Emergency and Remedial Response ("DERR")[5] is responsible for overseeing site investigations, risk assessments, and remediation activities at contaminated hazardous waste sites in Ohio that are not participating in the state's Voluntary

---

[1] ORC § 3734.20(A).

[2] *See* Comprehensive Environmental Response, Compensation, and Liability Act ("CERCLA"), 42 USC §§ 9601 - 9675.

[3] ORC § 3734.20 - .24.

[4] ORC § 3734.28.

[5] *See* http://www.epa.state.oh.us/derr.

Action Program (see Part 3.0 below). Through its Remedial Response Program, the division determines whether contaminated sites represent a risk to human health or the environment, and whether they are safe for their intended uses. If remedial action is necessary, the program oversees the remediation.

DERR also provides outreach to communities in which contaminated properties are located, raising awareness of technical and financial assistance available for site assessment and revitalization of brownfields, including the Clean Ohio Revitalization Fund, and facilitating site assessments under appropriate state and federal programs.

For the performance of risk assessments and remediation activities, DERR uses U.S. EPA's "Risk Assessment Guidance for Superfund, Volume I, Human Health Evaluation Manual" ("RAGS") which comprises Parts A-D, as follows.[6]

2.1 Baseline Risk Assessment

The baseline risk assessment in RAGS, Part A, is an analysis of the potential adverse health effects caused by the release of a hazardous substance from a site in the absence of any actions to control or mitigate these releases. The assessment – including an initial planning stage, data collection and analysis, exposure assessment, toxicity assessment, and risk characterization – contributes to the site characterization and subsequent development, evaluation, and selection of appropriate response alternatives. Results are used to determine whether additional response action is necessary at the site, to modify preliminary remediation goals, to support selection of the "no-action" remedial alternative, and to document the magnitude and primary causes of risk at a site.

2.2 Risk-Based Preliminary Remediation Goals

U.S. EPA toxicity values and exposure information are used in RAGS, Part B, to derive risk-based preliminary remediation goals ("PRGs") for a site. Initially developed at the scoping phase, using readily available information, risk-based PRGs generally are modified based on site-specific data gathered during the remedial investigation/feasibility study ("RI/FS").

---

6 *See* http://www.epa.gov/superfund/programs/risk.

2.3 Human Health Risk Evaluations

Human health risk evaluations of remedial alternatives are conducted during the feasibility study, during selection and documentation of a remedy, and during and after remedy implementation. RAGS, Part C, provides general guidance to assist in site-specific risk evaluations and to maintain flexibility in the analysis and decision-making process.

2.4 Standardized Planning / Reporting / Review

RAGS, Part D, presents approaches to standardized risk assessment planning, reporting, and review, spanning the CERCLA remedial process from project scoping to periodic review of the implemented remedial action.

2.5 Ecological Assessments

Ecological risk assessment is an integral part of the RI/FS process, which is designed to support risk management decision-making for contaminated sites. The RI component characterizes the nature and extent of contamination as well as estimated risks to human health and the environment posed by the contamination. The FS component develops and evaluates remedial options. For conducting ecological assessments, DERR follows the procedures in U.S. EPA's "Ecological Risk Assessment Guidance for Superfund: Process for Designing and Conducting Ecological Risk Assessments."[7]

3.0 VOLUNTARY ACTION PROGRAM

In 1994, the Ohio General Assembly enacted legislation that established a voluntary reuse and cleanup program for contaminated property in the State.[8] Set out in Chapter 3746 of the Revised Code, the Voluntary Action Program ("VAP") allows owners of property contaminated with hazardous substances or petroleum to voluntarily clean up the property and to receive a Covenant Not to Sue from the Director of Ohio EPA. Implementing regulations for the program are contained in Chapter 3745-300 of the Administrative Code.

---

[7] *See* http://www.epa.gov/superfund/programs/risk/ecorisk/ecorisk.htm.

[8] SB 221, 120th General Assembly (Eff. Sept. 28, 1994).

The VAP is designed to encourage reuse of property for economic development; ensure that cleanups will improve the environment and protect public health; revitalize Ohio's urban industrial areas and create jobs; and encourage lending institutions to provide money for redevelopment without fear of liability.

3.1 Scope

"Voluntary action" is defined to include a Phase I Property Assessment, a Phase II Property Assessment, a sampling plan, a remedial plan, or remedial activities followed by the issuance of a No Further Action ("NFA") letter indicating that the property meets applicable standards.[9]

3.2 Eligibility For Participation / Exclusions

All real property in Ohio is eligible for participation in the VAP with the following exclusions:[10]

(1) National Priorities List ("NPL") sites;

(2) property subject to the underground injection control ("UIC") program, except for certain Class V wells;

(3) property subject to federal or state corrective action permit obligations under the Resource Conservation and Recovery Act ("RCRA");[11]

(4) property subject to federal enforcement;

(5) property where closure is required under Chapter 3734 of the Revised Code;

(6) petroleum underground storage tank ("UST") systems;[12]

(9) property subject to site assessment, removal, or remediation involving oil and gas wells under Chapter 1509 of the Revised Code; and

---

[9] *See* ORC § 3746.01(O); OAC 3745-300-01(50).

[10] ORC § 3746.02; OAC 3745-300-02.

[11] 42 USC §§ 6901 - 6992k.

[12] ORC §§ 3737.88, .882, .89.

(10) property subject to an enforcement letter from the Director relating to a release or threatened release of hazardous substances or petroleum, except when sufficient evidence of entry in the VAP is demonstrated prior to receipt of such a letter.

3.3 Phase I Property Assessment

The purpose and scope of a Phase I Property Assessment are to determine whether there has been a release of hazardous substances or petroleum at the site; to characterize the property for purposes of VAP participation; and to determine the necessity and initial scope of a Phase II Property Assessment.[13]

Phase I assessment requirements are set out in Rule 3745-300-06. The assessment, at a minimum, must include a review of the historic and current uses of the property; a review of the environmental history of the property, including the hazardous substance or petroleum release history; and a property inspection.[14]

The property owner ("volunteer") must identify all areas of contamination on suspected contamination by hazardous substances or petroleum. Areas involving *de minimis* releases do not need to be identified.[15]

In addition, the volunteer must complete a written Phase I Property Assessment report that provides detailed information.[16] In order for a Phase I assessment to be used in support of a NFA letter, the certified professional (see discussion in Section 3.12 below) must perform a walk-over of the property; ensure that all information is complete,

---

[13] OAC 3745-300-06(B).

[14] OAC 3745-300-06(D).

[15] OAC 3745-300-06(F). A *de minimis* release is one in which the constituent released does not exceed residential direct-contact soil standards established in Rule 3745-300-08(B). In addition, the release must be confined to the surficial soils on the property, with no release to surface water, sediments, or ground water; be confined to an area not exceeding nine square feet of the soil surface and one foot in depth; and not be part of a pattern of disposal or mismanagement. OAC 3745-300-06(G).

[16] The Phase I report must include: (1) property identification, including a legal description, dates of the assessment and report, identification and title of investigators, and a summary of the current and intended use of the property; (2) conclusions regarding whether a release occurred and, if indicated, identification of the hazardous substances or petroleum to be evaluated in the Phase II Property Assessment and the areas where they are known or suspected to be present; (3) maps; (4) explanation of all procedures used; (5) summary of all relevant information, including the historic and current uses of the property, adjoining properties, and areas surrounding the property; the environmental history; interviews and property inspections conducted; and the release history on or adjoining the property; (6) statement of any limitations or qualifications impacting the Phase I assessment; (7) recommendation either that a NFA letter can be issued or that a Phase II assessment is required; (8) bibliography of references; (9) colored and dated photographs of the property's current condition; and (10) appendices for all supporting documentation. OAC 3745-300-06(I).

reliable, and current, and that the assessment has been performed in accordance with, and meets, all applicable requirements; and include the Phase I report and a written description of any additional relevant information in the NFA letter.[17]

If the Phase I assessment establishes the release of hazardous substances or petroleum, excluding *de minimis* releases, the volunteer must conduct, at a minimum, a Phase II Property Assessment prior to obtaining a NFA letter from a certified professional.[18]

3.4 Phase II Property Assessment

A Phase II Property Assessment is required if the Phase I assessment for the property involved established the release of hazardous substances or petroleum at the site.[19] If any of the following are discovered on the property, further analysis must be conducted to determine if all or a portion of a property is ineligible for participation in the VAP: hazardous substance or petroleum USTs, UIC wells in Classes I - IV, oil and gas wells, PCBs, any hazardous wastes treated, stored, or disposed of at the property on or after November 19, 1980, and solid waste facilities.[20]

The purpose of a Phase II assessment is to conduct an investigation that determines whether applicable standards are met in all identified areas and affected media, or whether remedial activities conducted in accordance with Rule 3745-300-15 achieve applicable standards.[21]

Phase II assessment activities are described in Rule 3745-300-07. They include data collection, pathway completeness determinations, provisions for protecting ground water meeting potable use standards, determination of applicable standards, determination of the concentrations of chemical(s) of concern in identified areas, determination of ground water yield, classification of ground water, and determination of ground water contamination sources or source areas located both on and off the property. If

---

[17] OAC 3745-300-06(J) - (L).

[18] OAC 3745-300-06(C).

[19] OAC 3745-300-07(A)(1).

[20] OAC 3745-300-07(A)(2).

[21] OAC 3745-300-07(C).

concentrations of chemical(s) of concern are found to exceed the applicable standards, the volunteer must implement a remedy in accordance with Rule 3745-300-15.[22]

Rule 3745-300-07 also sets out detailed requirements for sampling procedures, use of modeling to describe the saturated and unsaturated zones or concentration of chemical(s) of concern emanating to ground water, data analysis, determination of background levels in soil and water, and the Phase II Property Assessment report.[23]

3.5 Generic Numerical Standards

"Generic numerical standard" is defined as "a concentration of a hazardous substance or petroleum that exists on a property that ensures protection of public health and safety and the environment for the reasonable exposures associated with a residential, commercial, or industrial land use or potable ground water use.[24] Ohio EPA has established generic numerical standards for direct-contact soils, ground water, and surface water.[25] Standards for sediments and protection of ecological receptors have not yet been developed.

3.5.1 Direct-Contact Soil Standards

"Generic direct-contact soil standard" means "a generic numerical standard based on an exposure resulting from ingestion of soil, dermal contact with soil or inhalation of volatile and particulate emissions from soil."[26] Rule 3745-300-08(B) (1)-(3) discusses the applicability of these standards, relevant assumptions for both a single chemical and multiple chemicals, petroleum standards, reporting limits for certified laboratories, and applicable standards.

---

[22] *See* OAC 3745-300-07(D)(1) - (9).

[23] *See* OAC 3745-300-07(F) - (J). The Phase II report must include the following: (1) property identification, including a legal description, dates of the assessment and report, and identification and title of investigators; (2) summary of any amendment to the Phase I assessment; (3) statement of any limitations or qualifications impacting the Phase II assessment; (4) summary of data and data collection activities; (5) summary of rationale for sampling and testing activities; (6) summary of determinations involving pathway completeness, protection of potable ground water, applicable standards, concentrations of chemical(s) of concern and remedies implemented, ground water yield, classification of ground water, and sources of ground water contamination; (7) summary of sampling procedures; (8) summary of background level determination activities; (9) summary of models used and description of calibration and field-validation; (10) indication of whether the property met applicable standards or whether remedial activities were required to meet standards; (11) bibliography of references; (12) appendices for supporting documentation; (13) copy of written risk assessment report, if conducted; and (14) property map. OAC 3745-300-07(J).

[24] OAC 3745-300-08(A)(2).

[25] *Id.*

[26] OAC 3745-300-08(A)(1).

The standards themselves are set out in tables – one for each type of land use: residential, commercial, and industrial. Each table identifies the chemical of concern and lists values for single chemical noncarcinogens, single chemical carcinogens, soil saturation, and the single chemical generic direct-contact standard.[27]

3.5.2 Unrestricted Potable Use Standards For Ground Water

"Unrestricted potable use standards" are defined as "standards based on the assumption that ground water will be used as a source of water for drinking, cooking, showering, or bathing," and include both generic and risk-derived standards.[28] Rule 3745-300-08(C)(l)-(3) discusses the applicability of these standards and relevant assumptions. The standards are set out in tables that identify the chemical of concern and lists values for noncarcinogens, carcinogens, the MCL, and the generic unrestricted potable use standard.[29]

3.5.3 Standards For Surface Water

All point source and other regulated discharges of pollutants into surface waters must comply with all permit or other applicable State and federal requirements. Storm water associated with industrial activity must comply with applicable requirements in 40 CR. 122.26.[30]

3.6 Property-Specific Risk Assessment

If a volunteer chooses not to apply the generic numerical standards under Rule 3745-300-08, a property-specific Risk Assessment must be used to develop applicable standard for the chemical(s) of concern.[31] Under certain circumstances, such an assessment

---

[27] *See* OAC 3745-300-08(B)(3), Tables II - IV. Standards for PCBs are set out in Table V; lead standards are in Table VI.

[28] OAC 3745-300-01(A)(33)(a).

[29] OAC 3745-300-08(C)(3), Table VII.

[30] OAC 3745-300-08(D).

[31] OAC 3745-300-09(B)(1).

also is mandatory for determining an applicable standard in lieu of or in addition to using the generic direct-contact soil standards.[32]

The applicable standards developed from a property-specific Risk Assessment must be determined in accordance with risk goals related to carcinogenic risk, noncarcinogenic risk, and risk to important ecological resources.[33]

A property-specific Risk Assessment is comprised of four parts: selection of chemical(s) of concern, exposure assessment, toxicity assessment, and characterization of risk. Each of these is discussed at length in the governing regulations.[34] Rule 3745-300-09 also sets out specific procedures for ecological risk assessment, assessment and remediation of sediments, and surface water assessment, as well as requirements for compliance with applicable standards and for the Risk Assessment report.[35]

3.7 Ground Water Classification And Response

The level of cleanup required for ground water under a property that is contaminated with hazardous substances or petroleum depends on how the ground water is classified, whether the property has an urban setting designation, and the source of contamination.

3.7.1 Classification System

Ground water is classified as either critical resource, Class A, or Class B ground water in accordance with specific criteria unless it does not contain concentrations of chemical(s) of concern in excess of unrestricted potable use standards, or remedial actions

---

[32] *See* OAC 3745-300-09(B)(2). If a Phase II Property Assessment determines that radioactive materials are at a property, the volunteer must comply with the Atomic Energy Act of 1954, 42 USC §§ 2011 *et seq.*, and other applicable State and federal laws. OAC 3745-300-09(B)(3).

[33] OAC 3745-300-09(C).

[34] *See* OAC 3745-300-09(D)(3)(a) - (d).

[35] *See* OAC 3745-300-09(E) - (I). The Risk Assessment report must include the following: (1) circumstances under which the assessment was conducted; (2) list of institutional and engineering controls implemented at the property; (3) list of chemicals of concern not considered in the assessment because they met the criteria under Rule 3745-300-09(D)(3)(a)(i) and (ii) and written documentation of how those criteria were met; (4) list of receptor populations and exposure pathways and written justification for their selection or elimination; (5) documentation supporting derivation and application of exposure factors used to quantitate intake; (6) list of all toxicity values used in the assessment and their sources; (7) characterization of risk; (8) uncertainty analysis; (9) ecological risk report; (10) sediment assessment report; (11) surface water assessment report, if applicable; and (12) summary of compliance with applicable standards. OAC 3745-300-09(I).

consistent with those for critical resource ground water are implemented for ground water exceeding the same potable use standards.[36]

Critical resource ground water is ground water that is being used by a public water system and is part of a wellhead protection area; is part of an unconsolidated saturated zone capable of yielding water at a time-weighted average rate greater than 100 gallons per minute over a twenty-four-hour period; or is a consolidated saturated zone that is part of a sole source aquifer.[37]

Class A ground water does not meet the criteria for the critical resource classification and either is in a saturated zone currently utilized as a source of potable water on the property or within one-half mile of the property boundary, or has a background level of total dissolved solids of less than 3,000 milligrams per liter and meets specific requirements related to saturation zones.[38]

Class B ground water does not meet any of the criteria for either critical resource ground water or Class A ground water.[39]

3.7.2 Urban Setting Designation

If the property being cleaned up for reuse is designated as being in an urban setting, the underlying ground water that is classified as critical resource or Class A ground water may require a lower level of cleanup. The designation may be used only for purposes of eliminating the potable use pathway and may be requested from the Director of Ohio EPA only through a certified professional, providing that the property meets threshold criteria.[40]

---

[36] OAC 3745-300-10(B)(1) - (2); *see* OAC 3745-300-07(D)(8), (D)(9).

[37] OAC 3745-300-10(C)(1).

[38] OAC 3745-300-10(C)(2).

[39] OAC 3745-300-10(C)(3).

[40] OAC 3745-300-10(D)(1). The threshold criteria are: (1) the property is entirely within the corporate boundaries of a city or the boundaries of a township with a population of 20,000 in its unincorporated area; (2) the city or township has a community water system that is capable of meeting its future water supplies, with certain exceptions; (3) the property is not located in an Ohio EPA-approved wellhead protection area, unless the owner of the community water system has a wellhead protection plan for the area and consents in writing to the designation; (4) potable water supply wells are not located within one-half mile of the property boundary, with certain exceptions; (5) if the property is over a sole source aquifer and meets certain saturated zone criteria, the certified professional requesting the designation demonstrates that there is not a reasonable expectation that potable water wells will be installed within one-half mile of the property boundary. *Id.*

The Director must approve the designation, which must be used solely for purposes of determining applicable standards.[41]

3.7.3 Ground Water Protection

When ground water in a saturated zone underlying the property meets the unrestricted potable use standards of Rule 3745-300-07, the volunteer must undertake remedial activities which ensure that migration of hazardous substances or petroleum from sources on the property will not cause the standards to be exceeded anywhere within a saturated zone.[42]

If the ground water exceeds a standard for residential potable use, based on a Phase II Property Assessment, the volunteer must meet specific response requirements based upon the ground water's classification and whether the property has an urban setting designation.[43]

3.8 Remediation

If a Phase II Property Assessment reveals that concentrations of chemical(s) of concern in any environmental media exceed applicable standards as determined from either generic numerical standards, a property-specific risk assessment, background levels, or any other applicable standard, the volunteer must undertake remedial activities.[44] Remediation must have been conducted and documented in the No Further Action letter or addressed as part of an Operations and Maintenance Plan contained in the letter. It may be passive (*e.g.*, natural attenuation processes) or active (*e.g.*, air sparging or soil washing), and may involve institutional or engineering controls, critical resource ground water activities, interim measures, or risk mitigation measures.[45] Detailed information on Operation and Maintenance Plans and agreements, as well as Risk Mitigation Plans, may be required for particular remedial activities.[46]

---

[41] OAC 3745-300-10(D)(2).

[42] OAC 3745-300-10(E).

[43] *See* OAC 3745-300-10(F).

[44] OAC 3745-300-15(A)(1).

[45] *See* OAC 3745-300-15(B), (D).

[46] *See* OAC 3745-300-15(F) - (G).

When remedial activities are completed, the property owner (volunteer) must conduct verification in accordance with Rule 3745-300-07 to confirm that the remedy conducted has resulted in the meeting of applicable standards.[47]

3.9 Variances From Remediation Standards

A property owner undertaking voluntary action may apply to the Director for a variance from the applicable remediation standards. The variance will be granted only if the applicant makes all the following demonstrations:[48]

(1) it is technically infeasible to comply with the applicable standards or the costs of complying with the standards substantially exceed the benefits;

(2) the proposed alternative standards will result in an improvement of the conditions at the property and will sufficiently protect public health; and

(3) the proposed alternative standards are necessary to promote, protect, preserve, or enhance employment opportunities or the reuse of the property.

Before the variance may be granted, the Director must hold a public meeting and seek comment from adjacent property owners and local officials in the area where the property is located.[49]

3.10 Inspections And Investigations

At least once every five years, the Director or his representative must visually inspect each property for which a Covenant Not to Sue has been issued that involved institutional controls restricting the use of the property.[50] In addition, the Director or his representative may enter property that is the site of a voluntary action or property owned by someone involved in a voluntary action for purposes of inspection or investigation. The inspection or investigation must be at a reasonable time, but may be conducted for almost

---

[47] OAC 3745-300-15(E).

[48] ORC § 3746.09(A); OAC 3745-300-12(E).

[49] ORC § 3746.09(B) - (D); OAC 3745-300-12(H) - (K).

[50] ORC § 3746.171.

any relevant purpose including the inspection of records, documents, or the credentials and facilities of a certified laboratory, or to examine data or other information regarding remediation of the property.[51]

3.11 Consolidated Permits

To facilitate voluntary actions, Chapter 3746 provides for the granting of consolidated standards permits. When a volunteer undertakes a voluntary action that otherwise would require permits, licenses, or approvals due to other applicable State or federal requirements, the volunteer may apply for a consolidated permit.[52] This permit contains all the substantive requirements for the voluntary action and obviates the need to apply for permits for individual activities. Before the Director may issue such a permit, however, he must schedule a public meeting in the county where the voluntary action will take place and consider public comments on the proposal.[53]

3.12 Certified Professionals / Laboratories

A property owner participating in the VAP must utilize the services of a certified professional to verify that both the property and remedial activities undertaken at the property comply with applicable standards, and to issue a No Further Action ("NFA") letter for the property. The volunteer also must utilize the services of a certified laboratory to perform the analyses that form the basis for the NFA letter.[54]

A certified professional is an individual certified by the Director of Ohio EPA to issue a NFA letter on behalf of a VAP participant (see discussion in Section 3.13 below).[55] To be certified, an applicant must submit to the Director information detailing his experience, competence, proficiency, and moral character; pay a fee; and provide any additional information that the Director deems appropriate.[56] Once the Director issues a certification,

---

[51] ORC § 3746.21.

[52] ORC § 3746.15(A).

[53] ORC § 3746.15(B).

[54] ORC § 3746.10(B)(1).

[55] ORC § 3746.071; *see* OAC 3745-300-05.

[56] OAC 3745-300-05(B), (C); *see* OAC 3745-300-03.

the certified professional must apply annually for recertification.[57] In doing so, the certified professional must demonstrate satisfaction of the standards of conduct and the continuing education requirements set out in Rule 3745-300-05. Failure to satisfy these requirements may result in the suspension or revocation of certification.[58]

Laboratories performing analysis to support a NFA letter must be certified by the Director of Ohio EPA.[59] Certified laboratories may perform analyses for parameter groups or analytes using only the methods set out in the certificate.[60]

Rule 3745-300-04 sets out certification requirements for laboratories and discusses approved methods for analysis, performance evaluation programs, compliance and system audits, and special procedures for laboratory certification for analyses of asbestos and sediment toxicity.[61] Certificates are subject to renewal requirements, standards of performance and conduct, and revocation or suspension by the Director.[62]

Listings of certified professionals and laboratories are available from Ohio EPA.[63]

3.13 No Further Action Letters

A NFA letter may be issued by a certified professional for a VAP property only under the following circumstances:[64]

(1) after completion of a Phase I Property Assessment and the certified professional determines that there is no information establishing any reason to believe that a release of hazardous substances or petroleum occurred on the property;

(2) after completion of a Phase I Property Assessment and the certified professional determines that there was only a *de*

[57] OAC 3745-300-05(D).

[58] OAC 3745-300-05(G).

[59] *See* OAC 3745-300-04(A)(5), (B)(1). Certification is applicable only to analyses conducted to support NFA letters and does not constitute certification to perform analyses under any other State or federal laboratory certification program. OAC 3745-300-04(B)(2).

[60] OAC 3745-300-04(B)(1).

[61] *See* OAC 3745-300-04(C) - (G), (J), (K), (P) - (S).

[62] *See* OAC 3745-300-04(E)(2), (G), (I), (P).

[63] *See* http://www.epa.state.oh.us/derr/cp.pdf, http://www.epa.state.oh.us/derr/pdf _doc_wpd/lab.pdf.

[64] OAC 3745-300-13(A).

minimis release of hazardous substances or petroleum on the property;

(3) after completion of a Phase II Property Assessment and the certified professional determines that the concentrations of chemical(s) of concern do not exceed applicable standards; or

(4) after completion of a Phase II Property Assessment and the certified professional determines that the concentration of chemical(s) of concern exceed the applicable risk-based standards, but that those standards have been achieved through remedial activities or will be achieved through an operation and maintenance plan or agreement.

To obtain a NFA letter, a volunteer must submit to a certified professional all relevant investigatory and remedial information pertaining to the property.[65] The certified professional then must perform work or review the work of others to support the NFA request or ensure that the work has been performed and reviewed by others with the requisite relevant experience and competence necessary for issuance of the NFA letter.[66] If the certified professional concludes that a property meets or will meet applicable standards, he may prepare a NFA letter for the property that contains prescribed information.[67]

Upon completion of the NFA letter, the certified professional must send a copy of the letter to the volunteer, along with a written notice informing the volunteer that the original NFA letter may be submitted to the Director of Ohio EPA only by a certified professional and that the Director will issue a Covenant Not to Sue only if the original letter is submitted to the Director on behalf of the volunteer by the certified professional. The

[65] OAC 3745-300-13(B).

[66] OAC 3745-300-13(D).

[67] OAC 3745-300-13(E). The NFA must contain the following: (1) a legal description of the property; (2) site maps; (3) the Phase I Property Assessment report; (4) the Phase II Property Assessment report; (5) identification of the ground water classification for the property and the basis for that classification; (6) identification of all applicable standards; (7) summary of information submitted by the volunteer in the request for a NFA letter; (8) notification that a risk assessment was performed, if one was used in lieu of or in addition to generic numerical standards, and the report of that assessment; (9) information demonstrating that the property conforms with the exposure assumptions used to calculate the generic numerical standards or other applicable standards; (10) identification of all contaminants addressed or identified at the property, including their source, location, and concentration levels prior to and after any remediation; (11) name and qualifications of other persons who performed work in support of the NFA letter, and the nature and scope of the work performed; (12) list of all documents and their dates reviewed by the certified professional in preparing the NFA letter; (13) copy of any deed restriction on use of property, if applicable; (14) copy of any consolidated standards permit and supporting document, if applicable; (15) copy of any operation and maintenance plan or agreement, if applicable; (16) identification of tax parcel number and taxing district for the property; (17) affidavits prepared in connection with the

certified professional also must request in writing that he be notified if the volunteer wants the NFA letter to be submitted to the Director.[68] Promptly after receiving the NFA letter, the volunteer must provide written notice to the certified professional, with a copy to the Director, regarding his intent to have the letter submitted to the Director.[69]

If a Covenant Not to Sue is issued, the certified professional must ensure that a summary of the NFA letter, along with the covenant and any land-use restrictions, are filed with the appropriate country recorder. The NFA letter will be made available by Ohio EPA.[70]

NFA letters are transferable to another person by assignment or in conjunction with acquisition of title to the property.[71] Any information, data, documents, or reports submitted by a volunteer, certified laboratory, certified professional, or any other person for purposes of conducting or completing a voluntary action must be submitted by affidavit.[72]

3.14 Audits In Connection With NFA Letters

Ohio law requires the Director of Ohio EPA to conduct audits in connection with NFA letters and to issue audit findings.[73] The purpose of these audits is to determine the sufficiency of the voluntary action and to review both the qualifications and work of the certified professional and certified laboratory.[74] Rule 3745-300-14 provides for mandatory, priority, and random audits. At a minimum, audits must be conducted in connection with at least twenty-five per cent of the NFA letters involving remedial activities, and twenty-give percent of the letters not involving remedial activities, received during the previous calendar year, in accordance with specific procedures.[75]

---

voluntary action; and (18) any other information considered relevant. *Id.* at (1) - (18). *See also* OAC 3745-300-13(H) - (I).

68 OAC 3745-300-13(F).

69 OAC 3745-300-13(G).

70 OAC 3745-300-13(J).

71 OAC 3745-300-13(K).

72 *See* OAC 3745-300-13(L) - (P).

73 ORC § 3746.17; OAC 3745-300-14(B), (O).

74 ORC § 3746.17(A)(1) - (3); OAC 3745-300-14(B)(1) - (3).

75 ORC § 3746.17(B); OAC 3745-300-14(C) - (F), (H); *see* OAC 3745-300-14(A)(3) - (5).

Following the conclusion of all investigatory auditing activities, but prior to issuance of audit findings, the person responsible for maintaining compliance at the property subject to an audit may request one informal meeting with Ohio EPA to discuss technical aspects of the audit.[76]

The Director may contract for the completion of these audits but is restricted from selecting a contractor with any ties to the voluntary action performed.[77] The Director also may conduct an audit of a property if the certification of a certified professional or certified laboratory was revoked following the completion of a NFA letter for that property.[78]

3.15 Covenant Not To Sue

Once a voluntary action has been completed and a certified professional has submitted a NFA letter to the Director of Ohio EPA, the Director shall issue a Covenant Not to Sue to the property owner.[79] The covenant releases a volunteer from all civil and injunctive liability to perform additional activities relating to a release of hazardous substances or petroleum at the property.[80] Certain limitations apply if the release involves potential claims by the State under CERCLA or if the voluntary action used engineering controls to contain the release of hazardous substances or petroleum.[81] The covenant must be filed in the office of the county recorder of the county in which the property is located and must be recorded in the same manner as a deed.[82]

The covenant remains in effect only as long as the affected property remains in compliance with the applicable standards.[83] The Director may revoke a covenant if a volunteer fails to return a noncompliant property to compliance in accordance with the schedule provided by the Director.[84] In addition, the Director may deny a covenant for

---

[76] OAC 3745-300-14(J).

[77] ORC § 3746.17(E).

[78] ORC § 3746.19(B).

[79] ORC § 3746.12(A).

[80] ORC § 3746.12(A)(1).

[81] ORC § 3746.12(A)(2).

[82] ORC § 3746.14(A).

[83] ORC § 3746.12(B)(1).

[84] ORC § 3746.12(B)(4).

reasons including fraud and the insufficient protection of public health.[85] If the covenant is not revoked, it stays in effect for as long as the volunteer complies with the requirements that were in effect when he undertook the voluntary action.[86] Covenants are transferable to another person by assignment or in conjunction with acquisition of title to the property.[87]

3.16 MOA Track

In 2001, Ohio EPA and U.S. EPA signed a Memorandum of Agreement ("MOA"), establishing an alternative approach to cleanup, known as the "MOA Track." Participants may decide if they want to follow the original VAP or the MOA Track. The primary differences between the two approaches are that investigation and cleanup activities of MOA Track projects will be overseen directly by Ohio EPA personnel and include opportunities for public review of, and comment on, site documents as they are produced by the cleanup volunteer. There are no differences in the cleanup standards for the two approaches.

Participants effectively completing the MOA Track, as determined by Ohio EPA, may receive a Covenant Not to Sue, and have the comfort of knowing the cleanup was conducted under a program approved by U.S. EPA.

3.17 Immunity From Tort Actions

Chapter 3746 provides immunity from tort actions for harm caused by the release of hazardous substances or petroleum at a property participating in the VAP.[88] Immunity is provided specifically for the following, including their officers and employees: persons working as a contractor; a State agency conducting a voluntary action or maintenance activity; a State agency providing technical assistance; and a public utility performing work in an easement or right-of-way across property where voluntary action takes place, or performing necessary maintenance work on property where a voluntary action

---

85 ORC § 3746.12(C).

86 ORC § 3746.12(E).

87 OAC 3745-300-13(K).

88 ORC § 3746.24(B). Immunity is not provided for any action or omission that constitutes willful or wanton misconduct or intentionally tortious conduct. *Id.*

is being conducted.[89] When the State conducts an inspection, investigation, removal, or remediation of hazardous substances, no officer or employee shall be liable unless their actions constitute willful, wanton, or intentionally tortious conduct.[90]

3.18 Exemptions From Liability

Persons holding evidence of a security interest in a VAP property are exempted from liability for costs of conducting a voluntary action or investigating a release, but only if they do not participate in its management of the property.[91] Such evidence may include liens, mortgages, deeds of trust, or other indicia of ownership.[92] The exemption, however, applies only if the evidence is held primarily to protect a security interest in the property.[93]

A liability exemption also exists for fiduciaries or trustees who acquire ownership or control of property without having owned, operated, or participated in the management of the property, providing that the fiduciary or trustee must not have acted in a way that caused or contributed to a release of hazardous substances or petroleum at the property, and must conduct all activities on the property not related to the remediation of releases in accordance with applicable requirements.[94] An exemption does not preclude the filing of claims against the assets that constitute the estate or corpus held by the trustee.[95]

3.19 Penalties

The reckless violation of a consolidated standards permit and the knowing falsification or alteration of documents submitted to Ohio EPA constitute felonies under Chapter 3746. Violators will be subject to a maximum fine of $25,000 and imprisonment for

---

[89] *Id.*

[90] ORC § 3746.25(B).

[91] ORC § 3746.26(A)(1).

[92] ORC § 3746.26(B).

[93] ORC § 3746.26(A)(1).

[94] ORC § 3746.27(A).

[95] ORC § 3746.27(C).

up to four years. Each day of violation is a separate offense. The fine may increase to $50,000 for subsequent violations.[96]

[96] ORC § 3746.99.

Chapter VIII

NONHAZARDOUS SOLID WASTE MANAGEMENT

1.0 OVERVIEW OF FEDERAL AND STATE REGULATION

Subtitle D of the federal Resource Conservation and Recovery Act ("RCRA")[1] gave authority to the U.S. EPA to develop an Office of Solid Waste for the purpose of regulating the disposal of nonhazardous solid wastes and specifically to oversee state solid waste management planning and programs.[2] RCRA's primary purpose is to reduce the generation of solid waste and ensure the proper treatment, storage, and disposal of solid waste that is nonetheless generated so as to minimize the present and future threat to human health and the environment.

Chapter 3734 of the Ohio Revised Code creates an even more comprehensive program, giving the Director of Ohio EPA broad authority to regulate the management and disposal of solid wastes in Ohio, including the supervision of local solid waste management planning and creation of a special regulatory program for infectious waste management and disposal. Additionally, Chapter 3714 of the Revised Code sets out special requirements for construction and demolition debris.

---

1 42 USC §§ 6901 - 6992k.

2 42 USC §§ 6941 - 6956.

2.0 SOLID WASTE MANAGEMENT

Under Ohio law, "solid waste" means:[3]

> such unwanted residual solid or semisolid material as results from industrial, commercial, agricultural, and community operations, excluding earth or material from construction, mining, or demolition operations, or other waste materials of the type that normally would be included in demolition debris, nontoxic fly ash and bottom ash, including at least ash that results from the combustion of coal and ash that results from the combustion of coal in combination with scrap tires where scrap tires compromise not more than fifty per cent of heat input in any month, spent nontoxic foundry sand, and slag and other substances that are not harmful or inimical to public health, and includes, but is not limited to, garbage, scrap tires, combustible and noncombustible material, street dirt, and debris. "Solid wastes" does not include any material that is an infectious waste or a hazardous waste.

Unlike Ohio's rules governing hazardous waste, those governing solid waste do not necessarily have to be consistent with and equivalent to RCRA regulations.[4] In 1988, the Ohio General Assembly enacted legislation that amended and greatly expanded the State's solid waste management program.[5] Under Chapter 3734 of the Revised Code, the Director must promulgate uniform rules to ensure that solid waste facilities will be located, constructed, maintained, and operated, and will undergo closure and post-closure care in a sanitary manner so as not to create a nuisance, cause or contribute to water pollution, create a health hazard, or violate federal applicable standards. These rules may include financial assurance requirements for closure and post-closure care, as well as requirements for taking corrective action in the event of the discharge or release of explosive gases or leachate from a solid waste facility, or the contamination of ground water associated with transfer or disposal activities.[6]

---

[3] ORC § 3734.01(E).

[4] ORC § 3734.12.

[5] HB 592, 118th General Assembly (Eff. June 24, 1988).

[6] *See* ORC § 3734.02(A). The construction and operation of new facilities must employ the best available technology ("BAT"). OAC 3745-31-05(A)(3).

Revised rules implementing Ohio's approved Subtitle D program became effective in June 1994. Ohio EPA revised its BAT standards for sanitary landfills to incorporate changes mandated under the Subtitle D rules adopted by U.S. EPA in October 1991. The sanitary landfill rules in Chapter 3745-27 of the Administrative Code were approved by U.S. EPA on June 13, 1994, when U.S. EPA made its final determination of adequacy for Ohio's solid waste program.[7] Ohio EPA adopted changes in Chapter 3745-29 of the Administrative Code for "residual" industrial waste landfills, improving the flexibility for landfill operators to tailor landfill design and operating requirements based on the composition of the wastes destined for disposal at a particular facility.

By June 1990, Ohio EPA also was required to promulgate rules establishing a mandatory comprehensive training and certification program for employees of local health boards responsible for enforcing the solid waste laws and regulations, and for all persons responsible for the operation of solid waste facilities.[8] Although training for local health board employees was required to be completed by 1995,[9] lack of funding has delayed the rulemaking from going forward. However, those local health departments that do not have programs approved by the Ohio EPA are not permitted to enforce solid waste laws as outlined in Chapter 3734 of the Ohio Revised Code and those rules promulgated under it.[10]

Solid waste facilities in operation prior to 1968, which had been "grandfathered" under solid waste laws existing prior to 1988, were required to submit a permit application and engineering detail plans to the Director in accordance with a schedule established as part of HB 592 in 1988.[11] Facilities that commenced operations after 1968, but prior to 1980, are also subject to a permit call-in schedule established by the Director.[12] Ohio law subjects existing solid waste facilities to the prospect of being forced to retrofit BAT in order to continue to operate, or closing these older facilities.[13]

---

[7] 59 *Fed. Reg.* 30353 (June 13, 1994).

[8] ORC § 3734.02(L).

[9] ORC § 3734.02(L)(6)(a).

[10] ORC § 3734.08.

[11] ORC § 3734.05(A)(3) - (4).

[12] OAC 3745-27-97.

[13] ORC § 3734.05(A)(3) - (4).

Revisions to Ohio's solid waste laws in 1995[14] exempt solid waste incinerators that were placed in operation before October 12, 1994 and that are not authorized to treat infectious wastes from the permit-call in schedule established by HB 592 in 1988.[15] Ohio EPA may issue an order directing any existing solid waste facility to submit updated engineering detail plans, specifications, and information regarding the facility and its method of operation for approval under the BAT rules to be promulgated, if the Agency believes that conditions at the facility constitute a substantial threat to public health or safety, or are contributing to or threatening to contribute to air or water pollution or soil contamination.[16]

In addition to establishing performance and management standards, Ohio's statutory scheme for the control of solid wastes includes permit and license requirements and provision for the development of solid waste management plans, as described below. Ohio law grants the Director of Ohio EPA the authority to exempt any person from complying with any solid waste requirement if the Director determines that the exemption is unlikely to have an adverse effect on the public health or safety or the environment.[17]

2.1 Permit Requirements

No person may establish a solid waste facility in Ohio without submitting an application for a permit to install ("PTI") with accompanying detail plans, specifications, and information regarding the facility and method of operation, and receiving a PTI from the Director of Ohio EPA.[18] Applicants may submit requests for variances along with a PTI application. If an applicant requests a variance from any standard, the Director may hold a public hearing in the county in which the facility is to be located.[19] A variance can be granted only if the applicant demonstrates that any terms or conditions of the variance will not create a nuisance or hazard to public health or safety or environment.[20]

---

[14] HB 685, 121st General Assembly (Eff. Mar. 30, 1995).

[15] ORC § 3734.05(A)(10)

[16] ORC § 3734.05(A)(5).

[17] ORC § 3734.02(G).

[18] ORC § 3734.02(C).

[19] ORC § 3734.02(A).

[20] *Id.*

The Director will issue a PTI on the basis of the information in the application, as well as information gathered by or furnished to Ohio EPA, if the Director determines that the installation and operation of the facility will: (1) not prevent or interfere with the attainment or maintenance of applicable ambient air or ambient water quality standards; (2) not result in a violation of any applicable laws; and (3) employ BAT.[21] In deciding whether to grant or deny a PTI, the Director may consider the social and economic impacts resulting from its issuance.[22] The Director may impose such special terms and conditions as are appropriate or necessary to ensure compliance with applicable laws and to ensure adequate protection of environmental quality.[23]

Within 180 days after a completed PTI application is filed, the Director must issue or propose to issue or deny the PTI.[24] The Director may issue a PTI as a proposed or a final action. If the Director issues a proposed action and receives a written objection within thirty days, he must hold an adjudication hearing.[25] Although Ohio law does not require Ohio EPA to hold a public hearing prior to the issuance of a permit, current Agency policy is to hold a public hearing regarding the PTI application for a solid waste facility. In addition, Ohio EPA gives public notice of receipt of a PTI application and, upon request, conducts public informational sessions.

2.1.1 Sanitary Landfill BAT Standards

A PTI or plan approval for a new or expanded solid waste facility will terminate within eighteen months of the effective date of the PTI or plan approval unless the owner or operator undertakes a continuing program of installation or modification or enters into a binding contractual obligation to undertake and complete within a reasonable time a continuing program of installation or modification. The Director may extend this period under certain circumstances for up to twelve months if the applicant submits within a

---

21 OAC 3745-31-05(A).

22 OAC 3745-31-05(C).

23 OAC 3745-31-05(D).

24 OAC 3745-31-05(H).

25 ORC § 3745.07.

reasonable time before the termination date an application for an extension.[26] A PTI or plan approval may be revoked if the Director concludes at any time that any applicable laws have been or are likely to be violated.[27]

The BAT standards for sanitary landfills, which became effective in March 1990, set forth detailed technical information requirements for permit applications and minimum standards that must be satisfied for a PTI to be issued for a new landfill facility or the expansion of an existing facility.[28] These standards were revised in June 1994 to incorporate the requirements under the federal Subtitle D rules.[29] The approval criteria include location restrictions to protect national and state parks and scenic or sensitive areas, drinking water supplies, surface waters, and areas subject to seismic stress; they also have incorporated the federal siting standards for airports, floodplains, fault areas, and unstable areas.[30] Design, construction, and operational criteria require the use of recompacted soil and geomembrane liners, ground water monitoring networks, leachate collection and removal systems, methane gas monitoring and removal systems, and daily cover.[31] Standards for closure and post-closure care and a demonstration of financial assurance to provide for closure and post-closure care and corrective actions also are required.[32]

2.1.2 Industrial Landfill Standards

As part of its revision of the BAT standards for sanitary landfills, and the adoption of rules equivalent to the federal Subtitle D rules for municipal solid waste landfills, Ohio EPA created Chapter 3745-29 of the Administrative Code to govern the installation, construction, operation, closure, and post-closure care of industrial solid waste landfills. Generally, this Chapter retains all the BAT criteria that previously applied to any sanitary landfill in Ohio, regardless of whether the facility accepted residential, commercial, or

---

[26] OAC 3745-31-06.

[27] OAC 3745-31-07.

[28] *See generally* OAC 3745-27-06 to -07.

[29] In 2002, Ohio EPA proposed stricter criteria for approving new or expanded landfill facilities, including new construction requirements. The rules have not been approved and are tabled for an effective date of January 2003.

[30] OAC 3745-27-07(H), -20(C).

[31] OAC 3745-27-08 to -10.

industrial solid waste. Now, however, these standards apply exclusively to facilities that accept "industrial wastes," which are defined as:[33]

> a type of solid waste generated by manufacturing or industrial operations and includes, but is not limited to, solid waste resulting from the following manufacturing processes: electric power generation; fertilizer/ agricultural chemicals; food and food-related products/ by-products; inorganic chemicals; iron and steel manufacturing; leather and leather products; nonferrous metals manufacturing; plastics and resins manufacturing; pulp and paper industry; rubber and miscellaneous plastic products; stone, glass, clay, and concrete products; textile manufacturing; and transportation equipment.

Solid waste facilities that accept only industrial solid wastes may be reclassified as "industrial waste facilities," instead of sanitary landfills, simply by submitting a notification of intent to comply with Chapter 3745-29 of the Administrative Code.[34]

2.1.3 Residual Waste Landfill Standards

Ohio EPA has established graduated BAT standards for landfill facilities that do not accept general residential, commercial, or industrial solid waste, but that are used exclusively for the disposal of certain types of high volume nonhazardous industrial processing wastes, defined in the regulation as "residual wastes."[35] "Residual wastes" include certain wastes generated by foundry operations, pulp and papermaking operations, steelmaking operations, gypsum processing plants, lime processing operations, cement operations, and those that result from the combustion of coal as a primary fuel.[36] Residual waste landfill facilities are subject to classification based on the highest concentrations of certain toxic constituents in the leachate produced by any of the wastes disposed of at the landfill facility.[37] Facilities are classified as Class I, Class II, Class III, or Class IV. Class I

---

[32] OAC 3745-27-11, -14 to -18.

[33] OAC 3745-29-01(A).

[34] OAC 3745-29-02(C).

[35] *See generally* OAC Chapter 3745-30.

[36] OAC 3745-30-01(B).

[37] OAC 3745-30-03, -04.

facilities must meet the equivalent of the BAT standards for an industrial waste landfill set out in Chapter 3745-29 of the Administrative Code. The general requirements for each of the other classifications are basically the same, but the design and construction standards are gradually relaxed. For example, a Class IV residual waste facility may require a recompacted soil liner that is only one and one-half feet thick, and the post-closure care period may be reduced to as few as five years.[38] The same procedural requirements for obtaining a permit and an annual operating license that apply to solid waste facilities also apply to residual waste facilities.

2.1.4 Solid Waste Transfer Facility Standards

Solid waste transfer facilities must obtain a permit and are subject to similar requirements governing their location, design, construction, operation, and final closure.[39] Restrictions governing the acceptance of yard waste by transfer facilities were last amended in 1999.[40] "Solid waste transfer facilities" are defined to specifically exclude portable containers that have an aggregate volume of fifty cubic yards or less, legitimate recycling facilities, and scrap tire facilities.[41] A solid waste transfer facility cannot accept hazardous waste, asbestos or asbestos-containing material, wastes containing liquids which can be readily released under normal conditions, and any untreated infectious wastes.[42] "Legitimate recycling facilities" are defined as those facilities where recycling of material, other than scrap tires, is the primary activity and only source-separated recyclables are accepted, or, if mixed solid wastes and recyclable materials are accepted, those where at least sixty percent of the materials received each month is recycled for at least eight months in a calendar year.[43]

---

[38] OAC 3745-30-10(A), -04(C).

[39] OAC 3745-27-21 to -24.

[40] OAC 3745-27-23.

[41] OAC 3745-27-01(C)(13).

[42] OAC 3745-27-23(O)(1)-(4).

[43] OAC 3745-27-01(C)(2).

2.1.5 Solid Waste Incinerator Standards

Solid waste incinerators are subject to BAT standards.[44] These standards are similar to the standards for other solid waste management facilities and are in addition to the standards established under the air pollution control laws.[45] However, incinerators, other than those used for treatment of infectious waste, located on the premises where the wastes incinerated are generated are exempt from the BAT requirements found in OAC 3745-27.[46] Waste-to-energy facilities are no longer exempt from the solid waste permitting requirements.[47]

2.1.6 Scrap Tire Facilities

In order to operate a scrap tire collection, storage, monofill, monocell, or recovery facility in Ohio, the owner or operator must submit to the Director of Ohio EPA an application for either a registration certificate or a permit and apply for a license to the local Board of Health or Ohio EPA, as appropriate.[48] Ohio EPA has substantively changed its scrap tire rules effective March 29, 2002. For further discussion, see Part 7.0 of this chapter.

2.2 License Requirements

No person may operate or maintain a solid waste disposal or transfer facility without a valid and unexpired license issued by the Board of Health of the health district in which the facility is located, or the Director of Ohio EPA.[49] The Board of Health or the Director shall not issue a solid waste license unless: (1) the applicant has obtained a PTI; (2) the Director has approved the detail plans for the facility; (3) in the case of a previously or currently operating facility, the applicant operated the facility in compliance with all applicable laws; (4) the facility is adequately prepared for operations and has been inspected by the Health Commissioner and the Ohio EPA Director; and (5) the operator is competent

---

[44] OAC 3745-27-50 *et seq.*

[45] *See* OAC 3745-17-09.

[46] OAC 3745-27-03(E)

[47] *See* OAC 3745-27-03.

[48] ORC §§ 3734.75 - .78; *see* ORC § 3734.81.

[49] ORC § 3734.05(A)(1).

and qualified to operate the facility in substantial compliance with Ohio law and regulations.[50]

The Board of Health must either grant or deny a solid waste facility license within ninety days after a completed application has been approved unless detail plans have not been approved and a PTI has not been issued prior to the expiration of the ninety-day period. For new facilities, a license shall be issued or denied following the Director's issuance of the PTI, but not later than thirty days after the site has been inspected.[51] All solid waste facility licenses expire on December 31 of the year in which they become effective.[52] The license must be renewed on an annual basis during the month of December for the following year. Applications for a renewal license must be submitted in September.[53]

In granting or denying a solid waste license, the Board of Health must comply with Sections 3709.20 and 3709.21 and Chapter 3734 of the Revised Code,[54] which requires an opportunity for an adjudication hearing before the Environmental Review Appeals Commission.[55] Before the Board of Health may issue a license, it must inspect the solid waste disposal facility. Within thirty days after the issuance of a license, the Board of Health must certify to the Director that the facility has been inspected and is in substantial compliance with the statutory provisions.[56]

2.3 Inspection And Enforcement

Ohio law grants the Board of Health or the Ohio EPA Director, or their authorized representatives, the authority to enter at reasonable times upon any public or private property to inspect or investigate, obtain samples, and examine or copy any records, to determine compliance with the statute. If entry is refused, or if inspection or investigation is refused or hindered, the Board of Health or the Director, or their authorized

---

[50] OAC 3745-37-03.

[51] OAC 3745-37-04(A).

[52] OAC 3745-37-05.

[53] ORC § 3734.05(A).

[54] OAC 3745-37-07(B).

[55] ORC § 3745.04.

[56] ORC § 3734.07(A) - (B).

representatives, may apply for, and any judge of a court of record may issue, an appropriate inspection warrant necessary to achieve the purposes of the statute within the court's territorial jurisdiction. The court also may order the owner or operator to reimburse the Board of Health or the Director for costs associated with obtaining the warrant.

In addition, the Director or Board of Health may revoke or suspend a facility's operating license or permit.[57] Ohio EPA may request the Ohio Attorney General to bring a civil action to enforce Chapter 3734 or any rule adopted thereunder, or the terms of any permit issued thereunder. A civil penalty of up to $25,000 may be assessed for each day of each violation.[58]

2.4 Solid Waste Management Plans

As amended by HB 592, Chapter 3734 of the Revised Code establishes an elaborate planning process for State and local solid waste management. Under this law, each county must either establish its own Solid Waste Management District ("SWMD") or participate in establishing a joint SWMD made up of two or more counties.[59] Each district must prepare, adopt, submit for Ohio EPA approval, and then implement a Solid Waste Management Plan that conforms to the statutory requirements, the State Solid Waste Management Plan,[60] and Ohio EPA guidelines.[61]

The general requirements for all district Solid Waste Management Plans include: inventories of the sources, composition, and quantities of solid waste generated in the district; inventories of solid waste collection systems, transfer and disposal facilities, recycling activities, and open dumps, including those open dumps that contain scrap tires; projections for population, solid waste generation rates, and solid waste disposal rates; identification of any additional facilities required to serve the district and a siting strategy for

---

[57] ORC § 3734.07(C).

[58] ORC § 3734.13(C).

[59] ORC §§ 343.01, 3734.52.

[60] *See* http://www.epa.state.oh.us/dsiwm/pages/stateplan.html.

[61] *See* ORC §§ 3734.50 - .56.

such additional facilities; financial analyses; forecasts of potential liability to affected communities; and an implementation schedule.[62]

District plans also must establish the disposal or generation fees to be collected at solid waste disposal facilities, allocate the revenues from these fees, and provide the necessary authority for the district to establish rules.[63] District rules may affect the use of solid waste management facilities by generators outside the district and may impose additional requirements for the establishment of new facilities or the expansion of existing facilities.[64]

Requirements for solid waste management plans were first amended in 1996 to reflect the goals of the State Solid Waste Management Plan. In general the plans must include strategies to provide technical and informational assistance on waste reduction, reuse, recycling, and composting activities to solid waste generators within the district, and to manage household hazardous waste and scrap tires.[65] In particular, solid waste management plans that are due for their triennial amendment after August 1996 or that need to be amended due to material changes in circumstances, must demonstrate that their waste reduction and recycling programs are complying with Ohio law.[66]

In 2001, Ohio EPA updated the State Solid Waste Management Plan. Although the revised plan does not substantively depart from the goals of the initial plan, it:

(1) increases the industrial waste reduction and recycling goal from fifty percent to sixty-six percent;

(2) adds a goal that directs a SWMD to evaluate the feasibility of incorporating economic incentives into its source reduction and recycling programs; and

---

[62] ORC § 3734.53(A).

[63] ORC § 3734.53(B) - (C).

[64] ORC §§ 343.01(G), 3734.53(C).

[65] OAC 3745-27-90(D).

[66] The district must demonstrate either: (1) that its solid waste reduction, reuse, or recycling programs will be available to the residential and commercial sectors for at least seven of eleven materials (cardboard, office papers, newspapers, glass food and drink containers, steel food and drink containers, aluminum containers, plastic containers, wood packaging, lead acid batteries, major appliances, and yard wastes); residential solid waste generators must have access to the same recycling programs for at least four of the seven materials designated by the district; or (2) that its programs will reduce or recycle at least twenty-five percent of the municipal solid wastes and at least fifty percent of the industrial solid wastes generated by the year 2000, and that it will develop other waste reduction programs if the district relies on incineration or composting to manage more than fifty percent of its solid waste. OAC 3745-27-90(E)(1) - (2).

(3) establishes a statewide reduction and recycling goal of fifty percent by 2005.

Under the original deadlines established by HB 592, all SWMDs should have developed an initial plan by June 24, 1992, and should have begun implementation of the plan no later than December 24, 1993.[67] The law provides for periodic plan review and amendment at regular three-year intervals. The procedure for a plan amendment is the same as that for the adoption of the initial plan and involves ratification of the plan by county boards of commissioners, the largest municipalities within a district, and local legislative authorities representing at least sixty percent of the district's population.[68]

Initially, Ohio's solid waste management laws included a three-tiered fee system of both state and SWMD disposal fees, which imposed higher fees on wastes received at a land disposal facility from outside its "host" district, and still higher fees on wastes received from outside the State of Ohio.[69] The fee system was challenged as an impermissible burden on interstate commerce in a lawsuit filed by the National Solid Waste Management Association.[70] As part of a settlement agreement in that case, the disposal fee system was revised to provide for a flat state fee and a restricted range of SWMD disposal fees.[71] The statutes were revised to allow solid waste districts to levy a "generation fee" on solid wastes generated within their boundaries regardless of whether they are disposed of within or outside the district,[72] and to provide for contractual arrangements between solid waste management firms and districts to provide for the collection of a fee to support the activities within the district.[73]

Districts were given the authority to "designate" or limit the facilities that could dispose of solid wastes generated within their boundaries to augment their planning authority and provide for more definitive capacity assurance. Subsequent legislation revised

---

[67] ORC § 3734.55.

[68] *See* ORC §§ 3734.55 - .56.

[69] Former ORC § 3734.57(A) - (B).

[70] National Solid Waste Mgmt. Assn. v. Voinovich, 763 F. Supp. 244 (S.D. Ohio 1991), *reversed*, 959 F.2d 590 (6th Cir. 1992).

[71] ORC § 3734.57(A) - (B).

[72] ORC § 3734.574.

this authority and allowed districts the option of either "designating" facilities and exercising control over the flow of wastes from the district, or merely "identifying" facilities and allowing new or different facilities to be selected as needed by generators within the district.[74]

Following these legislative changes, on May 16, 1994, the United States Supreme Court ruled that a local ordinance requiring all solid wastes within the town of Clarkstown, New York, to be delivered to a transfer station operated for the town by a private contractor was invalid.[75] In a majority opinion written by Justice Kennedy, the Court held that the ordinance regulated interstate commerce and was invalid because it discriminated by favoring one local operator to the exclusion of any other providers in the same market. The Court further reasoned that there were less restrictive means to protect any legitimate local interest in public health and safety, such as developing uniform safety regulations. Finally, the Court ruled that the town's desire to support the construction and purchase of the transfer station through tipping fees did not justify the flow control ordinance, since the transfer facility could be financed through general taxes or municipal bonds without discriminating against interstate commerce.

Shortly after the *Carbone* decision, on May 27, 1994, Ohio's designation provisions were challenged when Mid-American Waste Systems, Inc., filed a complaint and a request for a temporary restraining order in federal district court in Columbus, seeking to delay the effective date of a new generation fee established by the Solid Waste Authority of Central Ohio ("SWACO").[76] The district, which relied upon publicly owned transfer stations, a waste-to-energy facility, and landfills to supply the majority of its required capacity, adopted two resolutions to maximize the utilization of these facilities and to assure a stable source of revenues for their continued operation.

Mid-American, which operates a materials recovery facility ("MRF") and hauling company from its facility in Canal Winchester, Ohio, had signed a designation

---

[73] ORC § 343.022.

[74] ORC §§ 343.013 - .015.

[75] C & A Carbone, Inc. v. Town of Clarkstown, NY, 511 U.S. 383, 114 S. Ct. 1677 (1994).

[76] Mid-American Waste Systems, Inc. v. Fisher, Case No. C-2-94-493, 1994 U.S. Dist. LEXIS 20966 (S.D. Ohio May 31, 1994).

agreement with SWACO which required Mid-American to utilize Ohio facilities for the disposal of residues from its MRF. Mid-American challenged the SWACO resolutions as an undue restraint on interstate commerce.

The district court granted Mid-American's request for a temporary restraining order, but delayed the enforcement of that order for a period of ninety days, until September 1, 1994. Relying extensively upon the United States Supreme Court's decision in *Carbone*, the court found that SWACO's resolutions affected interstate commerce by limiting the facilities that can compete for in-district wastes, and discriminated against interstate commerce without demonstrating that there is no other means to advance the local interests served by the resolutions.

In a more recent decision by the United States Court of Appeals for the Sixth Circuit, however, an Ohio SWMD's designation resolution was upheld on the grounds that it did not discriminate or advance local interests.[77] In *Maharg*, the Van Wert SWMD passed a resolution requesting proposals by operators of solid waste facilities. The request for bids required the successful designee to enter into a "designation agreement" and to pay a "contract fee" for each ton of solid waste generated within the district and delivered to the designated facility. The request for bids was for all facilities in Northeastern Indiana and Northwestern Ohio. Maharg, Inc. collects solid waste from residential and industrial customers, some of which are located in Van Wert County, Ohio. All the waste collected is hauled to a solid waste facility in Indiana that refused to enter into a designation agreement with the Van Wert solid waste management district. Maharg brought suit against the district claiming that the contract fee constitutes a "direct regulation" of interstate commerce.

The Sixth Circuit held in *Maharg* that the Van Wert SWMD's designation scheme was constitutional, did not violate the interstate commerce clause, and did not discriminate between local or instate facilities from those located across state lines. Additionally, the court found that unlike the "flow control" plan in *Carbone*, the district's scheme did not place an excessive burden on interstate commerce in comparison to the supposed local benefits achieved by the scheme.

---

[77] Maharg, Inc. v. Van Wert Solid Waste Management District, 249 F.3d 544 (6th Cir. 2001).

2.5 Affected Communities

Legislation enacted in 1996[78] amended Chapter 3734 of the Revised Code to provide that a community affected by a new or modified public landfill may seek compensation for any expenses it incurred as a result of the siting, operation, or closure of the landfill, through negotiations with the solid waste management district in which the landfill is located.[79]

The expenses that an affected community may be compensated for are: road improvements and maintenance; emergency services; litter prevention and reduction; collection and analysis of water wells; and enforcement of public health codes and environmental laws.[80] If an agreement cannot be reached, then either party can request binding arbitration. Arbitration awards may be appealed to the court of common pleas in the county in which the affected community is located.[81]

3.0 TRANSPORTATION OF SOLID WASTES FROM OUTSIDE STATE

Revisions to Chapter 3734 of the Revised Code in 1994[82] prohibit the transportation of solid waste from outside the State to a facility inside the State unless the transporter has first irrevocably consented in writing to the jurisdiction of the courts of Ohio by filing Consent-to-Jurisdiction forms with the Director of Ohio EPA and the owner or operator of the receiving waste facility.[83] All Consent-to-Jurisdiction documents must have been refiled in December 1995 and during the month of December of every fourth year thereafter.[84]

---

[78] HB 122, 121st General Assembly (Eff. Oct. 31, 1996).

[79] ORC § 3734.35(A). To be "affected," a community must: (1) be located one kilometer or less from the property boundary of the landfill; (2) not be a municipal corporation, township, or county in which the landfill is located; and (3) not be located in the same solid waste management district as the landfill. *Id.*

[80] ORC § 3734.35(C)

[81] ORC § 3734.35(E)

[82] HB 647, 120th General Assembly (Eff. July 22, 1994).

[83] ORC § 3734.131(A)(1) - (2). The prohibition does not apply to the transportation, transfer, or disposal of solid waste from residential premises located less than ten miles outside the boundaries of Ohio. *Id.* at (D)(1). Neither does it apply to Ohio or foreign corporations or nonresident motor carriers that have designated agents under applicable sections of the Revised Code, or to other residents of Ohio. *Id.* at (D)(2).

[84] ORC § 3734.131(A)(3).

4.0 QUALIFICATIONS OF LICENSEES AND RELATED PERSONS

Section 3734.40 of the Revised Code states that off-site treatment, storage, and disposal of solid and hazardous waste is "critical" to Ohio's economic structure and, when properly controlled, makes "substantial contributions" to the general welfare, health, and prosperity of the State and its inhabitants. Pursuant to its goal of fostering and justifying the "public confidence and trust in the credibility and integrity" of these activities, the Ohio General Assembly adopted a scheme that prevents "persons who are not competent and reliable or who have pursued economic gains in an occupational manner or context violative of the criminal code or civil public policies" of Ohio from operating off-site facilities.[85] The statutory scheme then requires the submission of a disclosure statement by applicants for a permit for a solid, hazardous, or infectious waste permit, grants the Ohio Attorney General authority to conduct background investigations, and sets out the criteria for disqualification from receipt of a permit or license.

4.1 Disclosure Statement

Section 3734.42 of the Revised Code provides that every application for an off-site facility permit must include a "disclosure statement," submitted on forms provided by Ohio EPA, the contents of which are more fully described in rules adopted by the Attorney General.[86] This statement must disclose extensive specified information regarding the applicant and, if a business, its officers, directors, partners, or key employees, as well as holders of equity in the business. The statement must include a description of the credentials and experience of these persons (excluding equity holders). Applicants also must list and explain the following: any civil or criminal prosecution by government agencies, administrative enforcement actions resulting in the imposition of sanctions, or license revocations or denials issued in the ten years immediately preceding the filing of the application, that are pending or have resulted in a finding of a violation of any environmental protection statute; and any judgment, liability, or conviction under any federal, state, or local law, that resulted in a sanction against the applicant, or, if a business, against the business or

---

[85] ORC § 3734.40.

[86] OAC Chapter 109:6-1.

any of its officers, directors, partners, or key employees. The applicant must list all agencies outside Ohio that have or have had regulatory responsibility over the applicant in connection with solid, infectious, or hazardous waste-related activities. In addition, the Attorney General or the Ohio EPA Director may require the applicant to disclose other information "that relates to the competency, reliability, or good character of the applicant."[87]

Anyone who already holds a permit or license for an off-site facility must file a disclosure statement according to a schedule developed by the Attorney General covering a five-year period.[88] Whenever there is a change of ownership of any off-site facility, the prospective owner must file a disclosure statement with the Attorney General and the Director of Ohio EPA at least 180 days prior to the proposed change.[89]

4.2 Background Investigation

Within a specified time after receipt of the disclosure statement, the Attorney General will prepare and submit to Ohio EPA an investigative report. The Attorney General will base this report on the information revealed in the disclosure statement, but also may receive criminal history information from the Federal Bureau of Investigation or any other law enforcement agency.[90]

With regard to this investigation, the Ohio Attorney General has several important information-gathering and enforcement powers. First, all applicants and permittees must provide any assistance or information requested by the Attorney General or the Ohio EPA Director. Refusal to cooperate in an investigation or inquiry may result in denial or revocation of a permit or license.[91] Second, the Attorney General may issue an "investigative demand" upon persons or businesses believed to possess documentary materials relevant to an investigation. This demand may require production of documents, answers to interrogatories, appearance, and testimony.[92] Finally, the court of common pleas

---

[87] ORC § 3734.41(D).

[88] ORC § 3734.42(E).

[89] ORC § 3734.42(F)(1).

[90] ORC § 3734.42(A)(3) - (4).

[91] ORC § 3734.42(B).

[92] ORC § 3734.43(B).

has authority to modify, set aside, and enforce investigative demands; unless the information is confidential, privileged, or otherwise subject to immunity, the Attorney General may use the disclosed information as evidence in any other proceeding.[93]

4.3 Disqualification

The Revised Code also sets out the possible grounds for disqualification from receipt of a license or permit. No permit or license may be issued or renewed unless Ohio EPA, the Hazardous Waste Facility Board ("HWFB"), or the Board of Health finds that the applicant's prior performance record in the handling of solid, infectious, or hazardous waste demonstrates "sufficient reliability, expertise, and competency" to operate a waste facility. If no prior record exists, the permitting or licensing authority must find that the applicant is "likely to exhibit" that reliability, expertise, and competence.[94]

No permit or license may be issued or renewed if any individual or business listed in the disclosure statement or shown to have a beneficial interest in the business, other than an equity interest or debt liability, has been convicted of any of twenty-one enumerated crimes. These crimes vary from murder and kidnapping to crimes relating to firearms and controlled substances.[95] Notwithstanding this list of crimes, no one may be denied the issuance or renewal of a permit or license on the basis of a conviction if the applicant "has affirmatively demonstrated rehabilitation" of the individual or business by a preponderance of the evidence.[96] If the offense disclosed is a felony, a permit "shall be denied" unless five years have elapsed since discharge from imprisonment, probation, or parole.[97] Section 3734.44(C) sets out the criteria by which the Director, the HWFB, or the Board of Health may determine that an applicant has affirmatively demonstrated rehabilitation.[98]

Finally, no one may receive a permit or license unless the Director, the HWFB, or the Board of Health finds that the applicant has a history of compliance with

---

93 ORC § 3734.43(H) - (R).

94 ORC § 3734.44.

95 *See* ORC § 3734.44(B).

96 ORC § 3734.44(C).

97 *Id.*

98 *See* ORC § 3734.44(C)(1) - (9).

environmental laws and is currently in substantial compliance with, or on a schedule that will ensure compliance with, environmental laws.[99]

4.4 Revocation / Denial

With regard to holders of existing permits, if the Director of Ohio EPA determines that the disclosure statement and investigative report contain information that would require the denial of a permit application, the Director may revoke any previously issued permits or may deny any application for a renewal.[100] With regard to prospective owners, if the Director determines that the disclosure statement and investigative report contain information that would require the denial of a permit application, the Director may disapprove the change in ownership. If the parties proceed with the change prior to the Director's approval, the parties must include in the contract language expressly making the change in ownership subject to the approval of the Director and expressly negating the change if approval is not given.[101]

The Director of Ohio EPA or the Board of Health may revoke a permit or license for any of the following causes: (1) any cause that would disqualify an applicant from receiving a permit; (2) fraud, deceit, or misrepresentation in securing a permit or in conducting permitted activities; (3) inducement of another individual to violate any law relating to the handling of solid, infectious, or hazardous waste; (4) coercion of any customer to utilize the services of the permittee; or (5) prevention of the transfer or disposal of solid or hazardous waste, or the treatment of infectious waste, at a facility not owned or operated by the applicant or licensee.[102]

5.0 INFECTIOUS WASTE MANAGEMENT

Infectious waste was first recognized as a separate waste type by Ohio with the enactment of legislation in 1988.[103] SB 243 required the Director of Ohio EPA to develop

---

[99] ORC § 3734.44(D).

[100] ORC § 3734.42(E).

[101] ORC § 3734.42(F).

[102] ORC § 3734.45.

[103] *See* SB 243 and HB 592, 118th General Assembly (Eff. Aug. 10, 1988 and June 24, 1988, respectively).

regulations governing the proper handling of infectious wastes and establishing standards for generators, transporters, and treatment facilities. HB 592 created a separate category of nonhazardous wastes for infectious wastes. In response to these legislative directives, Ohio EPA developed a comprehensive regulatory program that became effective May 1, 1990.

5.1 Definition

"Infectious wastes" are defined generally as waste materials contaminated with an infectious agent that causes or contributes to increased disease or mortality in human beings.[104] There are nine specific categories of these wastes: cultures and stocks of infectious agents; laboratory wastes; pathological wastes; isolation wastes; blood and blood products; animals used in research and related bedding; sharp wastes such as hypodermic needles, syringes, scalpel blades, and glass articles; waste from biological research; and radioactive infectious waste.[105]

5.2 Generator Standards

Producers of infectious waste are categorized as either small or large generators.[106] Small generators – those producing less than fifty pounds of infectious waste per month – are typically doctors, dentists, and veterinarians. These generators are required to quantify and record the amount of infectious waste generated each month; treat all specimen cultures produced or transport such cultures, via a licensed transporter, to a licensed treatment facility; and, prior to disposal, contain all sharp infectious wastes in packages designated "SHARPS."[107]

Producers of fifty pounds or more of infectious waste must comply with additional regulatory requirements. In accordance with the standards in Rule 3745-27-36(A) of the Administrative Code, large generators must obtain a registration certificate from Ohio EPA. A separate registration certificate is required for each premises owned or operated by

---

[104] *See* OAC 3745-27-01(U) - (V).

[105] OAC 3745-27-01(V)(1) - (10).

[106] *See generally* OAC 3745-27-30.

[107] OAC 3745-27-30(A).

the generator, and is valid for three years.[108] Large generators are required to segregate infectious wastes from other solid wastes at the point of generation.[109] These segregated wastes must then be further separated and placed in containers that are designated as either infectious waste or as sharp infectious waste. Packaging and labeling standards are detailed in Rule 3745-27-34.

If infectious wastes are transported off-site for treatment, "shipping papers" specifically identifying each package of waste must accompany the shipment. These shipping papers must meet the requirements of Rule 3745-27-33 and contain the following information: name and signature of the generator; name and phone number of the premises where the waste was generated; name and signature of the transporter; transporter registration number; name of the treatment facility; brief description of the infectious waste being shipped; type and quantity of containers being shipped; and certification by the generator that the wastes are packaged and labeled in accordance with applicable requirements.[110]

Large generators also are required to prepare spill containment and cleanup plans that must be maintained on-site.[111] A copy of these procedures must be available on the premises to persons likely to handle the infectious wastes, including janitorial employees or services. Generators must record any spill or release incidents involving infectious wastes.[112]

5.3 Transporter Standards

Transporters of infectious wastes are also subject to stringent regulatory restrictions.[113] Any person transporting infectious waste must register with Ohio EPA as an infectious waste transporter and obtain a vehicle registration decal for each vehicle used for infectious waste transportation.[114] Licensed transporters can accept for shipment only

---

[108] OAC 3745-27-36(A).

[109] OAC 3745-27-30(B)(1).

[110] OAC 3745-27-33.

[111] OAC 3745-27-30(B)(11).

[112] OAC 3745-27-30(B)(10).

[113] *See* OAC 3745-27-31.

[114] OAC 3745-27-31(A)(1), (F).

infectious wastes that are accompanied by shipping papers and that are packaged and labeled in accordance with the standards of Rules 3745-27-30 and 3745-27-33.[115]

Infectious wastes may be transported in only leak-resistant, fully covered vehicle compartments.[116] If the wastes are to be left within the transporting vehicle for more than thirty-six hours, they must be refrigerated at a temperature between two and eight degrees centigrade.[117] The wastes must be secured within the transporting vehicle and be transported with only other infectious wastes. Further, the wastes must be delivered to a licensed treatment facility in Ohio, a treatment facility owned or operated by the generator, or a treatment facility located in another state operating in compliance with applicable state and federal regulations, within ten consecutive calendar days. The transporter must carry a spill containment kit and certain emergency response equipment, and disinfect any surfaces that may have come in contact with the wastes.

5.4 Infectious Waste Treatment Facilities

Ohio EPA's infectious waste regulatory scheme includes the permitting and operation of infectious waste treatment facilities. With certain facility exceptions, infectious waste treatment facilities require a separate and valid license to operate.[118] New or modified off-site infectious waste treatment facilities must obtain a PTI from Ohio EPA and an annual operating license issued by an approved health district or the Director in accordance with Chapter 3745-27 of the Administrative Code.

The Director may not approve any PTI application if the facility will violate Chapters 3704 or 6111 of the Revised Code; the facility is located in a floodway; the person responsible for management or operation has not managed the facility in substantive compliance with the applicable provisions of Chapters 3704, 3734, and 6111 of the Revised Code; or the applicant does not meet the requirements of Sections 3734.40 and 3734.43.[119] Rule 3745-27-37 also includes location restrictions for infectious waste facilities.

---

[115] OAC 3745-27-31(A)(2) - (3).

[116] OAC 3745-27-31(A)(4).

[117] OAC 3745-27-31(A)(5).

[118] OAC 3745-37-01(A).

[119] OAC 3745-27-37(D).

Standards for the operation of infectious treatment facilities are outlined in Rule 3745-27-32. Licensed infectious waste facilities are inspected quarterly by either the local approved health district or Ohio EPA to assure compliance with the operational standards. Approved treatment methods include incineration and autoclaving as specified in the rule. The treatment facilities must comply with additional operational restrictions, certain quality control procedures, shipping paper requirements, and infectious waste storage requirements. Off-site incinerators are subject to special provisions under the air pollution control regulations.

Upon proper notification and approval, an infectious waste facility's license may be transferred from one person to another. No license may be transferred between facilities.[120]

6.0 CONSTRUCTION AND DEMOLITION DEBRIS

Construction and demolition debris ("C&DD") is expressly excluded from the definition of "solid wastes" in Chapter 3734 of the Revised Code.[121] It was largely unregulated until 1990, when the Ohio General Assembly passed legislation creating a new regulatory program.[122]

Set out in Chapter 3714 of the Revised Code, the C&DD program is administered jointly by Ohio EPA and local Boards of Health. It requires annual licensure of C&DD disposal facilities and the establishment of standards governing their location, construction, design, operation, and inspection. Although Ohio EPA drafted implementing rules for the program in 1992, it was not until 1996 that final rules were published in Chapter 3745-400 of the Administrative Code.[123] In August 2002, Ohio finalized amendments to these rules, making helpful clarifications.

"Construction and demolition debris" is defined as "materials resulting from the alteration, construction, destruction, rehabilitation, or repair of any manmade physical

[120] OAC 3745-37-06.

[121] ORC § 3734.01(E).

[122] HB 366, 118th General Assembly (Eff. July 24, 1990).

[123] The rules do not apply to a construction site where construction debris, and trees and brush removed in clearing the site, are used as fill material on-site, or to any site where clean hard fill is used. OAC 3745-400-03.

structure, including, without limitation, houses, buildings, industrial or commercial facilities, or roadways."[124] The definition specifically excludes materials that are otherwise identified as solid, infectious, or hazardous waste; materials from mining operations, nontoxic fly ash, spent nontoxic foundry sand, and slag; and all concrete, asphalt, or building or paving brick or stone that is stored for less than two years for recycling as usable construction material.[125] Also excluded from the definition are materials required to be removed prior to demolition, materials that are contained within or exist outside the structure, and liquids including containerized or bulk liquids and other closed or filled containers, tires, and batteries.[126] The 2002 amendments to these rules clarify the reuse, recycle, and storage exclusions to the definition of "construction and demolition debris" by defining these terms and providing an distinct exclusion for materials being reused, recycled, and temporarily stored.[127] Moreover, the amendments provide a definition of "disposal," making it clear that the C&DD rules do not apply to materials that have not been disposed.[128]

6.1 Licensing Of Construction And Demolition Debris Disposal Facilities

Section 3714.06 of the Revised Code, created in 1990, established initial licensing requirements for the installation, modification, and operation of C&DD disposal facilities. However, in 1996 Ohio EPA promulgated more detailed application requirements that are contained in Chapter 3745-37 of the Administrative Code.

The application for a C&DD facility license must be submitted at least ninety days prior to the proposed operation of a new or expanded facility. The facility owner or operator must submit the application, along with an annual $3,000 licensing fee, to the local Board of Health or Ohio EPA, as appropriate.[129]

---

[124] ORC § 3714.01(C); OAC 3745-400-01(F).

[125] *Id.* The exclusion of infectious waste is found in the rule, not the statute.

[126] OAC 3745-400-01(F).

[127] OAC 3745-400-01(II), (LL), and (OO). *See* OAC 3745-400-03, revised to provide precise language excluding those materials being reused, recycled, and stored.

[128] OAC 3745-400-01(N).

[129] ORC §§ 3714.06(A), .07. *See* OAC 3745-37-01(C), -02(A), (B), (D).

The license application must include a facility design plan; a letter from the local fire department stating that it will respond to fires at the C&DD facility; a plan drawing delineating the active, inactive, and unfilled disposal areas; the acreage for each area; the remaining life of the facility; financial assurance documentation; and a debris placement plan prepared by a professional engineer that includes operation plan drawings, drawings of the surface water run-on and run-off control structures, a pre-acceptance debris screening program narrative, and, for an existing facility, plan drawings showing horizontal limits of any soil barrier layer for construction over placed debris.[130]

The local Board of Health or Ohio EPA must grant or deny the application for a C&DD license within ninety days of its receipt.[131] The licensing authority will not issue a license unless all portions of the proposed facility meet the location requirements of Rule 3745-400-06 and other applicable statutory and regulatory requirements.[132] Any facility may seek an exemption from the rules governing C&DD facilities, except rules prohibiting new facilities within the boundaries of a sole source aquifer and rules requiring ground water monitoring.[133]

All C&DD facility licenses expire on December 31 of the year in which they become effective. Applications for renewal licenses must be submitted during the month of September.[134] Upon proper notification of and approval by the licensing authority, a license may be transferred to another person. The license holder must publish, at four-week intervals, prominent notice of the request for transfer in a paper of general circulation in the county in which the facility is located. No license may be transferred between facilities.[135]

A C&DD facility license may be suspended, denied, or revoked for a violation of Chapter 3714, any rules adopted thereunder, or the terms and conditions of a current license. A written order must be issued denying, revoking, or suspending a license, and must

---

[130] OAC 3745-37-02(E).

[131] OAC 3745-37-04(D).

[132] OAC 3745-37-03(C).

[133] ORC § 3714.06(C).

[134] OAC 3745-37-02, -05.

[135] OAC 3745-37-06.

state the findings upon which the action is based. Except in cases of emergency, the facility operator must receive prior written notice of such an order.[136]

C&DD facility modifications and exemptions are addressed in Rule 3745-400-15.

6.2 Siting Criteria

No C&DD facility constructed or in operation after July 24, 1990, may be located within the boundaries of a 100-year floodplain or a sole source aquifer.[137] The Board of Health or Ohio EPA may issue an exemption from this restriction if the exemption is unlikely to adversely affect the public health or safety or the environment. If the exemption would create an increase of more than one foot in the flood stage elevation upstream or downstream from the facility, the exemption will not be granted.[138] These siting criteria do not apply to facilities under construction or in operation prior to July 24, 1990, or to the expansion of such facility onto land owned by the facility owner or operator on the date the initial license application for that facility was submitted to the licensing authority.[139]

6.3 Design Requirements And Construction Specifications

The owner or operator of the C&DD facility must submit with the license application a facility design plan that includes the site characterization report outlined in Rule 3745-400-09(C); the facility construction design plan, including the soil liner and leachate collection system plans, outlined in Rule 3745-400-07(F); the final cap system design plan outlined in Rule 3745-400-07(G); and the ground water monitoring system plan outlined in Rule 3745-400-10.[140] The facility owner or operator must meet all the construction and performance specifications of Rule 3745-400-07, with certain exceptions involving recompacted soil liners and leachate collection systems.[141]

---

[136] ORC § 3714.10; *see* OAC 3745-37-07.

[137] ORC § 3714.03.

[138] ORC § 3714.04.

[139] ORC § 3714.06(C); OAC 3745-400-06.

[140] OAC 3745-400-07(A).

[141] OAC 3745-400-07(C).

Upon completion of each engineering component required by Rule 3745-400-07, the installation of ground water monitoring wells, or construction of the final cap system, the facility owner or operator must submit a certification report to the licensing authority. The purpose of the report is to certify that construction or installation complies with all applicable specifications. Each construction certification report must be certified by a professional engineer; the report on the installation of monitoring wells must be certified by a ground water scientist.[142]

6.4 Site Characterization

Rule 3745-400-09 sets out requirements for site characterization related to employment of a recompacted soil liner for all unfilled areas in a facility, requirements for site characterization related to a ground water monitoring well system, and requirements for the site characterization report required to be submitted as part of the facility design plan.[143]

6.5 Ground Water Monitoring

Ground water monitoring, assessment, and reporting requirements are set out in Rule 3745-400-10. The facility owner or operator must have a ground water monitoring well system unless the limits of debris placement meet specific criteria.[144] The number, spacing, and depth of wells included in the system shall be capable of determining the quality of the ground water under the facility and be based on site-specific hydrogeologic information contained in the site characterization report. The monitoring well system is not required to be capable of determining the impact of the facility on the quality of the ground water.[145]

[142] OAC 3745-400-08(A) - (B).

[143] *See* OAC 3745-400-09(A) - (C).

[144] OAC 3745-400-10(A); *see* OAC 3745-400-09(B).

[145] OAC 3745-400-10(A).

6.6 Operation Of Facilities

C&DD may be disposed of only by landfilling or by other approved methods that are capable of disposing of the debris without creating a nuisance or health hazard, causing water pollution, or violating any applicable requirements related to air pollution control and solid and hazardous wastes. Open burning of debris is permitted only as consistent with Chapter 3745-19 of the Administrative Code.[146]

Rule 3745-400-11 outlines the operational requirements of a licensed C&DD facility relating to compliance with all applicable requirements; records management; debris placement; construction maintenance; waste acceptance; equipment availability; fire prevention and control; access restrictions; inclement weather precautions; scavenging; litter control and disposal; management of the cap system, leachate system, and surface water; and ground water monitoring.[147] The 2002 amendments made several changes to the operational requirements found in Rule 3745-400-11 including: requiring that the owner or operator place and maintain markers defining the limits of the active licensed disposal area, and not divert surface water under, over, or through disposal areas of a facility.[148]

6.7 Closure Of Facilities

Closure of a C&DD facility is mandatory when the owner or operator declares that debris will no longer be accepted; a license has expired without renewal; a license has been denied, suspended or revoked; or all approved limits of debris placement and final elevations have been reached.[149] Except where a license is denied, suspended, or revoked, the owner or operator must provide written notification of closure intent and the anticipated date of ceasing acceptance of debris to the licensing authority and the solid waste management district in which the facility is located.[150]

Final closure activities must begin within seven days of ceasing to accept debris and must be completed in such a way as to minimize further maintenance at the

---

146 OAC 3745-400-04.

147 *See* OAC 3745-400-11(B) - (R).

148 *See* OAC 3745-400-11(D), (Q).

149 OAC 3745-400-12(B).

150 OAC 3745-400-12(C).

facility, as well as the formation and release of leachate to the air, soil, surface water, or ground water, to the extent necessary to protect human health and the environment.[151]

The 2002 rule changes to 3745-400-12 provide a timeline for completion of each closure activity. Required closure activities including written notification to the licensing authority and blocking all entrances and access roads to the facility must be completed within seven days of ceasing to accept debris.[152] Within thirty days of ceasing acceptance of debris, the owner or operator must post signs that the facility is closed and no longer accepting debris.[153] Within sixty days of ceasing to accept debris for disposal the owner or operator must cover all uncapped disposal areas with at least six inches of recompacted soil and grade the soil so that there is no ponding of water.[154] The construction of the cap system must be completed within one year of ceasing to accept debris for disposal.[155] Once the cap system is completed, all ground water monitoring wells are to be plugged and abandoned, and the owner or operator shall file with the appropriate County Recorder a plat of the facility and information describing the acreage, exact location, depth, volume, and nature of the placed debris.[156] Upon final closure, the owner or operator must submit to the licensing authority a final closure report that verifies compliance with all closure requirements.[157] Final closure is complete upon the licensing authority's written concurrence with the final closure report.[158] The licensing authority may enter a facility at reasonable times during final closure for purposes of determining compliance with closure requirements.[159]

---

151 OAC 3745-400-12(A).

152 OAC 3745-400-12(E)(1) and (2).

153 OAC 3745-400-12(E)(3).

154 OAC 3745-400-12(E)(4).

155 OAC 3745-400-12(E)(5).

156 OAC 3745-400-12(E)(6), (7).

157 OAC 3745-400-08(D).

158 OAC 3745-400-12(G).

159 OAC 3745-400-12(H).

6.8 Financial Assurance

Owners or operators must establish and maintain financial assurance for final closure of C&DD facilities. Rule 3745-400-13 requires that financial assurance be established and maintained through a variety of methods.[160] Alternate options may be sought if the licensing authority is satisfied that the alternate option will guarantee funding for final closure. Each new facility must provide $12,000 for each active licensed disposal acre, plus $2,000 per ground water monitoring well. For existing sites, financial assurance may begin at $2,400 per active acre, plus $400 per monitoring well. Financial assurance must be reviewed and adjusted annually for each license application.[161]

6.9 Inspections And Enforcement

The Board of Health or Ohio EPA, as appropriate, must make an annual inspection of each licensed C&DD facility and may enter any property to inspect, investigate, obtain samples, and examine or copy records in order to determine compliance with the provisions of Chapter 3714 of the Revised Code. A court may issue a search warrant, if necessary, but if inspection or entry by the licensing authority is refused or thwarted at a C&DD facility, the facility's license may be suspended or revoked. In addition, the facility may be charged for expenses, salaries, and fringe benefits for the personnel assigned to conduct the investigation, the attorneys necessary to obtain any search warrant, and the law enforcement personnel necessary to execute the search warrant.[162]

The Attorney General, prosecuting attorney, or city law director, within whose jurisdiction a C&DD facility is located, may commence a civil enforcement action for injunctive relief to abate any violation of Chapter 3714 or the rules adopted thereunder, or may commence an action for civil penalties for such violations at the request of the local Board of Health or Ohio EPA. The court may impose a penalty of not more than $10,000 for each day of each violation.[163]

---

[160] *See* OAC 3745-400-13(B) - (G).

[161] *See* OAC 3745-400-13 to -14.

[162] ORC § 3714.08.

[163] ORC § 3714.11(A) - (B).

The Board of Health or Ohio EPA may issue administrative orders to abate a violation, requiring that specific actions be taken within a specified, reasonable time. If an imminent hazard exists, an emergency order may be issued, to be effective immediately, but will remain effective for only ninety days. An emergency order must permit the recipient to request a hearing within thirty days.[164] Knowing violations of Chapter 3714 are second degree misdemeanors, with each day of violation treated as a separate offense.[165]

7.0 SCRAP TIRES

The General Assembly enacted legislation in 1993 that created a completely new regulatory program for scrap tires as a type of solid waste under Chapter 3734 of the Revised Code.[166] Rules implementing the program were established by Ohio EPA in 1996 and amended in 2002. Contained in Chapter 3745-27 of the Administrative Code, they cover transportation, collection, storage, disposal, and recovery of scrap tires, as well as their beneficial use.

"Scrap tire" is defined simply as "an unwanted or discarded tire."[167] Entities regulated under the scrap tire laws include transporters and collection, monocell, monofill, and recovery facilities. All must comply with requirements related to permitting or certification, licensing, operations, record-keeping, closure, post-closure, and financial assurance.

7.1 Transporters

The Director of Ohio EPA is granted authority under Section 3734.74 of the Revised Code to establish rules governing the transportation of scrap tires and the registration of persons engaged therein.

---

[164] ORC § 3714.12.

[165] ORC § 3714.99.

[166] SB 165, 120th General Assembly (Eff. Oct. 29, 1993).

[167] ORC § 3734.01(Z); OAC 3745-27-01(I)(5). "Unwanted" means that the owner or manufacturer no longer wants, or is able, to use the tire for its original purpose. "Discarded" means that the owner or manufacturer has disposed of the tire. OAC 3745-27-01(I)(5)(a). Excluded from the definition of "scrap tire" are retreaded or regrooved tires, spare tires carried on motor vehicles or trailers, or tires from bicycles or small equipment such as lawnmowers or wheelbarrows.

7.1.1 Annual Registration Requirements

Any person who transports scrap tires within Ohio must register with Ohio EPA and transport, store, and handle the tires so as not to create a nuisance, a hazard to public health or safety, or a fire hazard.[168] Transporters must file an application for an annual registration certificate at least ninety days prior to the date that the tires are to be transported and pay a registration fee of $300.[169] Registration renewal applications must be submitted by January 31 of each year and must be accompanied by the transporter's annual report required by Rule 3745-27-56.[170] Rule 3745-27-54(B)-(D) sets out information and signatory requirements for certificate applications. Criteria for the Director's approval, denial, suspension, or revocation of an annual registration certificate application are contained in Rule 3745-27-55.

7.1.2 Standards For Registered Transporters

Registered scrap tire transporters may deliver tires to only: (1) a licensed scrap tire collection, storage, monocell, monofill, or recovery facility; (2) a regulated solid waste incinerator or energy recovery facility; (3) premises where the scrap tires will be beneficially used; (4) another registered transporter; (5) a facility in another state that is in compliance with the rules of that state; or (6) a premises operating as an exempt scrap tire facility under Rule 3745-27-61(A), such as a tire retail dealer or tire retreader.[171]

Rule 3745-27-56 contains additional requirements for transporters, including temporary storage and transfer of tires, mosquito control, pre-positioning and pickup of trailers, use of shipping papers, and annual reporting.[172]

---

[168] ORC § 3734.83; OAC 3745-27-54(A)(1), -56(C)(6). Although registration may not be required depending on the number of tires transported, the reason for transportation, and the tires' intended uses, *see* OAC 3745-27-54(A)(2)(a) - (j), exempt (non-registered) transporters still must comply with the transportation, storage, and handling requirements as outlined in Rule 3745-27-56(B).

[169] ORC § 3734.83(A); OAC 3745-27-54(A)(1)(b).

[170] OAC 3745-27-54(A)(1)(b).

[171] OAC 3745-27-56(C)(1)(a) - (f).

[172] *See* OAC 3745-27-56(C)

7.1.3 Standards For Nonregistered Transporters

Transporters exempt from registration requirements must deliver scrap tires only to destinations in compliance with Rule 3745-27-56(C)(1). Before transporting the tires, they must either remove all water from the tires; arrange for all tires to be shredded or cut; or treat the tires with a larvacide approved by the Ohio Department of Agriculture.[173]

7.2 General Storage And Handling Of Scrap Tires

Rule 3745-27-60 regulates the storage and handling of tires at premises that are not required to be, or are not yet, registered or permitted and licensed. Standards address both inside and outside storage of tires and include requirements on water drainage, size of storage piles, distancing and clearance of storage piles, separation of portable containers, widths of fire lanes or aisles, and mosquito control.[174]

7.3 Collection, Storage, And Recovery Facilities

The Director of Ohio EPA is granted authority under Revised Code Sections 3734.70, 3734.71, and 3734.73 to establish rules for scrap tire collection, storage, and recovery facilities to ensure that they are located, maintained, operated, and closed in a manner that does not create a nuisance, hazard to public health or safety, or fire hazard. Sections 3734.81 and 3734.82 set out licensing and fee requirements for these facilities.

"Scrap tire collection facility" is a facility where whole scrap tires are temporarily stored in portable containers prior to transportation of the tires to a storage, monocell, monofill, or recovery facility or to a beneficial use site. The collection facility's aggregate storage area cannot exceed 5,000 cubic feet.[175]

"Scrap tire storage facility" is a facility where whole scrap tires are stored prior to their being transported to a monocell, monofill, or recovery facility or to a beneficial

---

[173] OAC 3745-27-56(B).

[174] *See* OAC 3745-27-60(A) - (B).

[175] OAC 3745-27-01(C)(5).

use site. Class I storage facilities have a *permitted* capacity of more than 10,000 square feet; Class II facilities have a *registered* capacity of 10,000 square feet or less.[176]

"Scrap tire recovery facility" means any site that is used for processing scrap tires for the purpose of extracting or producing usable products, materials, or energy. Class I recovery facilities have a *permitted* design input capacity of 200 or more tons of scrap tires per day; Class II facilities have a *registered* design input capacity of less than 200 tons per day.[177]

7.3.1 Registration / Permitting

Registration requirements and approval criteria for collection, Class II storage, and Class II recovery facilities are contained in Rules 3745-27-61 and 3745-27-62.[178] Permitting requirements and approval criteria for Class I storage and Class I recovery facilities are contained in Rules 3745-27-62 and 3745-27-63.[179] Mobile scrap tire recovery facilities, which must be registered, are regulated under Rule 3745-27-67.

7.3.2 Facility Operations

Owners or operators of licensed and registered or permitted scrap tire collection, storage, or recovery facilities must comply with requirements and operational criteria specified in Rule 3745-27-65. Included are standards for general scrap tire management, storage area size, contingency plans, mosquito and vector control, fire response and prevention, record keeping and reporting, facility compliance plans, and ash management plans, if applicable.[180]

7.3.3 Facility Closure

Final closure activities are mandatory for a scrap tire collection, storage, or recovery facility if: the facility no longer accepts scrap tires; the facility's license has

---

[176] OAC 3745-27-01(C)(10).

[177] OAC 3745-27-01(C)(9).

[178] *See* ORC §§ 3734.75 - .76, .78.

[179] *See* ORC §§ 3734.76, .78.

[180] *See* OAC 3745-27-65(A) - (L).

expired and no renewal application is pending; the license has been suspended or revoked; or the registration application has been denied.[181] Closure plan and closure certification requirements are set out in Rule 3745-27-66(B)-(D). The local Board of Health or Director of Ohio EPA may enter any closed scrap tire collection, storage, and recovery facility at any reasonable time for the purpose of determining compliance with closure requirements.[182] The facility is deemed closed when the owner or operator receives written concurrence from the Board of Health or Ohio EPA that the facility has completed closure.[183]

7.4 Monocell And Monofill Facilities

The Director of Ohio EPA is granted authority under Revised Code Section 3734.72 to establish rules for scrap tire monocell and monofill facilities to ensure that they are located, maintained, operated, and closed in a manner that does not create a nuisance, hazard to public health or safety, or fire hazard. Sections 3734.81 and 3734.82 set out licensing and fee requirements for these facilities.

"Scrap tire monocell facility" is a segregated section of a sanitary landfill that is used exclusively for the environmentally sound storage or disposal of scrap tires that have been shredded, chipped, or otherwise mechanically processed.[184] The permitting, construction, operation, closure, post-closure care, and financial assurance requirements for a scrap tire monocell are identified in Rule 3745-27-69.[185]

"Scrap tire monofill facility" is a specialized sanitary landfill facility that is used exclusively for the environmentally sound storage or disposal of scrap tires that have been shredded, chipped, or otherwise mechanically processed.[186] The permitting, construction, operation, closure, and post-closure care requirements for a scrap tire monofill are contained in Rules 3745-27-70 through 3745-27-75.[187] Final closure activities are

---

[181] OAC 3745-27-66(A).

[182] OAC 3745-27-66(F).

[183] OAC 3745-27-66(G).

[184] OAC 3745-27-01(C)(7), (E)(6).

[185] *See* ORC § 3734.77.

[186] OAC 3745-27-01(C)(8), (E)(7).

[187] *See* ORC § 3734.77.

mandatory for a scrap tire monofill if: the facility no longer accepts scrap tires; the facility's license has expired and no renewal application is pending; the license has been suspended or revoked; or the license application has been denied.[188] The local Board of Health or Director of Ohio EPA may enter any closed scrap tire monofill facility at any reasonable time for the purpose of determining compliance with closure requirements.[189]

7.5 Beneficial Use Of Scrap Tires

"Beneficial use" of scrap tires refers to the use of such tires in a manner that results in a product for sale or exchange, or in any other manner authorized under Rule 3745-27-78 of the Ohio Administrative Code.[190] The term does not include any use of a scrap tire at a scrap tire recovery facility nor does it apply to products manufactured from scrap tires and sold to a customer.[191]

The authorized beneficial uses of whole scrap tires include: dock bumpers; race track crash barriers; tire swings, sandboxes, or other children's playground equipment; rifle range backstops; agricultural use to hold down covers over such things as hay; and erosion control barriers at ends of culvert pipes. For shredded tires, the beneficial uses are: construction material in a landfill; lightweight fill in public road and embankment construction, under certain conditions; and covering material for playgrounds or bulking agent for compost, but only if use is restricted to shredded bias ply tires or tire shreds with all metal removed.[192] In addition, the Director of Ohio EPA may approve plans for beneficial uses not specifically authorized in the regulations.[193]

A person may beneficially use scrap tires only after notifying Ohio EPA.[194] Tires being stored prior to use at a beneficial use site must comply with storage standards set out in Rule 3745-27-60(B).[195]

---

[188] OAC 3745-27-73(C).

[189] OAC 3745-27-73(L).

[190] *See* OAC 3745-27-01(I)(1).

[191] *Id.*

[192] OAC 3745-27-78(D) - (E).

[193] OAC 3745-27-78(F).

[194] OAC 3745-27-78(B), (I).

7.6 Financial Assurance For Scrap Tire Facilities And Transporters

Rules 3745-27-15 through 3745-27-17 of the Administrative Code address financial assurance requirements for scrap tire facilities and scrap tire transporters.

7.7 Remediation

Rule 3745-37-79 provides guidelines and self-implementing characterization and remediation procedures to be followed after the open burning or open dumping of scrap tires has caused contamination or degradation of soil, surface water, ground water, or other natural resources.

7.8 Management Fund

Chapter 3734 of the Revised Code, as amended by SB 165, created a Scrap Tire Management Fund, to be funded by a $.50 per tire fee on the sale of tires (see Section 7.10 of this chapter).[196] The Director is authorized to expend monies in the fund to clean up properties where scrap tires have been accumulating and thereafter to recover those costs from either the person responsible for the scrap tires or the landowner. A landowner who is not responsible for accumulating tires, but who has paid the costs incurred by the Director in cleaning up his property, may recover those expenses from the responsible person in a civil action.[197]

7.9 Enforcement And Removal Actions

Under the authority of Revised Code Section 3734.85, the Ohio EPA Director may take action to abate accumulations of scrap tires. If the Director determines that the tires constitute a danger to the public health or safety or to the environment, he may order removal and transportation of the tires from the accumulation site to a licensed scrap tire storage, monocell, monofill, or recovery facility in Ohio, or to a similar facility in another state that is

---

[195] OAC 3745-27-78(C); *see* ORC э 3734.84.

[196] ORC §§ 3734.901 *et seq.*

[197] ORC § 3734.85(A).

in compliance with the laws of that state.[198] If the person responsible for the accumulation fails to comply with the order, the Director may refer the matter to the Ohio Attorney General for civil action.[199]

7.10 Fee On Sale Of Tires

Section 3734.901 provides for the levying of a $.50 per tire fee on the sale of tires in the State, through June 30, 2006, for the purpose of providing revenue to defray the cost of administering and enforcing the scrap tire program. Fee administration and enforcement provisions are set out in Section 3734.902; liability of the wholesale distributor, retail dealer, and other parties is covered in Sections 3734.903, 3734.907, and 3734.908.

7.11 Penalties

Reckless or knowing violations of scrap tire laws or an order issued under Section 3734.13 are punishable by fines of up to $25,000, or imprisonment for up to four years, or both. Each day of violation constitutes a separate offense. For convictions on subsequent violations, the fine may be doubled.[200]

---

[198] *Id.*

[199] *Id.* at (A) - (B).

[200] ORC § 3734.99.

Chapter IX

REGULATION OF UNDERGROUND STORAGE TANKS

1.0 INTRODUCTION

1.1 Background

Petroleum products, liquid chemicals, and flammable substances commonly are stored in underground storage tanks ("USTs") to reduce the chances of fire, explosion, and other hazards. Leaks from USTs often develop slowly as a result of tank corrosion and result in relatively small amounts of product loss. Similarly, spillage due to overfilling or poor housekeeping, while contaminating surrounding soil, is usually a minor discharge in terms of the amount of lost product. However, ruptures – *i.e.*, structural failures of the tank or piping – may result in substantial product loss and immediate detection. All such incidents can lead to contamination of soil and ground water.

The large number of USTs in use in the United States and the potential they represent for significant soil and water contamination, combined with the lack of voluntary leak detection activity, led Congress in 1984 to enact federal legislation mandating aggressive leak prevention, detection, and corrective action requirements, and to authorize states to administer regulatory programs for underground tanks.

1.2 Federal Legislation Regulating USTs

In 1984, as a part of the Hazardous and Solid Waste Amendments,[1] Congress added a new subtitle to the Resource Conservation and Recovery Act ("RCRA"),[2] creating a regulatory program governing USTs used for the storage of "regulated substances," which included both "hazardous substances" as defined in the federal Superfund law, and petroleum.[3]

RCRA's original UST program was aimed at identifying the tanks subject to the program, and establishing regulatory standards to assure that tank leaks could be prevented, or at least identified and controlled. Congress defined the regulated facilities as those tanks and associated pipeline facilities, ten percent or more of which, by volume, are located underground, and which are used to store "regulated substances."[4] Hazardous wastes, as defined in RCRA, are excluded from the UST program since tank storage, treatment, and disposal systems for hazardous wastes already were regulated under RCRA. The focus of the UST program is on underground tanks that contain products which, if released to the environment, may contaminate soil, ground water, or surface waters.

Congress required U.S. EPA to develop regulations establishing technical standards that would protect against corrosion of new and existing tanks; provide for leak prevention, detection, and corrective action once a leak is discovered; govern installation of new tanks; and provide financial assurance for corrective actions and compensation for third parties injured by a release.[5] The agency was given responsibility for inspection and enforcement as well as authority to approve state programs.[6] In addition, Congress prohibited the installation of bare steel tanks after May 7, 1985,[7] and required owners of USTs to notify a state agency of the location, age, size, and contents of all tanks in use on November 8, 1984, and abandoned tanks that were taken out of service after January 1, 1974,

---

1 Pub. L. 98-616, 98 STAT. 3277 (1984).

2 42 USC §§ 6901 - 6992k.

3 42 USC § 6991(2); *see generally*, 42 USC §§ 6991 - 6991i (sometimes referred to as "Subtitle I"); *see also* 42 USC § 9601(14).

4 42 USC § 6991(1).

5 42 USC § 6991b.

6 42 USC §§ 6991c, 6991d.

7 42 USC § 6991b(g).

but still in the ground.[8] Notifications were to be received by the designated state agency by May 8, 1986.[9]

In 1986, as part of the Superfund Amendments and Reauthorization Act ("SARA"),[10] Congress added a Remedial Trust Fund to the UST program.[11] The trust fund provides monies with which U.S. EPA or the states can undertake remedial action at a leaking tank site, and then seek reimbursement from the tank owners or operators. The liability of owners and operators for leaking tanks is patterned after the strict liability provisions of the Federal Water Pollution Control Act.[12] The 1986 SARA Amendments also imposed a mandatory floor of $1,000,000 on the financial responsibility requirements for tank owners and operators.[13]

1.3 Ohio UST Regulation

Prior to 1987, the storage of flammable and combustible liquids in Ohio was regulated by the State Fire Marshal under the Ohio Fire Code.[14] The flammable and combustible liquids code prescribes certain location, separation, equipment, and monitoring standards with respect to the storage of flammable and combustible liquids in stationary tanks located above or below the ground, and in portable tanks, containers, or bulk storage facilities.

In 1986, the Governor designated the State Fire Marshal as the agency to which the notification forms required by the UST program should be directed. The Fire Marshal's office established the Bureau of Underground Storage Tank Regulation ("BUSTR") and began expanding its regulation of underground storage of regulated substances in order to implement the federal UST program under RCRA.[15] In 1987, the General Assembly passed amendments to Chapter 3737 of the Ohio Revised Code that

---

[8] 42 USC § 6991a(a).

[9] *Id.*

[10] Pub. L. 99-499, 100 STAT. 1613 (1986).

[11] 42 USC § 6991b(h).

[12] *Compare* 33 USC § 1321 *and* 42 USC § 6991b(h)(6).

[13] 42 USC § 6991b(d)(5)(A).

[14] ORC § 3737.82; OAC 1301:7-7.

[15] *See* http://www.com.state.oh.us/odoc/sfm/bustr.

delegate to the Fire Marshal full responsibility for administration of both the UST technical regulatory program and the petroleum UST release corrective action program.[16]

In 1988, the Fire Marshal adopted initial rules implementing the Ohio UST program; these rules have since been extensively revised and expanded. Today, the flammable and combustible liquids rule, Rule 1301:7-7-28 of the Administrative Code, is focused on fire safety standards that apply to USTs and other storage systems. A separate chapter of the Administrative Code, Chapter 1301:7-9, is specifically directed at USTs; it contains the majority of the technical standards and the financial responsibility requirements that apply to UST systems.

In 1989, the General Assembly passed legislation,[17] amending the existing authority of the Fire Marshal and enacting additional statutory provisions to expand the agency's authority over the installation, use, and removal of USTs. The bill also created the Petroleum Underground Storage Tank Financial Assurance Fund ("Fund"), a mandatory State insurance program designed to provide an affordable financial assurance mechanism for petroleum tank owners and operators; the Petroleum Underground Storage Tank Release Compensation Board, which oversees the Fund; and a linked deposit program to provide low interest rate loans to upgrade existing USTs. BUSTR revised the corrective action rule in 1999 to include a more comprehensive, risk-based approach to corrective action at petroleum UST release sites (see Section 5.7 below).

The following discussion focuses on the current Ohio UST program, including the basic definitions and requirements it shares with the federal program, as well as differences between the two programs.

2.0 STATUTORY DEFINITIONS AND EXEMPTIONS

2.1 Definitions

2.1.1 UST

The federal statute and regulations define an UST as a tank or combination of tanks (including connected underground pipes) used to contain regulated substances, of

---

[16] ORC §§ 3737.88, .882.

[17] HB 421, 118th General Assembly (Eff. July 11, 1989).

which at least ten percent is beneath the surface of the ground.[18] The Ohio law and regulations contain virtually identical definitions.[19]

2.1.2 Regulated Substances

Both Ohio and U.S. EPA define "regulated substances" to include petroleum and hazardous substances as defined in Section 101(14) of the Comprehensive Environmental Response, Compensation, and Liability Act ("CERCLA"),[20] except hazardous wastes regulated under Subtitle C of RCRA.[21]

2.1.3 Owners And Operators

The definition of "owner," for purposes of the federal UST program, turns on the operational status of the tank at the date of passage of the original RCRA UST program – November 8, 1984. If a tank was in operation on that date, or brought into use thereafter, the "owner" of the tank is the person who currently holds ownership in the tank. If the tank was taken out of operation before November 8, 1984, the "owner" is the person who owned the tank immediately before it was taken out of operation.[22]

Ohio's statutes and regulations, however, expanded the definition of "owner" to include: "... any person who holds, or, in the instance of an [UST] system in use before November 8, 1984, but no longer in use on that date, any person who held immediately before the discontinuation of its use, a legal, equitable, or possessory interest of any kind in an [UST] system or in the property on which the [UST] system is located, including, without limitation, a trust, vendor, vendee, lessor, or lessee. The term does not include any person who, without participating in the management of an [UST] system and without otherwise being engaged in petroleum production, refining, or marketing, holds indicia of ownership in an [UST] system primarily to protect the person's security interest in it."[23]

---

[18] 42 USC § 6991(1); *see* 40 CFR 280.12.

[19] ORC § 3737.87(P); OAC 1301:7-9-02(B)(52).

[20] 42 USC §§ 9601 - 9765.

[21] ORC §§ 3737.87(L), .88(D); OAC 1301:7-9-02(B)(39), -03. *See* 42 USC § 6991(2); 40 CFR 280.12; *see also* OAC 1301:7-9-02(B)(19).

[22] 42 USC § 6991(3); 40 CFR 280.12.

[23] ORC § 3737.87(H); OAC 1301:7-9-02(B)(32).

"Operator" is defined in the Ohio regulations consistently with the federal rules to mean a person in control of or responsible for daily operation of the UST system.[24]

2.2 Exempt UST Systems

2.2.1 RCRA Statutory Exclusions

Congress provided nine statutory exemptions from the federal UST program for tanks used for certain purposes, storing certain substances, of certain sizes, and/or regulated by other provisions of federal or state law. The exemptions are:[25]

(1) farm or residential tanks storing motor fuel for noncommercial purposes, and with a capacity of less than 1,100 gallons;

(2) tanks storing heating oil for consumption on the premises where stored;

(3) septic tanks;

(4) pipelines regulated under the Natural Gas Pipeline Safety Act or the Hazardous Liquid Pipeline Safety Act, or comparable state laws;

(5) surface impoundments, pits, ponds, or lagoons;

(6) stormwater or wastewater collection systems;

(7) flow-through process tanks;

(8) liquid traps or gathering lines used in oil or gas production and gathering operations; and

(9) storage tanks in an underground area (*i.e.*, basements, cellars, mineworks, drifts, shafts, or tunnels) if the tank is located upon or above the surface of the floor.

These same nine exemptions, which are part of Ohio law,[26] have been incorporated into both the federal regulations and the Ohio remedial program as part of the definition of "USTs."[27]

---

[24] OAC 1301:7-9-02(B)(30); 40 CFR 280.12.

[25] 42 USC § 6991(1).

[26] ORC § 3737.87(P).

[27] 40 CFR 280.12; OAC 1301:7-9-02(B)(52).

Both the federal and State regulations contain additional exemptions or defer regulation of certain tanks; these are discussed below.

2.2.2 Federal Regulatory Exemptions

The federal regulations contain six additional categories of exempt tanks, to which none of the federal UST program requirements apply, and six categories of deferred tanks, to which some, but not all, of the federal requirements apply. These exemptions apply to:[28]

(1) any UST system holding hazardous wastes listed or identified under Subtitle C of RCRA, or a mixture of such wastes and other regulated substances;

(2) a wastewater treatment tank system that is part of a wastewater treatment facility regulated under Section 402 or Section 307(b) of the Clean Water Act;

(3) operational equipment or machinery tanks such as hydraulic lift tanks and electrical equipment tanks;

(4) any UST system with a capacity of 110 gallons or less;

(5) any UST system that contains a *de minimis* concentration of regulated substances; and

(6) any emergency spill or overflow UST system that is expeditiously emptied after use.

None of the technical standards for installation, operation, release detection, monitoring, or closure apply to five additional categories of tanks. However, the release response and corrective action requirements, 40 CFR Part 280, Subpart F, *do* apply to these tanks. Technical requirements have been deferred for:[29]

(1) wastewater treatment tank systems;

(2) UST systems containing radioactive materials regulated under the Atomic Energy Act of 1954;

---

[28] 40 CFR 280.10(b).

[29] 40 CFR 280.10(c).

(3) UST systems that are part of an emergency generator system at a nuclear generating facility regulated by the Nuclear Regulatory Commission;

(4) airport hydrant fuel distribution systems; and

(5) any UST system with a field-constructed tank.

The technical requirements for release detection equipment, monitoring, and recordkeeping have been deferred for one additional special category of tanks: those UST systems that store fuel solely for use by emergency power generators.[30] All the other requirements apply to such tanks.

2.2.3 State Regulatory Exemptions

In general, Ohio has adopted the same categories of USTs and provided the same regulatory exemptions as set out in the federal program. Ohio has accomplished this by including a list of exempt UST systems within each technical standard or requirement.[31] Ohio has not exempted airport hydrant fuel distribution systems from the annual registration requirement, but has provided an exemption from the State's financial responsibility requirements for USTs owned by a federal government entity.[32]

3.0 APPLICABILITY

Under Ohio law, any UST system used to store a regulated substance must be installed and constructed to prevent releases of the stored substance due to corrosion or structural failure for the operating life of the system; be cathodically protected against corrosion, constructed of noncorrodible material, or designed to prevent releases of the stored substance; and be constructed or lined with material that is compatible with the stored substance.[33] Exemptions apply to certain UST systems.[34]

---

[30] 40 CFR 280.10(d).

[31] OAC 1301:7-9-04(A), -05(B)(3), -06(A), -07(A), -08(A).

[32] OAC 1301:7-9-05(B)(2).

[33] OAC 1301:7-9-01(B).

[34] OAC 1301:7-9-01(C).

4.0 REGISTRATION AND PERMITTING

The RCRA UST program required an initial registration or notification to be filed with a designated state agency by May 8, 1986. This initial notification served to identify, for the state regulatory agencies, the owners of USTs subject to the UST regulatory program, and the location, number, size, age, and contents of USTs throughout each state. This information, in turn, was required to be summarized by the states and provided to U.S. EPA in the form of state inventories.[35]

Ohio has adopted its own UST registration form, and requires renewal registration applications to be filed annually for existing tanks to monitor compliance with tank upgrading requirements and to demonstrate financial responsibility.[36] Owners of new tanks must file an application for registration within thirty days after installation and pay a $50 per-tank registration fee.[37]

In addition to registration, a permit must be obtained from the local fire official to take an UST permanently or temporarily out of service, or to place an out-of-service UST back into service.[38] Local permit applications and fees vary from jurisdiction to jurisdiction. If no permit is required by the local fire official, a permit must be obtained from the State Fire Marshal.[39] A permit also must be obtained before beginning the installation of an UST system; the Fire Marshal may place upon such a permit any terms or conditions necessary to assure compliance with the Ohio UST rules.[40] UST installers and inspectors are subject to extensive certification and training requirements.[41]

Owners of new USTs that are a source of emissions of certain air pollutants also are subject to the requirement to obtain a permit to install ("PTI") from Ohio EPA, as discussed in Chapter II of this Handbook. Depending upon the size and contents of the UST, Ohio

---

[35] 42 USC § 6991a.

[36] OAC 1301:7-9-04, -05.

[37] OAC 1301:7-9-04(C). *See* http://www.com.state.oh.us/odoc/sfm/bustr. Registered UST owners may use the "On Line Office" section of the web site to complete and submit registration and permit applications.

[38] OAC 1301:7-9-12(D).

[39] *Id.*

[40] OAC 1301:7-9-06(D).

[41] OAC 1301:7-9-11.

EPA may issue a permit to operate ("PTO") for the UST that is the source of certain air emissions or register the UST as a minor source.

5.0 TECHNICAL REQUIREMENTS FOR UST SYSTEMS

5.1 Fire Safety Requirements

The general fire safety rules in the Ohio Fire Code require that tanks and all piping, fittings, and appliances used for underground storage of flammable or combustible liquids must be constructed and tested in accordance with standards listed in Rule 1301:7-7-44 of the Administrative Code, and approved by the local fire official.[42] Such liquids cannot be dispensed by a device that operates through pressure within the tank, unless the tank has been approved as a pressure vessel.[43] Approved pumps connected to the top of the tank must be used to dispense flammable liquids.[44] Combustible liquids may be dispensed by gravity from tanks, unless the viscosity of the liquid makes it impractical, and self-closing valves or faucets must be used.[45] Fuel dispensing systems must be installed in accordance with Rule 1301:7-7-44.[46] Precautionary measures must be taken to prevent ignition in locations where flammable vapors may be present, by eliminating or controlling sources of ignition, including smoking, open flames, cutting or welding, and sparks.[47] Spills and leaks must be reported to the local fire official and immediate measures for cleanup commenced within twenty-four hours.[48]

Location restrictions apply to certain UST systems. USTs used to store flammable liquids must be a minimum of one foot from any wall and three feet from any lot line. USTs used for storing combustible liquids must be one foot from any wall or lot line.[49]

---

[42] OAC 1301:7-7-28(C)(2).

[43] OAC 1301:7-7-28(C)(5)(c).

[44] OAC 1301:7-7-28(C)(5)(a).

[45] *Id.*

[46] OAC 1301:7-7-28(E)(2).

[47] OAC 1301:7-7-28(C)(8); *see also* OAC 1301:7-7-28(F).

[48] OAC 1301:7-7-28(C)(9).

[49] OAC 1301:7-7-28(H)(2).

5.2 Installation Of New Tanks

5.2.1 Steel Tanks

New steel tanks must have an approved noncorrosive coating or a cathodic protection system, unless the tank is installed at a site that is determined by a soil corrosion expert to have soil that is not corrosive enough to cause a release during the operating life of the tank.[50] Metal piping must be similarly protected.[51] Equivalent corrosion protection may be provided by some other method, subject to prior approval by BUSTR.[52]

Steel tanks and piping used for petroleum must have met the new tank standards, upgraded according to one of the approved upgrading strategies, or closed in accordance with the federal and State closure requirements (including the corrective action requirements) on or before December 22, 1998. Tanks containing hazardous substances were required to have complied with this standard on or before December 22, 1995.[53] The approved methods of upgrading existing tanks to meet the corrosion protection standards include:[54]

(1) installing an internal lining and internally inspecting the tank within ten years and every five years thereafter;

(2) installing an approved cathodic protection system and conducting an internal inspection, or, if the tank is less than ten years old, conducting a series of tightness tests or monitoring the tank monthly for releases; or

(3) using both an internal liner and an approved cathodic protection system.

Piping must be upgraded to meet the new piping standards, and spill and overfill protection standards also must be met.[55] By December 31, 1998, any tank less than ten years old must have met the standards required for new tanks.

[50] OAC 1301:7-9-06(B)(1)(b), (d).

[51] OAC 1301:7-9-06(B)(2)(b) - (c).

[52] OAC 1301:7-9-06(B)(1)(e), (2)(d).

[53] OAC 1301:7-9-06(C)(1).

[54] OAC 1301:7-9-06(C)(2).

[55] OAC 1301:7-9-06(C)(3) - (4).

Cathodically protected tanks must be inspected within six months of installation, and every three years thereafter; impressed-current systems must be monitored every sixty days by the owner or operator.[56] The Fire Marshal has specified particular industry standards that must be followed to assure that alcohol blends are stored in tanks that are compatible with these materials.[57] Tank and piping repairs must not affect the cathodic protection system, must be conducted only after a permit is issued by the Fire Marshal or a certified safety inspector, and must comply with established national codes and standards. Repaired UST systems must be tightness-tested before bringing the system back into use.[58] All activities involving the installation, abandonment, or removal of USTs, and all upgrading of an UST system, must be done under the supervision of a certified installer and must be inspected by a representative from the Fire Marshal's office, a certified safety inspector, or a certified UST inspector.[59]

5.2.2 Fiberglass-Reinforced Plastic And Composite Tanks

Fiberglass-reinforced plastic and composite tanks may be used in lieu of steel tanks, and must be certified to meet industry standards.[60] Like steel tanks, fiberglass and composite tanks must be installed under the supervision of a certified installer and inspected by a representative from the State Fire Marshal's office, a certified safety inspector, or a certified UST inspector.[61]

5.3 Spill And Overfill Prevention Equipment

In addition to meeting the corrosion protection standards, new tanks must have spill and overfill protection equipment.[62] Petroleum tanks must have met the new tank standards by December 1998; tanks used for storage of hazardous substances were required

---

[56] OAC 1301:7-9-08(C)(2)(a), (3).

[57] OAC 1301:7-9-08(D).

[58] OAC 1301:7-9-08(E) - (F).

[59] ORC § 3737.881(F); OAC 1301:7-9-06(E).

[60] OAC 1301:7-9-06(B)(1)(a), (c).

[61] ORC § 3737.881(F); OAC 1301:7-9-06(E).

[62] OAC 1301:7-9-06(B)(3).

to have been upgraded by the end of 1995.[63] Specialized equipment is not required for tanks filled by transfers of no more than twenty-five gallons at a time.[64] All other tanks must be equipped with spill control equipment to prevent a release of product if the transfer hose is detached from the fill pipe (*i.e.*, a catch basin), and one or more of a combination of automatic shut-off devices, flow restricters, or audible alarms to alert the operator before the tank can be overfilled.[65] Alternate equipment may be substituted upon prior approval by BUSTR.[66]

5.4 Leak Detection And Reporting Requirements

Owners and operators of new tank systems must provide equipment or utilize a method capable of detecting a release from any portion of an UST system that is installed, maintained, calibrated, and operated in accordance with the manufacturer's instructions; has a 0.95 probability of detecting a release; and meets any specific performance criteria specified for that method or equipment.[67] New tanks must meet the leak detection standards prior to operation; existing tanks must have added leak detection equipment or monitoring.[68]

Existing petroleum tank systems that were not upgraded to meet the new requirements must have used a combination of inventory control practices and tightness testing consistent with the requirements of the final federal rules as of December 22, 1998.[69] Existing bare steel tanks that do not meet the corrosion protection standards for new tanks must perform annual tank tightness tests.[70] Tanks that have corrosion protection must be tested only every five years.[71] All hazardous substance tanks must provide secondary containment for the tank and use a thirty-day monitoring method.[72]

---

[63] OAC 1301:7-9-06 (C)(1), (4).

[64] OAC 1301:7-9-06(B)(3)(b)(ii).

[65] OAC 1301:7-9-06(B)(3)(a).

[66] OAC 1301:7-9-06(B)(3)(b)(i).

[67] OAC 1301:7-9-07(B)(1).

[68] OAC 1301:7-9-07(B)(3); 40 CFR 280.40 - .42.

[69] OAC 1301:7-9-07(C)(1)(b).

[70] *Id.*

[71] OAC 1301:7-9-07(C)(1)(a).

[72] OAC 1301:7-9-07(D)(2).

The Ohio regulations also provide detailed descriptions of other allowable release detection methods, including vapor monitoring, ground water monitoring, interstitial monitoring for double-walled tanks or tanks installed within a secondary barrier, and other equivalent methods.[73] Release detection also must be provided for piping, including leak detection for pressurized piping.[74] Release detection upgrades require a permit and must be supervised by a certified installer.[75] The federal rules require that certain release detection records be maintained for five years; inventory control or monitoring records must be retained for at least one year and, in the case of tightness testing results, until the next test is conducted.[76] The State rules contain similar requirements, except that documents pertaining to performance claims must be maintained for five years after the termination of an UST system; records that relate to the calibration, repair, or maintenance of a release detection system must be maintained for the life of the UST system.[77]

Releases or suspected releases must be reported to the State Fire Marshal's office and the local fire department within twenty-four hours of discovery by the owner or operator.[78] Both federal and State rules provide that suspected releases need not be reported if a monitor is defective, provided the defect is immediately corrected, or if, in the case of inventory control, a second month of data does not confirm the suspected release.[79] Owners and operators must report any discovery of released substances in the soils, nearby water supplies, or manmade structures in the surrounding area (*i.e.*, basements or utility and sewer lines), or unusual operating conditions, such as unexplained product loss, erratic equipment performance, or the unexplained presence of water in the tank.[80] Any spill or overfill of petroleum of twenty-five gallons or more, or which causes a sheen on surface water, also must be reported immediately. Spills of less than twenty-five gallons need not be reported if

---

[73] OAC 1301:7-9-07(E).

[74] OAC 1301:7-9-07(F), (B)(4).

[75] OAC 1301:7-9-07(H) - (I).

[76] 40 CFR 280.45(a) - (b).

[77] OAC 1301:7-9-07(G).

[78] 40 CFR 280.50; OAC 1301:7-9-13(D).

[79] 40 CFR 280.50(c); OAC 1301:7-9-13(C)(33)(a).

[80] 40 CFR 280.50(a), (b); OAC 1301:7-9-13(C)(33)(b).

they are contained on the owner's property, do not reach a surface water body, and are cleaned up within twenty-four hours.[81]

5.5 Sensitive Areas

In addition to adopting general requirements for new USTs and upgrading existing USTs, the General Assembly delegated authority to the State Fire Marshal to designate "sensitive areas" and to establish alternative release containment and detection requirements for USTs located in those areas.[82] The Fire Marshal has identified sensitive areas by rule as: (1) listed areas associated with federally declared sole source aquifers under the Safe Drinking Water Act; (2) areas within fifty feet of a private water supply well or developed spring not located on the same site as the UST system; (3) areas within specified linear distances from designated public water supply wells; (4) areas less than 1,000 feet upstream of a surface water intake for a public drinking water supply; (5) areas within 200 feet of a lake or reservoir; and (6) areas within 100 feet of a tunnel used for pedestrian or vehicular traffic.[83] New USTs located in sensitive areas must meet the leak detection and spill and overfill prevention requirements applicable to all new USTs, and be equipped with secondary containment.[84] Existing USTs installed after December 22, 1988, but prior to September 1, 1992, must have provided release detection for underground piping by December 22, 1998.[85] Existing USTs installed prior to December 22, 1988, must have provided release detection for underground piping, complied with the corrosion protection standards for tanks and piping, and provided active monthly monitoring for releases and spill and overfill protection by December 22, 1998.[86]

---

[81] 40 CFR 280.53; OAC 1301:7-9-13(D).

[82] ORC § 3737.88(A)(2).

[83] OAC 1301:7-9-09(B).

[84] OAC 1301:7-9-10(C).

[85] OAC 1301:7-9-10(D).

[86] OAC 1301:7-9-10(E).

5.6 Release Confirmation And Determination

Releases from USTs containing hazardous substances are subject to the reporting requirements and the investigative and remedial action requirements established under CERCLA and its Ohio counterpart.[87] However, CERCLA contains an exemption for petroleum products.[88]

In 1986, Congress added similar requirements to RCRA for the reporting, investigation, and remediation of releases from petroleum USTs.[89] A two-phased approach has been established to address suspected releases from petroleum USTs. First, based upon the nature of the information upon which the owner or operator suspects a release has occurred, an assessment phase is undertaken, including release investigation and confirmation. Once the nature and extent of the release are known, a specific series of corrective actions must be undertaken. If it appears likely that a substantial release has occurred, or if the Fire Marshal issues an order, an owner or operator may be required to proceed immediately to the corrective action phase. Ohio's release confirmation requirements are more stringent than the federal requirements.[90]

If a suspected release is discovered, a tightness test must be conducted within seven days. If a release may impact a drinking water well on the UST site or nearby property, the well water must be sampled and analyzed for petroleum constituents within three days of discovery. Within sixty days of a failed tightness test or a spill or overfill, owners and operators must conduct a site check to determine whether soil and ground water are contaminated, unless a Tier 1 evaluation (see below) has begun. The results of the site check must be submitted to the Fire Marshal.[91]

As part of the site check, owners and operators must determine the appropriate action levels – *i.e.*, non-site-specific concentrations for petroleum constituents that are protective of human health – for the UST site. If the concentrations at any location on the

[87] 42 USC §§ 9601 - 9675; ORC §§ 3734.26 - .28, 3750.06. For further discussion, see Chapter VII of this Handbook.

[88] 42 USC § 9601(14).

[89] 42 USC § 6991.

[90] *Compare* OAC 1301:7-9-13(E) *and* 40 CFR 280.52.

[91] OAC 1301:7-9-13(E).

site are above the determined action levels, owners and operators must proceed with a Tier 1 evaluation (see below).[92]

5.7 Corrective Action

BUSTR revised its rules in 1999 to include a more comprehensive, risk-based approach to corrective action at petroleum UST sites. For releases reported or confirmed prior to March 31, 1999, owners and operators must comply with either the corrective action rule that was in effect at the time of the release or the 1999 revised rule. Releases reported or confirmed after March 31, 1999, however, must be addressed under only the 1999 rule.[93] Primary differences between the 1992 and 1999 rules are found in three areas: subsurface investigation, chemicals of concern, and remedial options. The following discussion focuses on the 1999 rule.

Once a release is confirmed through testing and other evidence, the owner and operator must initiate specific response actions within twenty-four hours to minimize potential risks to human health and the environment: clean up spills and overfills; remove free product to the maximum extent practicable; prevent further release and migration of petroleum into the environment; monitor and mitigate hazards associated with the release; manage contaminated soils; and comply with applicable reporting requirements.[94]

Ohio has developed a matrix of common petroleum constituents to determine when corrective actions must be undertaken. Action levels are established for selected chemicals of concern based upon site features and exposure pathways (air, soil, and ground water).[95] In addition, Rule 1301:7-9-13 sets out a three-tiered evaluation process, including interim response actions, to assure that owners and operators undertake the most appropriate corrective actions for releases from UST systems.[96] Reports on evaluations and response actions are to be submitted to the State Fire Marshal within a specified number of days.

---

[92] OAC 1301:7-9-13(F).

[93] OAC 1301:7-9-13(B); *see also* Electing to Use the New 1999 Corrective Action Rule (BUSTR Fact Sheet, June 1999), and Technical Guidance Manual for 1999 Closure and Corrective Action Rules (BUSTR, July 2001), available at www.com.state.oh.us/odoc/sfm/bustr/Downloads.htm.

[94] OAC 1301:7-9-13(G).

[95] OAC 1301:7-9-13(I).

[96] *See* OAC 1301:7-9-13(H) - (O).

5.7.1 Tier 1 Evaluation

If the results of the site check exceed the action levels for an UST site, the owner or operator must conduct a Tier 1 evaluation. This involves collecting data on the potential sources of the confirmed release, the chemicals of concern, potential source areas, source and location of potable water supplies, potential drinking water use, and the regional geological, hydrogeological, and physical characteristics of the UST site and surrounding area. The Tier 1 also includes an assessment of the nature and extent of contamination.[97]

5.7.2 Tier 2 Evaluation

When Tier 1 action levels are not appropriate for site-specific conditions, UST system owners and operators may conduct a Tier 2 evaluation to assess exposure. The evaluation involves developing a site conceptual exposure model and conducting a site assessment that evaluates exposure pathways, determines the distribution of chemicals of concern, determines the geological and hydrogeological characteristics of the UST site, evaluates concentrations at the point of exposure, determines the point of demonstration, and evaluates the fate and transport of chemicals for completed pathways. Tier 2 also includes determining appropriate options; establishing land use restrictions to eliminate exposure pathways; and comparing the maximum concentrations of chemicals of concern to the action level or site-specific target level as applicable.[98]

5.7.3 Tier 3 Evaluation

The Tier 3 evaluation involves a more complex chemical fate-and-transport evaluation, using numerical models to develop site-specific target levels. It requires extensive data collection, use of complex modeling and analytical tools, and more sophisticated resources. Before beginning a Tier 3, the owner and operator must submit an evaluation plan and a Tier 2 evaluation report to the State Fire Marshal for approval.[99]

---

[97] OAC 1301:7-9-13(H).

[98] OAC 1301:7-9-13(M).

[99] OAC 1301:7-9-13(O).

5.7.4 Remedial Action

Based upon the full site evaluation, the owner and operator must submit to the State Fire Marshal a remedial action plan that includes proposed target levels identified by chemicals of concern and environmental media.[100] The Fire Marshal must provide reasonable public notice to those members of the public most directly affected by the release, and provide an opportunity for public review and comment before the plan is approved. The Fire Marshal may hold a public meeting to consider comments on the plan.[101] Once the plan is approved, the owner and operator must implement the plan, and monitor, evaluate, and report the results of plan implementation to the Fire Marshal. If an approved plan does not achieve the target cleanup levels identified in the plan within one year, the owner and operator must reevaluate the remedial action alternatives and submit a revised plan, return to the Tier 2 evaluation and submit a revised tier report, or submit a Tier 3 evaluation plan.[102]

5.8 Closure

Ohio regulations require an UST owner and operator to obtain a permit from the local fire official if the official has been delegated such authority, or the State Fire Marshal, prior to either temporary or permanent closure of an UST system.[103] If a permit is obtained from the Fire Marshal, a permit fee of $35 will be assessed, in addition to any inspection fees incurred. If the local fire official issues the permit, a local fee may be established by ordinance. The federal rules require written notice of intent to remove an UST system from service to be given at least thirty days in advance.[104] Removal or abandonment of an UST system must be performed under the supervision of a certified installer.[105]

Tanks taken out of service temporarily must have the fill line, gauge opening, and dispensing unit secured against tampering. Vent lines must remain open and

[100] OAC 1301:7-9-13(P).

[101] OAC 1301:7-9-13(Q).

[102] OAC 1301:7-9-13(R) - (T).

[103] OAC 1301:7-9-12(D); *cf.* 40 CFR 280.70, 280.71.

[104] 40 CFR 280.71(a).

[105] ORC § 3737.881(F); OAC 1301:7-9-13(C).

functioning.[106] If an UST remains out of service for more than twelve months, it must be permanently closed.[107]

Permanent closure requires either removal of the tank and restoration of the site, or abandonment in place.[108] Abandonment must be done in accordance with API Publication 2015-94; it is concluded by filling the tank completely with an inert, solid material.[109] Federal regulations additionally require that prior to closing, a tank must be completely emptied and thoroughly cleaned; the owner must maintain complete records of all closure activity.[110] The State rules also require owners and operators to perform a closure assessment to determine if the spills or leaks from the UST system have contaminated soils or ground water or if free product is present.[111] This requirement may be applied to UST systems permanently closed before December 22, 1988, if such systems are determined to pose a current or potential threat to human health or the environment.[112]

BUSTR's rules detail the sampling and analytical requirements necessary to complete an adequate closure assessment.[113] The rules also outline the contents of the closure assessment report that must be submitted to the Fire Marshal within forty-five days after receipt of the laboratory reports of sampling.[114]

6.0 FINANCIAL RESPONSIBILITY

The federal UST program contains financial responsibility rules for only petroleum UST systems. The rules establish the methods, minimum amounts of per-occurrence and aggregate coverage, and compliance deadlines for all petroleum UST systems. Owners and operators of USTs at petroleum marketing facilities (including any facility where petroleum

---

[106] OAC 1301:7-9-12(F)(1); *cf.* 40 CFR 280.70(a) - (b).

[107] OAC 1301:7-9-12(G)(2); 40 CFR 280.70(c). A request for an extension of the twelve-month limit on temporary closures may be submitted to the State Fire Marshal at least thirty days prior to the end of the initial twelve-month period. OAC 1301:7-9-12(G)(3)(b).

[108] OAC 1301:7-9-12(H) - (I).

[109] OAC 1301:7-9-12(H).

[110] 40 CFR 280.71(b), 280.74.

[111] OAC 1301:7-9-12(H)(1)(a), (K); *cf.* 40 CFR 280.72.

[112] OAC 1301:7-9-12(N); 40 CFR 280.73.

[113] OAC 1301:7-9-12(K).

[114] OAC 1301:7-9-12(L).

is produced, refined, transferred, or sold to other marketers or the public), or which handle an average of more than 10,000 gallons per month, must maintain annual per-occurrence coverage of $1,000,000. All other owners and operators must maintain per-occurrence coverage of $500,000.[115] The annual aggregate limits are based on the number of USTs owned. Owners of more than 100 petroleum USTs must maintain annual aggregate coverage of $2,000,000. Owners of 100 or fewer USTs must maintain annual aggregate coverage of $1,000,000.[116] Compliance with these rules was required for all entities by December 22, 1993.

In Ohio, HB 421 created the Petroleum Underground Storage Tank Financial Assurance Fund ("Fund"), which was designed to provide monies to reimburse owners and operators for the cost of corrective actions at leaking petroleum UST sites, and to create a fund to pay third party claims for bodily injury and property damage resulting from a leaking petroleum UST.[117] Coverage by the Fund is conditioned upon payment of annual premiums, and provides up to $1,000,000 of per-occurrence and aggregate coverage, less the deductible amount, which was initially established by statute at $50,000.[118] The Petroleum Underground Storage Tank Release Compensation Board ("Board") is authorized to increase the deductible under certain circumstances; it currently stands at $55,000.[119] Additional aggregate coverage is available for owners of more than 100 USTs. The annual premium also may be modified by the Board.[120] Supplemental fees may be assessed if the unobligated Fund balance falls below $15,000,000.[121] Fees may be assessed only under special circumstances in any year in which the unobligated balance exceeds $45,000,000 on the date the Board's annual determination is made.[122]

---

[115] 40 CFR 280.93(a).

[116] 40 CFR 280.93(b).

[117] ORC § 3737.91.

[118] ORC § 3737.91(E)(1).

[119] OAC 3737-1-15, -06.

[120] ORC § 3737.91(B), (E)(2). The current fee is $450 per tank. OAC 3737-1-04(H).

[121] ORC § 3737.91(C); OAC 3737-1-05(A).

[122] ORC § 3737.91(B); OAC 3737-1-04(A).

Owners and operators of six or fewer tanks may elect to reduce their deductible amount, upon payment of an additional premium.[123] An owner or operator is not eligible to receive payments from the Fund unless he has demonstrated adequate financial assurance for the deductible amount.[124] BUSTR has adopted a financial responsibility rule that requires either the owner or operator to demonstrate financial responsibility for the deductible amount, or a multiple thereof, based on the number of tanks located in Ohio.[125]

HB 421 also created a Linked Deposit Program to ensure that sufficient credit would be available at reasonable rates to finance improvements necessary to comply with the technical standards. The program is operated through lending institutions to make loans available at below-market rates.[126]

7.0 LEAKING UST CLEANUP AND COST RECOVERY

Releases from leaking petroleum UST systems are not subject to remediation through the federal Superfund program because of the express statutory exemption of petroleum products from the definition of "hazardous substance."[127] Releases from leaking UST systems containing hazardous substances are subject to action by U.S. EPA through its Superfund authority. Releases of a "reportable quantity" of any hazardous substance must be reported to the National Response Center.[128] Superfund remedial and/or response actions are not within the scope of this chapter; responses to releases from leaking tanks containing hazardous substances are not governed by the federal or State UST programs.

If the State Fire Marshal finds that a release of petroleum from an UST has occurred, he can take any action deemed necessary to correct the release, including one or more of the following:[129]

---

[123] ORC § 3737.91(F). The current reduced deductible of $11,000 is available to owners of six or fewer tanks who pay an additional $150 annual fee per tank. OAC 3737-1-06(B).

[124] ORC § 3737.91(E)(1).

[125] OAC 1301:7-9-05.

[126] ORC §§ 3737.95 - .98.

[127] 42 USC § 9601(14).

[128] 42 USC § 9603. *See* http://www.nrc.uscg.mil/nrchp.html.

[129] ORC § 3737.882(A).

(1) issue a citation and order requiring the owner or operator to undertake such actions as are necessary to protect human health and the environment;

(2) request the Ohio Attorney General to commence a civil action in the common pleas court to obtain the relief necessary to protect human health and the environment; or

(3) enter the premises where the UST is located and undertake such corrective action as is necessary to protect human health and the environment.

Any action taken by the Fire Marshal under the third option must conform to the federal and State corrective action rules, including the requirements for public participation.[130]

The owner or operator of any UST from which a release has occurred, or any "responsible person" who has an interest in the property on which the UST is located, is strictly liable to the State for any costs incurred for any corrective action or any enforcement action undertaken by the Fire Marshal or the Attorney General, unless the responsible person can demonstrate that the release was caused solely by an act of God, an act of war, an act or omission of a third party, or any combination of these three.[131] A civil action may be commenced to recover those costs. If a responsible party alleges that a release was caused solely by a third party, the responsible person is still liable to the State for response costs, and is entitled by subrogation to the rights of the State against the third party.[132] A responsible person may then request that the Attorney General bring an action to recover those response costs from the third party.[133]

Citations and orders issued by the Fire Marshal are issued without the necessity for issuance of a proposed order but are otherwise subject to appeal under the provisions of Chapter 3745 of the Revised Code, which governs actions of the Director of Ohio EPA.[134]

---

[130] *Id.*

[131] ORC § 3737.89(A).

[132] ORC § 3737.89(B).

[133] ORC § 3737.89(C).

[134] ORC § 3737.882(D).

Chapter 3745 provides for appeals to the Environmental Review Appeals Commission from the issuance of any order.[135]

8.0 ENFORCEMENT

In addition to instituting a cleanup in response to a leaking UST, the State Fire Marshal can enforce the requirements of the Ohio UST program through both civil and criminal proceedings. If a tank owner or operator fails to comply with a rule adopted by the Fire Marshal or an order issued to enforce such rule, or to respond to a leaking petroleum tank, a civil penalty of up to $10,000 for each day that the violation continues may be assessed by administrative order or through a civil action brought by the Ohio Attorney General.[136] An administrative order assessing a civil penalty is subject to appeal to the Environmental Review Appeals Commission. A knowing violation of rules or orders issued by the Fire Marshal is an unclassified felony, punishable by a fine of $25,000 or imprisonment for not more than fourteen months, or both.[137] A reckless violation is a first degree misdemeanor, punishable by a maximum sentence of six months or a fine of up to $1,000, or both.[138]

9.0 THE CLAIMS PROCESS

9.1 The Petroleum Underground Storage Tank Release Compensation Board

The General Assembly created the Petroleum Underground Storage Tank Release Compensation Board ("Board") in 1989 to facilitate recovery from the Petroleum Underground Storage Tank Financial Assurance Fund ("Fund") of certain costs of remediating petroleum releases from an UST.[139] The Board consists of the State Treasurer, the Directors of Commerce and Environmental Protection or their designees as members ex officio, and nine members appointed by the Governor with the advice and consent of the Senate. No more than five of the appointed members may be from the same political party.

---

[135] ORC § 3745.04. For further discussion, see Chapter XII of this Handbook.

[136] ORC § 3737.882(C).

[137] ORC § 3737.99(H).

[138] ORC §§ 3737.99(H), 2929.21.

[139] HB 421, 118th General Assembly (Eff. July 11, 1989).

Of the appointed members, there must be one representing the interests of each of the following groups: petroleum refiners, retail petroleum dealers, and local governments. Further, one must have experience in casualty and fire or pollution insurance, two must represent the interests of businesses that own USTs and are not primarily engaged in the sale of petroleum, and two must be registered professionals with experience in geology or environmental engineering who shall represent the interests of the public and must not be associated with the petroleum industry.[140]

The Board is charged with the task of administering the moneys in the Fund exclusively for:[141]

(1) payment of the expenses of administering the Fund;

(2) payment of the administrative expenses of the Board;

(3) payment to or reimbursement of responsible persons for the necessary cost of corrective action for and compensating third parties for bodily injury and property damage caused by accidental petroleum releases;

(4) deposit into any funds provided for in a resolution of the Board in connection with any revenue bonds; and

(5) placement of UST linked deposits.

9.2 Eligibility

Before awarding Fund payment of corrective action costs for an accidental release of petroleum, the Director of the Fund must determine that the owner or operator is eligible for the payment of such costs. This determination is made on the basis of:[142]

(1) receipt of a complete application for eligibility made within one year of the date the release is required to be reported;

(2) determination that, at the time the release was first suspected or confirmed, the responsible person possessed a valid certificate of coverage;

---

[140] ORC § 3737.90(A).

[141] ORC § 3737.92(A).

[142] OAC 3737-1-07(A).

(3) the corrective action performed or to be performed has been authorized by the Fire Marshal;

(4) the costs of performing the action are determined to be necessary in order to comply with the Fire Marshal's rules;

(5) either a determination that the tank was properly registered when the release was first suspected or confirmed, or a recommendation by the Fire Marshal that payment be made because good cause existed for the failure to have properly registered the tank system and the system was subsequently registered and all back fees have been paid;

(6) determination by the Fire Marshal that, when the claim was filed, a responsible person was in compliance with all orders issued regarding the tank system from which the release occurred;

(7) demonstration of financial responsibility for the deductible amount;

(8) determination that the responsible person has not falsified any attestation contained on a registration application;

(9) the responsible person has met release reporting requirements; and

(10) the tank system from which the release occurred was in compliance with applicable Fire Marshal rules adopted under Section 3737.88 of the Revised Code when the release was first suspected or confirmed.

9.3 Application For Reimbursement

The responsible person may apply for reimbursement of allowable costs that were actually incurred in conducting corrective action. The application must be made within one year of the completion of any program task and must include all records of:[143]

(1) immediate corrective action and free product removal reports;

(2) site assessment reports;

(3) remedial action plans and monitoring plans;

[143] OAC 3737-1-12(A), (E), (F).

(4) evaluation reports, notifications, plans, and interim response action notifications;

(5) invoices, payment records, and any other records documenting actual costs incurred related to corrective action;

(6) completion reports;

(7) extension requests and responses, and alternative technology requests and responses;

(8) any other information requested by the Director of the Fund; and

(9) certification by the responsible person and primary consultant or contractor that the information is true and represents actual costs incurred.

A responsible person also may apply for reimbursement for partial completion of a task, provided that the application for reimbursement is at least fifty percent of the responsible person's deductible and that the responsible person provides documentation of actual expenses incurred.[144]

Reimbursement or payment of third party claims from the Fund is limited to expenses associated with bodily injury or property damage. Judgments or settlements in third party lawsuits are subject to the same restrictions.[145]

9.4 Reimbursement Application Review

The Director must review the application for reimbursement and notify the responsible person of any apparent errors or omissions and request any additional information required to complete the application.[146] The Fire Marshal and the responsible person must be given written notice of the Director's determination to approve, approve with modifications, or deny the application.[147]

---

[144] OAC 3737-1-12(G).

[145] OAC 3737-1-16.

[146] OAC 3737-1-13(A).

[147] OAC 3737-1-13(C).

9.5 Third-Party Claims

In limited circumstances, a third party who has been injured bodily or whose property has been damaged by the accidental release of petroleum is eligible for reimbursement or payment from the Fund. A responsible person seeking coverage for third party injuries or damages must establish and maintain eligibility as if the claim were for a corrective action.[148]

9.6 Reimbursement Determination

The Director may approve or disapprove a claim administratively without a hearing. If the Director's determination is inconsistent with a recommendation or determination of the Fire Marshal, the Director must detail those inconsistencies in a written finding of fact prior to authorizing any disbursement from the Fund for payment of the claim.[149]

The responsible person may contest the Director's determination of the claim by filing an objection with the Board within thirty days of the mailing of the notification of the determination and finding of fact. The Board then appoints a hearing officer to conduct an adjudication hearing on the determination in accordance with Revised Code Section 119.09.[150]

Once the Board pays or reimburses a responsible person from the Fund, the Board is entitled by subrogation to all rights of the responsible person to recover those costs from any other person.[151]

9.7 Disbursements

Even when an eligible applicant for reimbursement from the Fund has submitted a complete application for reimbursement, the Fund will not be obligated to pay unless and until the applicable deductible or reduced deductible has been met.[152]

---

[148] OAC 3737-1-19.

[149] ORC § 3737.92(E).

[150] ORC § 3737.92(F). For further discussion, see Chapter II of this Handbook.

[151] ORC § 3737.92(I).

Obligations of the Fund for eligible claims are made on a first-come, first-served basis as determined by receipt of the completed application. An exception to this prioritization occurs when the Fire Marshal requests approval of a prioritization of an accelerated review on the basis of the threat posed to human health or the environment by the release at issue or if the Board grants an accelerated review.[153]

For any single release, the maximum disbursement from the Fund is $1,000,000, less the applicable deductible. For any fiscal year, the maximum disbursement on behalf of any responsible person is as follows:[154]

Tanks Owned	Maximum Disbursement
not more than 100	$1,000,000 less applicable deductible
not more than 200	$2,000,000 less applicable deductible
not more than 300	$3,000,000 less applicable deductible
more than 300	$4,000,000 less applicable deductible

The maximum disbursement from the Fund for any single release or for any fiscal year does not in any way limit the liability of the responsible person for a release of petroleum.[155]

9.8 Accelerated Review

A responsible person may file a request for accelerated review of a claim. Such a request must provide financial data demonstrating that approval of "hardship status" is necessary to prevent an imminent financial hardship from resulting to the responsible person.[156] The Director may seek additional justification from the responsible person to demonstrate the imminent financial hardship and, upon review of the financial data provided, recommend to the Board approval or denial of the request.[157] The Board may accept or reject such a recommendation. If the Board approves hardship status, that status remains in effect

---

[152] OAC 3737-1-08(A).

[153] OAC 3737-1-08(B).

[154] ORC § 3737.91(D)(3).

[155] *Id.*

[156] OAC 3737-1-08(D).

[157] *Id.*

for one year from the date of the Board's action.[158] The responsible person may file a subsequent request for hardship status on or before the expiration of a one-year period.[159]

9.9 Limitations Of Fund Coverage

The following expenditures may not be authorized for reimbursement from the Fund:[160]

(1) costs of corrective actions to remediate releases suspected or confirmed prior to July 1, 1989;

(2) costs of corrective action for a release for which the Director has issued a final order denying eligibility for reimbursement;

(3) litigation costs of any kind incurred by a responsible person including, but not limited to, litigation costs involving acquisition of site access; local, State, or federal permit decisions; any ordinance, rule, or regulation; or any order issued by the Fire Marshal;

(4) costs associated with:

(a) achieving compliance with the certification provision of the Revised Code, with the exception of costs associated with corrective action and compensation to third parties for bodily injury or property damages caused by an accidental release of petroleum;

(b) interest or carrying charges of any kind;

(c) insurance premiums other than specific policies or bonds required for corrective action;

(d) subsurface assessments performed in conjunction with site acquisition or sale where no release is confirmed; and

(e) corrective action costs that are determined to be nonreimbursable as a result of an audit;

---

[158] *Id.*

[159] *Id.*

[160] OAC 3737-1-09(A).

(5) costs incurred solely in cleaning up nonpetroleum product contamination or cleaning up petroleum or petroleum product contamination unrelated to a release from an assured UST system;

(6) costs incurred solely in cleaning up a release from an unassured UST system;

(7) costs not associated with cleanup program tasks completed in accordance with rules of the Fire Marshal or, where applicable, with an order that establishes cleanup procedures and criteria for the site;

(8) costs covered by other insurance policies;

(9) costs associated with closure or removal of UST systems;

(10) costs for corrective action other than those that are usual, customary, and reasonable for similar corrective action activities and under similar circumstances, as determined from the Fund's experience;

(11) costs for corrective action not submitted in accordance with Rule 3737-1-12;

(12) additional corrective action costs for a release after the Fire Marshal has issued a No Further Action ("NFA") letter for the release, unless the corrective action is required by the Fire Marshal due to discovery of chemicals of concern resulting from the original release but not reasonably discovered prior to issuance of the NFA letter; or

(13) for corrective action where preapproval is required but was not sought or granted, costs for corrective action greater than ninety percent of the usual, customary, and reasonable costs of the least expensive corrective action alternative for similar corrective action activities and under similar circumstances as determined from the Fund's experience.

The Board, upon payment to or reimbursement of a responsible person from the Fund for corrective action costs or cost of compensation to third parties for bodily injury or property damage, is entitled by subrogation to all rights of the responsible person to recover those costs from any other person.[161]

161 OAC 3737-1-09(B).

Chapter X

EMERGENCY PLANNING AND COMMUNITY RIGHT TO KNOW

1.0 FEDERAL REQUIREMENTS

On October 17, 1986, Congress enacted the Emergency Planning and Community Right-to-Know Act of 1986 ("EPCRA" or "Act")[1] as Title III of the Superfund Amendments and Reauthorization Act ("SARA").[2] Following closely on the heels of the chemical disaster in Bhopal, India, in which a release of methyl isocyanate from a Union Carbide plant killed almost 2,000 people,[3] EPCRA contains provisions concerning emergency planning for chemical disasters and notification requirements for all types of chemical spills.[4]

EPCRA required U.S. EPA to develop a list of extremely hazardous substances that, if present at a facility in amounts greater than a threshold planning quantity, would subject the facility to a myriad of emergency planning, hazardous chemical inventory reporting, and spill notification requirements. The list, codified at 40 CFR Part 355, Appendix A, may be revised at any time based on the toxicity, reactivity, volatility, dispersability, combustibility, or flammability of a substance.[5]

---

[1] 42 USC §§ 11001 - 11050.

[2] Pub. L. 99-499, 100 Stat. 1613 (1986).

[3] *See* Montgomery, Reducing the Risk of Chemical Accidents: The Post-Bhopal Era, 16 Envtl. L. Rep. 10300 (1986) (ramifications of the chemical incident in Bhopal).

[4] *See* 42 USC §§ 11001 - 11050.

[5] *See generally* http://yosemite.epa.gov/oswer/ceppoweb.nsf/content/epcraoverview.htm.

The Act also establishes reporting provisions requiring the disclosure of toxic chemical releases.[6] Facilities with ten or more full time employees that conduct operations within specified Standard Industrial Classification ("SIC") Codes and that either manufacture, process, or otherwise use a toxic chemical in excess of the threshold quantity established for each such use are subject to the toxic chemical reporting provisions of EPCRA.[7] Facilities that generate less than 500 pounds of a listed chemical that is released to the environment, treated, recycled, or used for energy recovery, and that use less than one million pounds of the chemical in a calendar year, qualify for a small-source exemption and need to file only a certification.[8] Releases of pollutants that are federally permitted also are exempt.[9] Otherwise, facilities subject to the reporting requirements must submit a Toxic Release Inventory ("TRI") report on Form R by July 1 of each year for each toxic chemical manufactured, processed, or otherwise used at a facility, disclosing the total amount of the toxic chemical released during the preceding calendar period.[10]

The list of toxic chemicals established pursuant to Section 313(c) may be revised at any time by U.S. EPA, either upon its own initiative or upon petition by any person, based upon the criteria set out in Section 313(d).[11] U.S. EPA expanded the list in 1994 to include an additional 282 chemicals and chemical categories.[12] At present, more than 600 toxic chemicals and twenty chemical categories are subject to reporting under Section 313.[13]

---

[6] 42 USC §§ 11021 - 11023.

[7] 42 USC § 11023(b). As originally enacted, EPCRA applied only to sources in SIC codes 20 through 39. Effective December 31, 1997, seven new industry were added to Section 313's EPCRA reporting requirements. 62 *Fed. Reg.* 23834 (May 1, 1997). For a discussion of the expanded reporting requirements, see Section 2.2 of this chapter.

[8] 59 *Fed. Reg.* 61488 (Nov. 30, 1994); *see* 40 CFR § 372.27.

[9] 42 USC §§ 9603(a), 11004(a).

[10] 42 USC § 11023(a), (g).

[11] 42 USC § 11023(d). Additions to the TRI list were unsuccessfully challenged on grounds that U.S. EPA did not consider data concerning the exposure to humans of a particular substance. National Oilseed Processors Ass'n v. Browner, 42 Envtl. L. Rep. 1641, 924 F. Supp. (D.D.C. 1996).

[12] 59 *Fed. Reg.* 61432 (Nov. 30, 1994). Of the 282 newly added chemicals, approximately 170 are active ingredients in pesticides.

[13] *See* http://www.epa.gov/tri.

2.0 STATE IMPLEMENTATION

The states play a critical role in the implementation of EPCRA. Under the Act, the governor of each state was required to establish a state emergency response commission and appoint its members no later than April 17, 1987.[14] The state commission is responsible for the development of emergency planning districts and the appointment of members to local emergency planning committees.[15] Membership on the local committees is to include, among others: elected officials; law enforcement, medical, and health personnel; members of the media; and representatives from facilities subject to the requirements of EPCRA.[16] The primary purpose of each local planning committee was the preparation of an emergency response plan for its district by October 17, 1988.[17]

2.1 State Emergency Response Commission

To comply with the mandates of EPCRA, the Governor of Ohio established the first State Emergency Response Commission ("SERC" or "Commission") in April 1987.[18] The SERC, in turn, created local emergency planning districts and appointed members to serve on local emergency planning committees. In December 1988, the State enacted the Ohio Right-to-Know Act,[19] which created an even broader framework for the implementation of EPCRA in Ohio.[20]

Ohio's Right-to-Know Act created a new SERC to carry out the responsibilities of the commission established earlier by executive order. The new SERC has nine ex officio members (the Directors of Environmental Protection, Health, Natural Resources, and Transportation; the Chair of the Public Utilities Commission; the State Fire Marshal; the Administrator of the Bureau of Employment Services; the Superintendent of the Highway Patrol; and the Attorney General), two nonvoting members (the chairmen of the

---

[14] 42 USC § 11001(a).

[15] *Id.*; ORC § 3750.02(B)(2).

[16] 42 USC § 11001(c).

[17] 42 USC § 11003(a).

[18] Executive Order 87-16.

[19] SB 367, 117th General Assembly (Eff. Dec. 14, 1988).

[20] *See* ORC Chapter 3750.

respective standing committees of the Senate and House of Representatives that consider environmental issues), and ten members appointed by the Governor. The appointed members must represent specific groups such as environmental advocacy coalitions, petroleum refiners or marketers or chemical manufacturers, another industry subject to regulation, municipal governments, county governments, chiefs of fire departments, professional firefighters, volunteer firefighters, and local emergency management agencies.[21]

The SERC developed a state emergency response plan that outlined the responsibilities of each of the various state agencies represented on the Commission.[22] At least once a year, the SERC is required to implement the state plan in conjunction with a local emergency response plan developed by a local planning committee. As a result of this exercise, the SERC must then revise the state plan as appropriate.[23] In 1995, the General Assembly enacted legislation[24] amending the SERC's discretionary powers by authorizing the Commission to require the Director of Ohio EPA and the Executive Director of the Ohio Emergency Management Agency to review the effectiveness of the implementation, administration, and enforcement of the chemical emergency response planning and reporting programs in Ohio and to report their findings.[25] Based on this review and report, the Commission may make recommendations for legislative or administrative action, as necessary, to effectuate the goals of Chapter 3750.[26]

The SERC is responsible for promulgating rules that conform to the scope, content, and coverage of EPCRA.[27] The SERC also may adopt rules that are more stringent than EPCRA, as long as the rules are not inconsistent with the Act.[28] As a result of these requirements, the Ohio program parallels the federal requirements closely. One exception is Rule 3750-30-20, which requires facility maps detailing on-site chemical storage areas as a

---

[21] ORC § 3750.02(A).

[22] *See* ORC § 3750.02(B)(13). A state emergency response plan was developed and submitted to the Governor's office on January 11, 1990.

[23] ORC § 3750.02(B)(13).

[24] SB 162, 121st General Assembly (Eff. Oct. 29, 1995).

[25] ORC § 3750.02(C)(6).

[26] *Id.*

[27] ORC § 3750.02(B)(1).

[28] ORC § 3750.02(B)(2).

mandatory component of the Ohio hazardous chemical inventory reporting form. The federal rules do not mandate the submission of a facility map.[29]

The SERC is supported by the Emergency Response, Site Investigation, and Radiological Safety Section ("ERSIS") of Ohio EPA's Division of Emergency and Remedial Response.[30] Ohio EPA's Right-to-Know Unit collects and compiles information from Hazardous Chemical Inventory forms submitted by industry. The Ohio Emergency Management Agency also provides support for SERC activities.

2.2 Ohio's Toxic Release Inventory Program

While the responsibility for emergency planning activities and hazardous chemical reporting resides with the SERC, Ohio EPA is responsible for the implementation of Ohio's Toxic Release Inventory ("TRI") program. The program, governed by Revised Code Chapter 3751, is managed by the TRI Unit in Ohio EPA's Division of Air Pollution Control. Pursuant to Section 3751.02 of the Revised Code, the Director of Ohio EPA is required to adopt rules "that are consistent with and equivalent in scope, content, and coverage to, and no more stringent than section 313" of EPCRA.[31] As a result of this statutory directive, Ohio's TRI program and the regulations codified at Chapter 3745-100 of the Administrative Code are consistent with Section 313 of EPCRA.

Since 1987, Ohio facilities in SIC codes 20 through 39, with ten or more full-time employees, which use, manufacture, or process any of the identified toxic chemicals in excess of applicable threshold quantities, have been required to report releases of these chemicals to both U.S. EPA and Ohio EPA. Releases that are federally permitted are

---

[29] Shortly after its adoption in 1990, the mapping rule was appealed to the Environmental Board of Review ("EBR") (now the Environmental Review Appeals Commission). Although neither EPCRA nor Chapter 3750 requires the submission of a site map, the EBR upheld the SERC regulation. When the EBR decision was appealed to the Franklin County Court of Appeals, the court reversed the EBR decision, upon a finding that the mapping requirement was more stringent than EPCRA. The case was reversed by the Ohio Supreme Court, which held that the statute permitting SERC to adopt rules consistent with and equivalent in scope, content, and coverage to EPCRA prescribes only the minimum regulatory requirements. This provision does not prevent the SERC from promulgating rules that impose stricter reporting requirements. Ohio Chamber of Commerce v. State Emergency Response Comm'n, 64 Ohio St.3d 619, 597 N.E.2d 487 (1992).

[30] *See generally* http://www.epa.state.oh.us/derr/ersis/ersis.html.

[31] ORC § 3751.02(A)(1).

exempt.[32] This information must be reported on Form Rs by July 1 of each year. As of December 31, 1997, seven non-manufacturing industry groups were added.[33]

U.S. EPA has since lowered the reporting threshold for lead and all lead compounds – except for lead contained in stainless steel, brass, and bronze alloys – to 100 pounds[34] and has changed the reporting thresholds for certain persistent, bioaccumulative chemicals.[35]

Since the inception of Ohio's TRI program, Ohio EPA's Division of Air Pollution Control has compiled the statistics from nearly 6,600 reports filed by more than 1,700 Ohio companies in Ohio annually. These annual reports summarize releases of listed toxic chemicals to the air, water, and land for each reporting year. The reports demonstrate that from 1987 to 1995, there was a sixty-one percent decrease in toxic chemicals released to the environment.[36] The most recent report shows that there was an additional thirteen percent decrease in toxic chemical releases between 2000 and 2001.[37]

2.3 Penalties

Ohio's Right-to-Know Act authorizes penalties for violations under Revised Code Chapters 3750 and 3751. Under the emergency planning provisions, facility owners or operators who fail to report the release of a hazardous or extremely hazardous substance may

---

[32] *See* 42 USC § 9603(a), incorporated by reference into 42 USC § 11004(a). For air releases, the "federally permitted release" exemption includes "any emission into the air *subject to* a permit or control regulation" under the Clean Air Act. In In re Mobil Oil Corp., EPCRA Appeal No. 94-2 (Sept. 29, 1994), the Environmental Appeals Board ("EAB") held that an air release is "subject to" a permit or control requirement only if it is in compliance with that permit or control requirement. Thus, emissions in excess of permit limits are not "federally permitted releases" and are subject to reporting if they exceed the reporting threshold, which for many pollutants is set at one pound. U.S. EPA has since issued guidance on how the "federally permitted release" exemption for air emissions should be interpreted. *See* 64 *Fed. Reg.* 71614 (Dec. 21, 1999).

[33] 62 *Fed. Reg.* 23834 (May 1, 1997). The groups are: metal mining (SIC code 10, except 1011, 1081, and 1094), electric utilities (SIC codes 4911, 4931, and 4939 – limited to facilities that combust coal and/or oil for the purpose of generating electricity for distribution in commerce), commercial hazardous waste treatment (SIC code 4953 – limited to facilities regulated under RCRA Subtitle C), chemicals and allied products-wholesale (SIC code 5169), petroleum bulk terminals and plants (SIC code 5171), and solvent recovery services (SIC code 7389 – limited to facilities engaged in solvents recovery services on a contract or fee basis). Under federal law, facilities in these seven groups were required to submit their first TRI reports by July 1, 1999, for the 1998 reporting year.

[34] 66 *Fed. Reg.* 4500 (Jan. 17, 2001); 66 *Fed. Reg.* 10585 (Feb. 16, 2001).

[35] 64 *Fed. Reg.* 58666 (Oct. 29, 1999).

[36] *1995 Toxic Release Inventory Annual Report*, Ohio EPA, Division of Air Pollution Control (April 1997).

[37] *2001 Toxic Release Inventory Annual Report*, Ohio EPA, Division of Air Pollution Control (May 2003).

be subject to a fine of not more than $25,000 for each day of violation.[38] Any person falsifying or tampering with information or records required under Chapter 3750 is also subject to a fine of not more than $25,000 for each violation.[39] Violations of the hazardous chemical inventory reporting provisions carry a maximum fine of $10,000 for each day of violation.[40] Upon the written request of the SERC executive committee, the affected local emergency planning committee, or the local fire department, an action under Section 3750.20 may be brought against an alleged violator by the Ohio Attorney General, the prosecuting attorney of a county, or the city director of law.[41]

Reckless violations of the release reporting provisions of Section 3750.06 carry criminal penalties.[42] A reckless violation is a felony and carries a possible prison sentence of two to four years in jail, and/or monetary penalties of at least $10,000 but not more than $25,000 for each violation. Subsequent violations carry a possible two- to four-year prison term and monetary penalties of $25,000 to $50,000 for each offense.[43]

For violations of the TRI reporting requirements of Chapter 3751, civil penalties of up to $25,000 for each day of violation are provided in Section 3751.10(B). Similar to the penalty provisions associated with Chapter 3750, Section 3751.10 authorizes an action against an alleged violator by the Attorney General, the prosecuting attorney of a county, or the city director of law upon the written request of the Director of Ohio EPA.[44] Release of reported confidential information to an unauthorized person by Ohio EPA is considered a felony and is subject to a fine up to $20,000 for each day of violation, or imprisonment for not more than one year, or both.[45]

---

[38] ORC § 3750.20(B)(1).

[39] ORC § 3750.20(B)(2).

[40] ORC § 3750.20(B)(3).

[41] ORC § 3750.20(B)(4).

[42] ORC § 3750.99.

[43] *Id.*

[44] ORC § 3751.10(B).

[45] ORC § 3751.99.

3.0 CESSATION OF REGULATED OPERATIONS

In 1994, the General Assembly enacted legislation creating Chapter 3752 of the Revised Code, which establishes procedures that a facility owner or operator must follow when the facility ceases regulated operations.[46] Cessation of regulated operations means the "discontinuation or termination of regulated operations or the finalizing of any transaction or proceeding through which those operations are discontinued."[47] Regulated operations in turn are defined as "the production, use, storage, or other handling" of "extremely hazardous substances, hazardous substances, flammable substances, and petroleum."[48]

3.1 Applicability

Under Chapter 3752 and Ohio EPA's implementing regulations set out in Chapter 3745-352 of the Administrative Code, the cessation of regulated operations program applies to facilities that are subject to EPCRA reporting requirements, Material Safety Data Sheet ("MSDS") requirements, and emergency and hazardous chemical inventory reporting requirements.[49] The law sets out a number of exceptions to these provisions,[50] and also provides for a waiver of requirements in connection with temporary discontinuance of regulated operations.[51]

3.2 "Contaminated With" Definition

Pursuant to Section 3752.03 of the Revised Code, the Director of Ohio EPA has defined "contaminated with" as "every stationary tank, vat, electrical transformer, vessel of any type, piping, nonstationary equipment and furnishing, nonstationary container, motor

---

46 HB 98, 120th General Assembly (initial effective date of July 1, 1995, delayed to July 1, 1996, by HB 117).

47 ORC § 3752.01(C).

48 ORC § 3752.01(T) - (U).

49 ORC § 3751.01; OAC 3745-352-10. *See* 42 USC §§ 11021, 11022; 29 USC § 651; OAC 3750-30-15, -20, -27.

50 The requirements do not apply to: (1) oil or gas production operations regulated under ORC Chapter 1509; (2) equipment, petroleum, or piping owned or operated by a public utility as defined in ORC Section 4905.02 or by any other electric light company as defined in ORC Section 4905.03; (3) any tank regulated under ORC Sections 3737.87 to 3737.98; (4) any facility not subject to ORC Sections 3750.07 and 3750.08 either after July 1, 1996 or for three consecutive years prior to ceasing regulated operations; or (5) any person subject to ORC Sections 3752.11, .111, .113. ORC § 3752.02; OAC 3745-352-10.

51 ORC § 3752.10.

vehicle rolling stock and all debris that contains or contained a regulated substance," with some exceptions, as explained below.[52]

Stationary tanks, vats, electrical transformers, vessels of any type, and piping, and nonstationary equipment and furnishings, nonstationary containers, motor vehicles, rolling stock, and debris are not considered to be contaminated with a regulated substance if they contained: only hazardous waste but are empty for purposes of Rule 3745-51-07; polychlorinated biphenyls ("PCBs") at a concentration less than fifty parts per million ("ppm"); or regulated substances other than hazardous waste or PCBs and the facility certifies that the substances have been removed and will not be released in amounts causing unreasonable risk to public health or safety or the environment.[53] If the regulated substance was a compressed gas, the facility must certify that the container's valves have been removed and that the container has been purged with an inert gas.[54]

All buildings, structures, or outdoor locations of operation are considered to be contaminated if they contain any contaminated stationary or nonstationary containers discussed above.[55]

3.3 Notice Requirements

A key objective of Revised Code Chapter 3752 is that the owner or operator of a reporting facility notify the Director of Ohio EPA that regulated operations are ceasing. Notice requirements vary depending on the length of cessation.

3.3.1 Temporary Discontinuance Of Operations

If operations at a facility will discontinue only temporarily (longer than thirty days but no more than 365 consecutive days), the owner or operator must submit to the Director a written certification of temporary discontinuance of regulated operations.[56] The

---

52 OAC 3745-352-05(I)(1).

53 OAC 3745-352-05(I)(2), (3).

54 OAC 3745-352-05(I)(2)(c)(ii).

55 OAC 3745-352-05(I)(4).

56 ORC § 3752.09(A)(1); OAC 3745-352-20(B)(1).

certification, which is to be submitted within forty-five days of discontinuance, must indicate the date of discontinuance and state that it will not exceed a period of 365 days.[57]

If a facility that temporarily discontinues operations does not resume regulated activity within the 365-day period, the owner or operator must designate and maintain a contact person in accordance with Section 3752.05 of the Revised Code and comply with the obligations set out under Section 3752.06(A).[58] In compliance with Section 3752.07, the owner or operator also must secure against the entry of unauthorized persons into each building, structure, or outdoor location at the facility where regulated operations occurred and that contains or is contaminated with regulated substances.[59]

If the Director determines that an owner or operator has failed to satisfy these requirements, the Agency may issue an order requiring the owner or operator to comply.[60] Coal mining, reclamation, and surface mining operations for which valid permits have been issued and temporary facilities located on a construction site that are idle due to weather or scheduling delays, but which eventually will be removed upon the completion of construction activities, are exempt from submitting a written certification of temporary discontinuance.[61]

3.3.2 Cessation Of Regulated Operations

Unless the owner or operator of a reporting facility has filed with the Director of Ohio EPA a notice of temporary discontinuance or a waiver application, the owner or operator must prepare a notice of cessation of all regulated operations at the facility. The notice must be sent, within thirty days of cessation, to the Director, the local emergency planning district, and the fire department having jurisdiction in the area.[62] Within 30 days, the owner or operator must secure the facility in accordance with OAC 3745-352-30 unless

---

[57] *Id.*

[58] ORC § 3752.09(A)(2).

[59] *Id. See also* OAC 3745-352-30. Any law enforcement officer as defined in ORC Section 2901.01 may arrest violators of the security provisions. ORC § 3752.07(D).

[60] ORC § 3752.09(A)(3).

[61] ORC § 3752.09(B).

[62] ORC § 3752.04.

the facility will continue to be operated without interruption so as to secure against unauthorized entry.[63]

3.4 Duties Of Owner Or Operator

Within ninety days of cessation of regulated operations, the facility owner or operator must do all of the following:[64]

(1) submit to the Director a copy of the most recent emergency and hazardous chemical inventory form required by Section 3750.08 of the Revised Code, along with a statement indicating the presence of any asbestos-containing materials at the facility; a copy of the current hazardous chemical list or MSDSs required under Section 3750.07; and a list of every stationary tank, vat, electrical transformer, and vessel of any type that contains or is contaminated with regulated substances and that is to remain at the facility; the location of each; and the identification of the regulated substances involved;

(2) drain or remove all regulated substances from each stationary container remaining at the facility and either transfer the substances to another facility under the same ownership or operation; transfer ownership of the substances to another person; or transport the substances off the premises and manage them in compliance with Chapter 3734 of the Revised Code and other applicable State and federal laws and regulations;

(3) remove all debris, nonstationary equipment and furnishings, containers, motor vehicles, and rolling stock that contain or are contaminated with a regulated substance and either transfer the items to another facility under the same ownership or operation; transfer ownership of the items to another person; or transport the items off the premises and manage them in compliance with Chapter 3734 of the Revised Code and other applicable State and federal laws and regulations; and

(4) certify to the Director in writing that these actions have been completed.

---

[63] ORC § 3752.07; OAC 3745-352-20(A)(1)(b).

[64] ORC § 3752.06(A)(1) - (6).

Upon written request by the facility owner or operator, the Director may extend the length of time required for compliance with these provisions if the owner or operator is unable to complete the actions due either to temporary and uncontrollable circumstances or to the facility's size, operational complexity, or other relevant factors.[65]

The removal and certification requirements do not apply to the owner or operator of a reporting facility that is permitted for the storage, treatment, or disposal of hazardous waste under Revised Code Section 3734.05, or that has obtained a generator identification number under Section 3734.12. In such instances, the owner or operator shall comply with the applicable closure and post-closure requirements established under Section 3734.12.[66]

Upon receiving a certification under Section 3752.06(A)(6), the Director of Ohio EPA will inspect the facility to determine if all applicable requirements have been met.[67]

3.5 Waivers

For a reporting facility that will discontinue all regulated operations for more than 365 consecutive days, the owner or operator may request a waiver from the requirements of Sections 3752.05 to 3752.07 of the Revised Code.[68] The written request must be submitted to the Director of Ohio EPA within forty-five days after discontinuance of operations and must be accompanied by an interim maintenance and operation plan for the facility that states the date by which regulated operations will be resumed, a demonstration that operations will resume, a plan to prevent unauthorized entry to the site, and a plan for preventing air and water pollution and soil contamination.[69]

The Director will approve the waiver application only if it meets all applicable requirements and ensures that regulated operations will resume on or before the date

[65] ORC § 3752.06(B).

[66] ORC § 3752.06(C).

[67] ORC § 3752.08.

[68] ORC § 3752.10(A).

[69] *Id.*

specified in the application.[70] The Director may include in the approval order any terms and conditions necessary to protect public health or safety during the temporary discontinuance of operations.[71]

If the Director disapproves a waiver application or revokes a waiver approval, the owner or operator must comply with the closure requirements within the specified timeframe.[72] The same requirements apply if a waiver is not renewed and operations at the facility do not resume within the time period specified in the application.[73]

3.6 Duties Of Other Parties

If a reporting facility owner abandons the facility and fails to carry out the requirements of Chapter 3752, or if a facility operator fails to comply with the security measures required by Section 3752.07, the law imposes certain duties on other parties.

3.6.1 Holder Of First Mortgage

Within fifteen days after an owner's abandonment of a facility, the holder of the first mortgage on real property at the facility must secure the facility and post warning signs that prohibit trespassing, and file a notice of the owner's abandonment and the holder's compliance with applicable security and posting requirements with the Director of Ohio EPA, the local emergency planning committee, and the fire department having jurisdiction in the area.[74]

The holder must continue security measures and maintain warning signs until title to the facility has been transferred or the holder files a release of the mortgage with the county recorder.[75] Within thirty days before the holder will cease to maintain security and

---

[70] *Id.*

[71] *Id.*

[72] *See* ORC § 3752.10(B).

[73] ORC § 3752.10(C)(1).

[74] ORC § 3752.11(B)(1); OAC 3745-352-25(B).

[75] *Id.*

warning signs at the facility, the holder must notify the Director, the local emergency planning committee, and the fire department with jurisdiction in the area.[76]

Actions taken by the holder to carry out these security and notification obligations do not subject the holder to liability or responsibility for compliance with other requirements under Chapter 3752.[77]

3.6.2 Fiduciary

If the facility operator fails to secure the facility as required under Section 3752.07, a fiduciary,[78] within sixty days after receiving actual notice of the cessation of regulated operations, must secure the facility and post warning signs that prohibit trespassing, and file a notice of cessation of regulated operations and the fiduciary's compliance with applicable security and posting requirements with the Director of Ohio EPA, the local emergency planning committee, and the fire department having jurisdiction in the area.[79] These requirements do not apply if there are insufficient assets in the trust or if the fiduciary is prevented from complying because of uncontrollable circumstances.[80]

The fiduciary must continue security measures and maintain warning signs until the fiduciary no longer holds legal title to or an equity or partnership interest in the facility or leases the facility, or until the fiduciary or another person has complied with Section 3752.06(A)(4)-(5) in connection with the regulated substances present at the facility.[81] Within thirty days before the fiduciary will cease to maintain security and warning signs at the facility, the fiduciary must notify the Director, the local emergency planning committee, and the fire department with jurisdiction in the area.[82] These requirements do not

---

[76] ORC § 3752.11(C).

[77] ORC § 3752.11(D).

[78] A "fiduciary" is a person who, for purposes of administering an estate or trust, holds legal title to, or an equity partnership interest in, or is a lessee of, a reporting facility, but who has not exercised direct control over the regulated substances at the facility. ORC § 3752.111(A)(1); OAC 3745-352-25(A).

[79] ORC § 3752.111(B), (B)(2).

[80] ORC § 3752.111(B).

[81] ORC § 3752.111(B)(1).

[82] ORC § 3752.111(C).

apply if the fiduciary rejects appointment as a fiduciary within sixty days after receiving actual notice of appointment.[83]

3.6.3 Action By Ohio EPA Or Political Subdivision

If a holder of first mortgage on real property or a fiduciary fails to undertake the required actions discussed above, the Director of Ohio EPA or any political subdivision in which the affected reporting facility is located has the authority to perform the required acts and to recover any costs incurred as a civil penalty under Revised Code Section 3752.17.[84] Upon receiving notification that a holder or fiduciary will cease to maintain security and warning signs at the facility, the Director or political subdivision may determine that security measures should continue and undertake appropriate actions for continuation. Any costs incurred are a lien upon the facility.[85]

3.6.4 Exemption Of Indenture Trustee

Generally, an indenture trustee for debt securities is exempt from Chapter 3752 if the trustee has not exercised direct or actual control over regulated substances at the reporting facility.[86] However, an indenture trustee may be obligated to act if: the operator of a reporting facility fails to comply with the security measures set forth in Section 3752.07; and the indenture trustee has foreclosed on its interest either formally or informally.[87] In that event, the indenture trustee must either petition the court for an appointment of a receiver or secure the facility against unauthorized entry and submit a notice of cessation of regulated operations at the facility to the Director, the emergency planning committee, and to the appropriate fire department.[88]

---

[83] ORC § 3752.111(D).

[84] ORC § 3752.112(A).

[85] ORC § 3752.112(B).

[86] ORC § 3752.113(A).

[87] ORC § 3752-113(B).

[88] ORC § 3752.113(B)(1) - (2).

3.7 Inspections And Investigations

To determine compliance with Chapter 3752 and implementing rules, the Director may enter and inspect or investigate any public or private property and any pertinent records, obtaining, if necessary, an administrative inspection warrant under Section 2933.21 of the Revised Code. If the Director obtains a search warrant, but entry into the facility premises is refused or the investigation is somehow hindered, the owner of the facility may be held liable for any expenses incurred.[89]

3.8 Ohio EPA Remedial Action

The Director of Ohio EPA may take remedial action if he determines that the conditions at a reporting facility present an imminent and substantial threat to public health or safety, or are threatening to cause or contribute to air pollution, water pollution, or soil contamination.[90] The agency may use money from the immediate removal fund[91] to take whatever remedial action is necessary to protect the public health and safety and the environment. However, the Director may act only in response to a violation or a failure to comply with the various sections of Chapter 3752.[92] If the Director takes remedial action, he may recover any costs incurred (in addition to any other liabilities imposed by law) from the owner or operator of the facility in question. The cost of the remedial action is a lien upon the facility.[93]

3.9 Prohibitions

Once a reporting facility or other party has posted warning signs on the facility's premises, no person may enter those premises without permission.[94] Falsification

---

[89] ORC § 3752.12(B).

[90] ORC § 3752.13(A).

[91] *See* ORC § 3745.12.

[92] *See* ORC § 3752.13(A)(1) - (10).

[93] ORC § 3752.13(B).

[94] ORC § 3752.14(A).

of or tampering with records kept or submitted under Chapter 3752 is punishable by fine and possible imprisonment.[95]

Violations of Chapter 3752 (excluding Sections 3752.07, 3752.11, 3752.111, and 3752.113) and implementing rules are subject to a civil penalty of $10,000 for each day of each violation. Violations of Sections 3752.07 or 3752.113 and implementing rules incur a $5,000 penalty for each day of each violation. Violators of Sections 3752.11 or 3752.111 and implementing rules must pay a penalty equal to the costs incurred as a result of the violations.[96]

Reckless violations of Chapter 3752 (excluding Sections 3752.07, 3752.11, 3752.111, 3752.113 and 3752.14) or implementing rules are subject to a fine of $10,000 to $25,000 per day, a maximum prison sentence of four years, or both. Each subsequent offense may be fined a maximum of $50,000.[97] A reckless violation of any of the excluded sections is a first degree misdemeanor.[98]

---

[95] ORC § 3752.99; *see* ORC § 3752.15.

[96] ORC § 3752.17(C).

[97] ORC § 3752.99(A).

[98] ORC § 3752.99(B) – (C).

Chapter XI

POWER SITING LAW

1.0 INTRODUCTION

Ohio's power siting law, codified at Chapter 4906 of the Ohio Revised Code, provides for comprehensive regulation of the siting of new major utility facilities, as well as substantial additions to facilities already in operation. If any person, as defined by law, proposes to construct a "major utility facility" or a "substantial addition" to an existing facility, the person must obtain a certificate of environmental compatibility and public need from the Ohio Power Siting Board before it may "commence to construct" the facility or addition.

2.0 OHIO POWER SITING BOARD

Section 4906.02 of the Revised Code establishes the Ohio Power Siting Board ("Board"). Led by the Chairman of the Public Utilities Commission of Ohio ("PUCO"), the Board is composed of the Directors of Environmental Protection, Health, Development, Natural Resources, and Agriculture, together with a public representative, who must be an engineer, appointed by the Governor. There also are four legislative members who participate in Board proceedings but do not vote. Under Revised Code Section 4906.03, the Board accepts or rejects applications for certificates and promulgates rules necessary to implement Chapter 4906.[1]

---

[1] *See* http://www.opsb.ohio.gov. The site includes Board rules, names of members, current cases, and publications.

The Board employs a small professional and administrative Staff for processing applications, participating in public and adjudication hearings, and monitoring compliance with the terms and conditions of certificates issued by the Board. PUCO hearing examiners serve as administrative law judges at the public and adjudication hearings for each application for certification of a major utility facility.

3.0 CERTIFICATE OF ENVIRONMENTAL COMPATIBILITY AND PUBLIC NEED

The centerpiece of Ohio's power siting law is the requirement that a utility or municipality proposing a major utility facility must obtain a certificate of environmental compatibility and public need before commencing construction.[2] The term "major utility facility" is defined in Section 4906.01(B) of the Revised Code to mean:

> (1) an electric generating plant and associated facilities designed for, or capable of, operation at a capacity of fifty megawatts or more;
>
> (2) an electric transmission line and associated facilities of a design capacity of one hundred twenty-five kilovolts or more; and
>
> (3) a gas or natural gas transmission line and associated facilities designed for, or capable of, transporting gas or natural gas at pressures in excess of one hundred twenty-five pounds per square inch.

A certificate is not required for "the replacement of an existing facility with a like facility,"[3] a facility in operation on October 23, 1972, or a facility on which construction had commenced prior to October 23, 1974.[4] However, a certificate is required for a "substantial addition to a facility already in operation," with "substantial addition" to be defined by the Board.[5] The Board has, by rule, defined what projects constitute "substantial addition" to a major utility facility.[6]

---

[2] ORC § 4906.04.

[3] *Id.*

[4] ORC § 4906.05.

[5] *Id.*; *see* OAC 4906-1-02(O), (T).

[6] *See* OAC 4906-1-01(N), (U).

Municipalities have successfully challenged the need for full compliance with Chapter 4906 in instances where they construct major utility facilities pursuant to authority granted by Section 4 of Article XVIII of the Ohio Constitution (the "Home Rule" provision, which, among other things, authorizes municipalities to acquire, construct, own, and operate public utilities). In *City of Columbus v. Ohio Power Siting Comm'n*,[7] the Ohio Supreme Court refused to require a municipality to obtain a certificate for the construction of a municipally owned trash-fired power plant. The court held, however, that the municipality was required to comply with the various State environmental laws, as mandated by Section 4906.10(A).[8]

An application for a certificate must be filed not less than two years (one year in the case of transmission lines) nor more than five years before the planned construction date, although it is possible to obtain a waiver of this requirement from the Board for "unforeseen emergencies."[9] The application for a certificate must contain detailed information, including a description of the facility and its location, a summary of environmental impact studies, a statement explaining the need for the facility, a statement of why the proposed location is best suited for the facility, and a statement of how the facility fits into the applicant's long-term forecast reports required to be filed under Section 4935.04 of the Revised Code. Extensive public notice requirements are triggered by filing of the application.[10]

Within sixty to ninety days of receiving a certificate application, the Board is to schedule hearings, which must be concluded as expeditiously as practicable. Not less than fifteen days prior to the initial hearing, the Staff will submit a written report of its investigation of the application.[11]

The Board has authority under Section 4906.10 to grant or deny an application, or to grant it with conditions or modifications deemed appropriate. The Board is not to grant a certificate unless it "finds and determines" certain statutory criteria, including: [12]

---

[7] 58 Ohio St.2d 435, 390 N.E.2d 1208 (1979).

[8] *Id.* at 441, 390 N.E.2d at 1212.

[9] ORC § 4906.06(A).

[10] ORC § 4906.06; *see* OAC 4906-5-06, -08.

[11] ORC § 4906.07.

[12] ORC § 4906.10(A).

(1) the basis of the need for the facility (the Board shall presume the need as it is stated in the application);

(2) the nature of the probable environmental impact;

(3) that the facility represents the minimum adverse environmental impact;

(4) that the facility is consistent with regional power grid expansion plans (transmission lines only) and will serve the interests of electric system economy and reliability;

(5) that the facility will comply with the air pollution, solid waste, and water pollution laws and regulations of the State of Ohio;

(6) that the facility will serve the public interest, convenience, and necessity;

(7) the facility's impact on the viability of agricultural land in existing agricultural districts; and

(8) that the facility incorporates maximum feasible water conservation practices, as determined by the Board.

Both the "minimum adverse environmental impact" and "water conservation practices" criteria specifically require consideration of the available technology and the nature and economics of "the various alternatives." Proper consideration of the alternatives may include a full evaluation and assessment of multiple sites for proposed facilities.[13] The hearing, appeal, and judicial review provisions of Ohio's statutes governing the PUCO – Revised Code Sections 4903.2 to 4903.16 and 4903.20 to 4903.23 – apply to the Power Siting Board as if it were the PUCO.[14]

4.0 RULES OF THE BOARD

Pursuant to its rulemaking authority, the Board has adopted rules that are codified in Chapters 4906-1 *et seq.* of the Ohio Administrative Code. Chapter 4906-1 contains definitions and general rules governing administrative matters such as filing procedures and

[13] *Id.*

[14] ORC § 4906.12.

fees. Various procedural requirements are set out in Chapters 4906-5 and 4906-7, including procedures governing the processing of applications and conducting of hearings before the Board. Chapters 4906-13 and 4906-15 provide instruction in the preparation of certificate applications for electric generating facilities and transmission (electric, gas, and natural gas) facilities, respectively.

4.1 Substantial Addition Definition

An important provision in the Board's rules is the definition of "substantial addition" set forth in Rules 4906-1-01(O) (transmission line) and 4906-1-01(T) (electric generating plant). With respect to an electric generating plant, a substantial addition is "any modification of a utility facility not operating under a certificate, which modification in itself constitutes a major utility facility." Generally, the addition of a generating unit of fifty megawatts or more, or adding a generating unit of fifty megawatts or more that is designed to operate in conjunction with existing capacity to establish a combined cycle unit, constitutes a substantial addition.[15] For transmission lines, a substantial addition is any addition or modification of line facilities as listed in the "Application Requirement Matrix" contained in Appendices A and B to the rule.[16]

4.2 Certificate Application

The Board's rules contain extensive descriptions of the type and amount of information to be submitted in support of a certificate application, including justification of need; site alternatives analyses; technical, financial, and environmental data; and the social and ecological impacts of the proposed facility.[17] The information for each area must be comprehensive yet detailed. For example, Rule 4906-13-07(A)(3) requires that the application for a generating facility identify construction noise impacts from dynamiting activities, operation of earth-moving equipment, driving of piles, erection of structures, truck traffic, and installation of equipment, as well as describe equipment and procedures to

---

[15] OAC 4906-1-01(T).

[16] OAC 4906-1-01(O).

[17] *See* OAC Chapters 4906-13, 4906-15; *see also* OAC 4906-1-01(U).

mitigate noise impacts during construction and operation of the facility. A full application for a generating plant facility typically contains multiple volumes.

4.3 Development Of Alternatives

Rule 4906-5-04 represents a significant element of additional complexity in the certificate application process involving transmission lines. The rule requires, in most cases, "fully developed information" on a preferred and an alternate site/route for transmission lines. Each site/route must be an actual and viable alternative on which the applicant could construct the proposed facility.[18] For good cause, the requirement for fully developed information on the alternate site/route may be waived.[19]

4.4 Letter Of Notification And Construction Notice

For certain transmission line projects identified in the "Application Requirement Matrix" contained in Appendices A and B to Rule 4906-1-01, the Board's rules provide for use of a letter of notification procedure or a construction notice procedure, each of which is more streamlined than the standard application procedure.[20]

4.5 Completeness Of Certificate Application / Staff Investigation

Formal proceedings on a certificate application do not commence until the Chairman of the Board has determined that an application meets the requirements of the statute and the rules and is accepted.[21] Certificate proceedings generally are conducted before an administrative law judge, who then presents a report and recommendations to the Board for appropriate action. As in the case of PUCO orders, final orders of the Board are reviewable only by the Ohio Supreme Court.[22]

---

[18] OAC 4906-5-04(A).

[19] OAC 4906-5-04(B).

[20] *See* OAC 4906-5-02.

[21] OAC 4906-5-05(A). An application for a major utility facility related to a coal research and/or development project as defined in Sections 1555.01 and 1551.30 of the Revised Code, submitted to the Ohio Coal Development Office for review under Section 1551.33 of the Revised Code, shall be accepted as complete. OAC 4906-5-05(B).

[22] State ex rel. Ohio Edison Co. v. Parrott, 73 Ohio St.3d 705, 654 N.E.2d 106 (1995).

5.0 ELECTROMAGNETIC FIELDS

The potential health effects of electromagnetic fields ("EMFs") are an additional consideration in the siting of electric transmission lines. Because of publicized concerns that EMFs, which are present wherever there is electric current, may cause adverse health effects, the Board has developed a strategy for dealing with EMFs.

5.1 Background: EMF Studies

Numerous scientific studies regarding EMFs have been published, with some suggesting a correlation between exposure to EMFs and the development of cancer, particularly in children. Other studies have concluded that there is no such link.[23]

In view of the uncertainty and ongoing public concern about health-related EMF issues, Congress – in the Energy Policy Act of 1992[24] – directed the U.S. Department of Energy ("DOE") and the National Institute of Environmental Health Sciences ("NIEHS") to determine whether exposure to EMFs produced by the generation, transmission, and use of electric energy affects human health; carry out research, development, and demonstration of technologies to mitigate adverse human health effects; and provide for dissemination of relevant information.[25]

Under the Electric and Magnetic Fields Research and Public Information Dissemination ("EMF-RAPID") Program established pursuant to the 1992 legislation, DOE requested the National Research Council ("Council") – the principal operating arm of the National Academy of Sciences, the National Academy of Engineering, and the Institute of Medicine – to undertake a comprehensive evaluation of published studies relating to the effects of EMFs on cells, tissues, and organisms. In an interim report on that review,[26] the Council's research committee concluded that the current body of evidence does not show that exposure to residential EMFs produces cancer, adverse neurobehavioral effects, or reproductive or developmental abnormalities. Although the Council found that an association between residential wiring configurations and childhood leukemia persists in

---

[23] *See* http://www.niehs.nih.gov/emfrapid.

[24] Pub. L. 102-486, 106 STAT. 2776 (1992).

[25] *Id.*, § 2118, at 3075, codified at 42 USC § 13478.

[26] Possible Health Effects of Exposure to Residential Electric and Magnetic Fields (National Academy Press, 1997).

multiple studies, it concluded that the causative factor responsible for that association has not been identified, and that "[n]o evidence links contemporary measurements of magnetic-field levels to childhood leukemia."[27] The Council's final report[28] stated that "[t]he results of the EMF-RAPID Program do not support the contention that the use of electricity poses a major unrecognized public-health danger." The Council recommended that "[b]asic research on the effects of power-frequency magnetic fields on cells and animals should continue, but a special research funding effort is not required."[29]

NIEHS, in fulfillment of the 1992 Congressional directive, was responsible for overseeing health effects research and evaluation. According to its report following completion of the EMF-RAPID Program, NIEHS found that although "[t]he scientific evidence suggesting that ELF-EMF exposures pose any health risk is weak ... the epidemiological studies demonstrate ... a fairly consistent pattern of a small, increased risk with increasing exposure that is somewhat weaker for chronic lymphocytic leukemia than for childhood leukemia.... No indication of increased leukemias in experimental animals has been observed."[30]

The electric utility industry itself continues to study EMF issues. Building on more than twenty years of research in EMF health science, the Electric Power Research Institute ("EPRI") maintains a central position on EMFs. EPRI's Internet website[31] indicates that current research emphasizes childhood leukemia, potential relationships between relevant occupational EMFs and contact current exposures, and guidelines for limiting exposure of electric utility employees and the public.

Additional information on EMF studies is available at EMF-Link[32] which summarizes current research, legislation, and litigation. The website provides "Questions and Answers" and "Hot Topics" as well as connections to other resources.

---

[27] *Id.* at 2.

[28] Research on Power Frequency Fields Completed Under the Energy Policy Act of 1992 (National Academy Press, 1999).

[29] *Id.* at 8.

[30] Transmittal letter from Kenneth Olden, Director of NIEHS (May 4, 1999), contained in Health Effects from Exposure to Power-Line Frequency Electric and Magnetic Fields (National Institute of Environmental Health Sciences, NIH Pub. No. 99-4493). The full report is available at http://www.niehs.nih.gov/emfrapid.

[31] http://www.epri.com.

[32] http://www.infoventures.com/emf.

5.2 Ohio Power Siting Board Consideration Of EMFs

In October 1990, the Ohio Power Siting Board passed a resolution calling for an investigation of EMFs emitted from high voltage transmission lines. The resolution provided, first, that the Board had the authority to initiate studies or investigations, and that those entities subject to its jurisdiction were required to provide information to assist such studies. Second, the Board was empowered to issue certificates for high voltage transmission lines known to produce EMFs. Third, in response to increasing public awareness, as well as to state and federal regulatory action regarding EMFs, the Board began a study of high voltage transmission lines to investigate the strengths of the associated EMFs. Staff were directed specifically to obtain on-site measurements of EMFs associated with typical transmission lines in Ohio, use computer models capable of calculating EMF strengths and evaluate the models' validity by comparisons with on-site measurements, develop a data base of EMF strengths associated with the conductor configuration of typical future transmission lines, ascertain the extent of the regulated electric utilities' knowledge of EMF measurements, and prepare recommendations of appropriate further action for the Board's consideration.

In 1996, the Board released the results of the Staff's six-year study.[33] The report stated that magnetic fields can be measured and calculated accurately, provided that sources are known. After 180 sets of measurements were taken, the Staff found that the strengths of EMFs associated with transmission lines in Ohio – where the maximum value measured was 30 milliGauss – were significantly lower than the limits imposed by New York (200 milliGauss) and Florida (150 and 200 milliGauss for 235 kV and 500 kV, respectively), which were the only states with established maximum limits at the time.[34] Although the Staff concluded that epidemiological data have failed to show a strong correlation between EMFs and health effects, it recommended to the Board that utilities in the state continue to calculate maximum field strength of proposed lines and monitor developments in EMFs related to

[33] Staff EMF Survey Report (Oct. 1996).

[34] *Id.* at 1-2.

potential health effects. The Staff also recommended that the utilities monitor developments in transmission construction design.[35]

In compliance with Staff recommendations, the Board has amended Chapter 4906-15 of the Administrative Code to require that utilities submit data on EMF strength levels as part of the certification process for electric transmission lines.[36] Accordingly, applications must discuss production of EMFs and their strength levels under conductors and at the edge of the right of way (given specified load conditions), current findings on possible health effects of EMF strength levels, consideration of EMF strength levels as a company policy and in designing and siting transmission line projects, and current public information procedures involving EMF strength levels.[37]

To date, the Board has considered one EMF-related case. In a proceeding involving an electric transmission project in Putnam County,[38] which was decided prior to the Board's promulgation of the EMF amendments to its rules, Ohio Power Company sought certification of its East Leipsic Extension. Intervening landowners claimed that since certain studies have raised a genuine concern about the effects of EMFs, the Board should avoid or mitigate any possible health risk to residents near the proposed transmission lines by ordering the company to locate its extension at an alternative site. Intervenors also asserted that failure to assess the potential health impacts in current and planned high density population areas is inconsistent with the statutory obligation of the Board. The Board found that Ohio Power's application was not in any way deficient due to a lack of information regarding EMFs, and further that the Staff had complied with its duty to submit the application to the Ohio Department of Health for comments and had extensively reviewed the EMF question during the proceeding.

---

[35] *Id.* at 41.

[36] In the Matter of the Power Siting Board's Investigation into the Strengths of Electric and Magnetic Fields Emitted from High Voltage Transmission Lines, Case No. 90-1609-EL-BIN (Mar. 22, 1993).

[37] OAC 4906-15-06(E)(2).

[38] In the Matter of the Application of Ohio Power Company for Certification of the East Leipsic 138 kV Extension Electric Transmission Line Project in Putnam County, Ohio, Case No. 90-1530-EL-BTX (June 17, 1991).

Chapter XII

ENVIRONMENTAL REVIEW APPEALS COMMISSION

1.0 STATUTORY AUTHORITY

The same legislation that created Ohio EPA in 1972[1] also created the Environmental Board of Review, now known as the Environmental Review Appeals Commission ("ERAC" or "Commission").[2] The ERAC is an administrative tribunal that hears appeals from final actions of the Director of Ohio EPA. One of the prevailing reasons given for creation of the tribunal, during the legislative debates, was to provide a check on the considerable powers proposed to be granted to the office of the Director.

The ERAC consists of three members appointed by the Governor, subject to confirmation by the Senate, for six-year terms.[3] Each member must have "extensive experience in pollution control and abatement technology, ecology, public health, environmental law, economics of natural resource development, or related fields."[4] No more than two members can be of the same political party.[5] At least one of the members must be an attorney and at least two of the members must "represent the public interest."[6]

---

1 SB 397, 109th General Assembly (Eff. Oct. 23, 1972).

2 The name was changed by the General Assembly in December 1996. *See* HB 670, 121st General Assembly (Eff. Dec. 2, 1996) at 296 *et seq.*

3 ORC § 3745.02.

4 *Id.*

5 *Id.*

6 *Id.*

The ERAC is authorized to hear appeals from "[a]ny person who was a party to a proceeding before the director" seeking an order "vacating or modifying the action of the director of environmental protection or local board of health, or ordering the director or board of health to perform an act."[7] The key jurisdictional term "action" or "act" is defined to include:[8]

> the adoption, modification, or repeal of a rule or standard, the issuance, modification, or revocation of any lawful order other than an emergency order, and the issuance, denial, modification, or revocation of a license, permit, lease, variance, or certificate, or the approval or disapproval of plans and specifications pursuant to law or rules adopted thereunder.

In addition, "any person who would be aggrieved or adversely affected" by the Director's issuance, denial, modification, revocation, or renewal of a permit, license, or variance without issuance of a proposed action may appeal to the ERAC within thirty days of issuance of the Director's final action.[9] However, only entities that appear, submit evidence, or otherwise participate in a rulemaking proceeding have standing to challenge that rulemaking to the Commission.[10]

Both statutory and case law in Ohio make it clear that the ERAC "has exclusive original jurisdiction over any matter which may ... be brought before it."[11]

2.0 APPEALS

Appeals to the ERAC by parties to proceedings before the Director of Ohio EPA must be filed within thirty days of notice of the action being appealed, must be in writing, and must "set forth the action complained of and the grounds upon which the appeal is based."[12] Appeals filed by aggrieved third parties must be filed within thirty days of issuance of a final

---

[7] ORC § 3745.04. Local boards of health issue solid waste licenses pursuant to Section 3734.05 of the Revised Code.

[8] *Id.*

[9] ORC § 3745.07. *See* Citizens Lobby for Environmental Action Now v. Schregardus, Case Nos. EBR 092958-092961 (Oct. 19, 1993).

[10] New Boston Coke Corp. v. Tyler, 32 Ohio St.3d 216, 218, 513 N.E.2d 302, 305 (1987).

[11] ORC § 3745.04. Cases that reinforce the exclusivity of ERAC jurisdiction include: State ex rel. Maynard v. Whitfield, 12 Ohio St.3d 49, 465 N.E.2d 406 (1984); Warren Molded Plastics, Inc. v. Williams, 56 Ohio St.2d 352, 384 N.E.2d 253 (1978); State ex rel. Williams v. Bozarth 55 Ohio St.2d 34, 377 N.E.2d 1006 (1978); Cincinnati ex rel. Crotty v. Cincinnati , 50 Ohio St.2d 27, 361 N.E.2d 1340 (1977).

[12] ORC § 3745.04.

action.[13] Procedural rules applicable to proceedings before the Commission are set forth in Chapter 3746 of the Ohio Administrative Code.

The filing of an appeal does not automatically stay the effectiveness of the action appealed from.[14] The ERAC is authorized to issue a stay "pending immediate determination of the appeal without interruption by continuances ...."[15] As a practical matter, however, the Commission rarely issues stays and will do so only upon a showing of "compelling reasons" justifying a stay.[16]

One of two distinct types of proceedings will occur before the ERAC, depending upon the procedures employed by the Director in the first instance. The Commission will hold a hearing *de novo* if the appeal concerns an action for which "no adjudication hearing was conducted [by the Director] in accordance with sections 119.09 and 119.10 of the Revised Code."[17] If the Director did conduct an adjudication hearing pursuant to Sections 119.09 and 119.10, then the Commission is "confined to the record as certified to it by the director."[18]

A hearing *de novo* is a hearing "anew," or a case tried over again, which means that all new testimony and other evidence are presented to the ERAC.[19] Since all Ohio EPA rulemakings involve a public hearing pursuant to Section 119.03 of the Revised Code, not an adjudication hearing pursuant to Sections 119.09 and 119.10, all rulemaking appeals to the Commission are subject to a hearing *de novo*. For most routine permit decisions – *i.e.*, those that are not expected to be controversial or of great public interest – Ohio EPA will issue a final permit without first conducting an adjudicatory hearing, which can be appealed to the Commission for a hearing *de novo*.[20] This procedure reduces the backlog of adjudicatory

---

[13] ORC § 3745.07.

[14] ORC § 3745.04.

[15] *Id.*

[16] OAC 3746-5-13(A).

[17] ORC § 3745.05.

[18] *Id.* Section 3745.04 of the Revised Code requires the Director or local Board of Health to certify to the ERAC, within seven days after notice of an appeal, "a record of the proceedings out of which the appeal arises, including all documents and correspondence, and a transcript of all testimony."

[19] *See* ORC § 3745.05.

[20] *See* ORC § 119.06(C).

hearings pending before the Director, and reduces Ohio EPA's need for hearing examiners and other resources to perform the adjudicatory function.

The standard of review applicable to ERAC appeals is whether the action appealed from is "lawful and reasonable."[21] The Commission is empowered to vacate or modify any action found to be unlawful or unreasonable.[22] In *Citizens Com. to Preserve Lake Logan v. Williams*,[23] the Franklin County Court of Appeals defined the term "unreasonable" in Section 3745.05 to mean "that which is not in accordance with reason, or that which has no factual foundation."[24]

3.0 DECISIONS

Final decisions rendered by the ERAC are in writing and set forth the findings of fact and conclusions of law upon which orders of the Commission are based.[25] ERAC decisions are appealable to the Franklin County Court of Appeals, or, if the appeal arises from an alleged violation of a law or regulation, to the court of appeals of the district in which the violation was alleged to have occurred.[26] The appropriate court of appeals is authorized to grant a suspension of an ERAC order if the court finds that "an unjust hardship to the appellant will result from the execution of the Commission's order pending determination of the appeal."[27] Normally confined to the record certified to it by the ERAC in an appeal, the court "may grant a request for the admission of additional evidence when satisfied that such additional evidence is newly discovered and could not with reasonable diligence have been ascertained prior to the hearing before the Commission."[28]

The standard of review in the court of appeals is whether the ERAC's order is "supported by reliable, probative, and substantial evidence and is in accordance with law."[29]

---

[21] ORC § 3745.05.

[22] *Id.*

[23] 56 Ohio App.2d 61, 381 N.E.2d 661 (1977).

[24] *Id.* at 70, 381 N.E.2d at 667.

[25] ORC § 3745.05.

[26] ORC § 3745.06.

[27] *Id.*

[28] *Id.*

[29] *Id.*

Decisions by the court of appeals affirming, reversing, vacating, or modifying orders of the ERAC may be appealed to the Ohio Supreme Court, in most cases, by filing a motion to certify the appeal.[30]

[30] An appeal as of right lies with the Ohio Supreme Court ("Court") in cases that involve a constitutional question. An appeal to the Court can be certified by the court of appeals if the judges thereof make an order finding that a judgment upon which they have agreed is in conflict with a judgment pronounced upon the same question by another court of appeals. Acceptance of jurisdiction in other appeals is discretionary with the Court, depending upon whether it finds that the case is of "public or great general interest."

Chapter XIII

ENFORCEMENT

1.0 INTRODUCTION

Ohio law provides strong remedies for violations of environmental statutes, regulations, permits, and orders. Penalties of up to $25,000 per day per violation, injunctive relief, criminal fines, and imprisonment for up to one year are authorized for most violations. Typically, Ohio EPA investigates environmental law violations and, when civil or criminal judicial enforcement is considered appropriate, refers cases to the Ohio Attorney General's Environmental Enforcement Section. Sometimes, the Agency is able to negotiate settlements through administrative orders without involving the Attorney General's Office.

Common types of environmental law violations include installation or operation of a pollution source without a permit or in violation of the terms and conditions of a permit; failure to report information required by a statute, regulation, or permit condition; submission of false information; and engagement in activity that is specifically prohibited under a particular regulatory scheme.

Information about environmental law violations usually comes to the attention of an enforcer in one of three ways: review of a report submitted to a regulatory agency; an inspection conducted by a regulatory agency; or a complaint to a regulatory agency from a third party – *e.g.*, a neighbor, employee, or competitor.

The purpose of this chapter is to review the distinctive characteristics and potential ramifications of the different statutory enforcement options that can be initiated by Ohio EPA: administrative orders, civil actions, and criminal prosecutions. Also discussed are

Ohio's new audit privilege statute, citizen suits, and verified complaints, and their role in shaping environmental regulation and enforcement.[1]

2.0 ADMINISTRATIVE ORDERS

Ohio environmental statutes empower the Director of Ohio EPA to issue administrative orders requiring compliance with the State's various pollution control regulatory schemes.[2]

Also known as "Director's Findings and Orders," administrative orders generally are the least confrontational and least severe of the various enforcement options; they provide the most expeditious means of resolving violations. Ohio EPA issues and negotiates administrative orders without involving the Attorney General's Office or the courts. Upon discovery of a violation, the Agency's standard practice is to issue Findings and Orders in draft form, setting out the violations and applicable laws, specifying a compliance schedule, and imposing a civil penalty. Civil penalties imposed under administrative orders are subject to statutory limitations discussed in Part 3.0 of this chapter. In a letter accompanying the order, the Ohio EPA Director invites the recipient to discuss the draft with Agency staff and advises the recipient that failure to reach prompt agreement with the Agency will precipitate referral to the Attorney General with risk of greater aggravation and escalated penalties.

The use of Findings and Orders has emerged as Ohio EPA's enforcement tool of choice. Under the Agency's program of negotiating compliance schedules and resolution of alleged violations with the source owner or operator, if an agreement is reached, the Agency issues an administrative order rather than referring the case to the Attorney General for judicial enforcement.[3] Agreed Findings and Orders cannot be appealed; included in each final order is a waiver of appeal rights to be signed by the owner or operator.

---

[1] For a discussion of enforcement under the federal environmental statutes, see *Environmental Law Handbook* (Thomas F.P. Sullivan ed., 16th ed. Government Institutes, Inc. 2001).

[2] *See* ORC §§ 3704.03(R) (air related orders), 3734.13(A) - (B) (waste related orders), 6111.03(H) (water related orders).

[3] U.S. EPA has approved the use of Findings and Orders for the air program on two conditions: (1) that every case include a penalty; and (2) that at least a portion of every penalty be cash. The federal agency has been silent regarding the use of Findings and Orders in water, solid waste, and hazardous waste enforcement programs.

3.0 CIVIL ACTIONS

Enforcement schemes under Ohio's air, waste, and water pollution control programs provide for civil enforcement actions to be brought by the Ohio Attorney General at the request of Ohio EPA.[4] The standard procedure in a civil action is for the Attorney General to file a complaint in the court of common pleas in the county where the alleged violation has occurred. The complaint, in addition to demanding civil penalties, sometimes seeks quick action by the court through injunctive relief – *e.g.*, a temporary restraining order or preliminary injunction – to compel the defendant to discontinue the allegedly unlawful conduct or take affirmative measures to bring the offending source into compliance with the applicable regulatory scheme.[5]

Under Ohio law, the Attorney General is not held to the traditional standard for obtaining injunctive relief – *i.e.*, a balancing of the equities. Rather, in order to obtain injunctive relief for violations of Ohio's environmental laws, the Attorney General need show only the existence of harmful environmental conditions against which the Ohio General Assembly has authorized prohibitory and mandatory relief.[6]

Ohio EPA's civil penalty policies are consistent with those established by U.S. EPA. The policies are designed to remove the economic benefit of noncompliance and reflect the gravity of the violation. Factors taken into account in calculating civil penalty demands include size of the violator, ability to pay, history of noncompliance, degree of cooperation, and actual or possible harm resulting from the violation.[7]

The amount of civil penalties that may be assessed for pollution control violations varies with the environmental programs. Penalties authorized under Ohio's air statute are a

---

4 *See* ORC §§ 3704.06(B), 3734.10, 6111.07(B), 6111.09; *see also* OAC 3745-49-04.

5 *See* ORC §§ 3704.06(B), 3734.10, 6111.07(B), 6111.09.

6 State ex rel. Brown v. Chase Foundry & Mfg. Co., 8 Ohio App.3d 96, 456 N.E.2d 528 (Franklin Cty. App. 1982), *cert. denied,* 464 U.S. 823 (1983). *Chase Foundry* arose under Ohio Revised Code Section 3704.06(B) which authorizes injunctive relief for violations of Ohio's air pollution control laws. However, the statutes authorizing relief for violations of Ohio's solid and hazardous waste laws and water pollution control laws are similarly worded. *See* ORC §§ 3734.10, 6111.07(B), 6111.09.

7 U.S. EPA has developed various computer models to assist in the calculation of settlement penalty figures. For instance, the BEN computer program is designed to calculate the economic benefit a violator derives from delaying or avoiding compliance with environmental statutes. (Except in extraordinary circumstances, the lowest settlement under the penalty policy will be the calculated economic benefit of noncompliance.) The ABEL computer program is designed to assess a violator's ability to finance civil penalties or new investments in pollution control equipment.

maximum of $25,000 per day per violation[8] The waste statute establishes a $10,000 maximum daily penalty for each violation except for violations involving PCBs, plastics, and scrap tires.[9] A violation of PCB storage and disposal requirements imposes a maximum daily penalty of $25,000 per violation.[10] For a violation of requirements governing the labeling of plastics, the maximum daily penalty is $250 per violation.[11] Violations involving scrap tires are punishable by a maximum daily penalty of $5,000 per violation unless there is open burning or open dumping of tires, or a violation of an emergency order of the Director, in which cases the penalty would increase to $10,000.[12] The water statute provides for daily civil penalties of up to $10,000 per violation.[13]

A summary of common violations that give rise to civil liability under Ohio's environmental laws is set out in Appendix A.

One of the more prominent civil actions in recent Ohio history is the *Dayton Malleable* case.[14] The Attorney General filed the initial action in the Montgomery County Court of Common Pleas in 1978, seeking an injunction to require Dayton Malleable, Inc. ("DMI") to comply with terms and conditions of its NPDES permit. The permit included a compliance schedule establishing dates for initiating and completing various stages of a construction project, with final compliance to be achieved in July 1977. The only issue at the trial was whether a penalty would be proper and, if so, in what amount.

The trial court found that a penalty was proper and set the amount at $493,500, using U.S. EPA's civil penalty policy and taking into consideration the economic benefit of noncompliance and the harm, or risk of harm, to public health or the environment, as well as several mitigating factors beyond DMI's control that delayed compliance.

The Montgomery County Court of Appeals held that DMI's failure to meet deadlines in the compliance schedule was not a violation of a term or condition in the NPDES permit. The court further held that the assessment of penalties for delays occurring before the final

---

[8] ORC § 3704.06(C).

[9] ORC § 3734.13(C).

[10] *Id.*

[11] *Id.*

[12] *Id.*

[13] ORC § 6111.09(A).

compliance date was in error, based on its conclusion that the schedule for compliance was an "agreement" between Ohio EPA and the company, and not a permit term or condition, and that a "strict construction" of the penalty provision in Revised Code Chapter 6111 would prohibit assessment of a penalty.[15]

The Ohio Supreme Court disagreed, holding that schedules of compliance are terms and conditions of NPDES permits, and further that a court may assess a civil penalty against a person who violates, or fails to perform a duty imposed by, a schedule of compliance.[16] With regard to the trial court's determination of the amount of the penalty, the court affirmed the use of the federal penalty policy.[17]

In a more recent case, an Ohio court rejected Ohio EPA's application of U.S. EPA's Clean Air Act Stationary Source Civil Penalty Policy.[18] In its 1991 decision in *State of Ohio v. Steel Processing Serv., Inc.*,[19] the Jefferson County Common Pleas Court upheld Ohio EPA's finding that Steel Processing's rail car salvage operation involved unpermitted air contaminant sources.

Ohio EPA, in its complaint, requested that a penalty of $78,050 be assessed against Steel Processing. The Agency arrived at that figure by utilizing U.S. EPA's penalty policy. Approximately $39,000 of the penalty amount was attributable to the "gravity component" of the penalty policy calculation; the additional $39,050 reflected an augmentation of the gravity component based upon Ohio EPA's determination that Steel Processing's violations were willful. The court rejected that determination, concluding that Steel Processing was neither recalcitrant nor uncooperative in its dealings with the Agency.

The court explicitly noted that the U.S. EPA penalty policy could provide useful information in quantifying a penalty, but concluded that "ultimately ... it is the function of

---

14 State ex rel. Brown v. Dayton Malleable, 1 Ohio St.3d 151, 438 N.E.2d 120 (Montgomery Cty. App. 1982).

15 *Id.* at 155, 438 N.E.2d at 123.

16 *Id.* at 156, 438 N.E.2d at 124.

17 *Id.* at 157-58, 438 N.E.2d at 125.

18 *See* http://www.epa.gov/compliance/resources/policies/civil/caa/stationary/penpol.pdf. A clarification of the policy is available at http://www.epa.gov/compliance/resources/policies/civil/caa/stationary/penpolappi.pdf.

19 No. 90-CIV-67 (Jefferson Cty. Comm. Pl. Jan. 24, 1991).

[the courts] to impose a penalty under Section 3704.06 of the Ohio Revised Code."[20] The court assessed a civil penalty of $25,000 and enjoined Steel Processing from conducting any unpermitted operations in the State.

The Ohio Attorney General's Office also will join with U.S. EPA, when appropriate, to bring a civil enforcement action, such as that filed against Hoge Lumber Co. ("Hoge") in 1995.[21] In their complaints, the United States and the State of Ohio alleged that Hoge was operating an air contaminant source (a boiler) without a permit to operate and in violation of both the emission limit established under Ohio's State Implementation Plan and the source-specific emission limit contained in Hoge's permit to install. The U.S. District Court granted the plaintiffs' motions for summary judgment on the issue of liability and applied Section 113 of the Clean Air Act to assess the civil penalty, recognizing that similar criteria are used under Ohio law. Hoge was ordered to pay a civil penalty of $650,000,[22] which by agreement between the plaintiffs was split evenly between the United States and Ohio.

Civil penalty figures have fluctuated over the years. After rising steadily in the early 1990s, as the State vowed to enforce environmental statutes aggressively,[23] by the mid 1990s penalty figures, for the most part, were not as great.[24] Between 2000 and 2002, however, the State stepped up environmental enforcement by issuing a total of 393 administrative orders, compared to 245 between 1997 and 1999.[25] Ohio EPA also began processing administrative cases more quickly; the average case age dropped almost by half (475 days to 261 days) from

---

[20] *Id.* at 11. For another example of a court considering the factors in the U.S. EPA civil penalty policy but ultimately exercising its own discretion in fashioning the penalty, *see* State ex rel. Celebrezze v. Thermal-Tron, Inc., 71 Ohio App.3d 11, 592 N.E.2d 912 (Cuyahoga Cty. App. 1992).

[21] United States v. Hoge Lumber Co., No. 3:95CV7044, 1997 U.S. Dist. LEXIS 22359 (N.D. Ohio May 7, 1997).

[22] *Id.* at 22353 (N.D. Ohio Nov. 5, 1997).

[23] *See, e.g.,* State ex rel. Montgomery v. Elano, No. C3-96-238 (S.D. Ohio June 26, 1996) (consent order imposing $1,000,000 penalty for hazardous waste violations and $188,000 for investigation costs); State ex rel. Fisher v. Phthalchem, No. A-8907973 (Hamilton Cty. Comm. Pl. Mar. 4, 1992) (consent order imposing $1,800,000 penalty for air, water, and hazardous waste violations); State ex rel. Fisher v. Wheeling-Pittsburgh Steel Corp., No. 91-CIV-473 (Jefferson Cty. Comm. Pl. Oct. 10, 1991) (consent order imposing $1,250,000 penalty for air pollution control violations); State ex rel. Fisher v. General Elec. Co., No. 90-CI-77 (Pickaway Cty. Comm. Pl. Aug. 30, 1991) (consent order imposing $1,600,000 penalty for air pollution control violations).

[24] *See, e.g.,* State ex rel. Montgomery v. Buckeye Steel Castings, No. CVH-6602 (Franklin Cty. Comm. Pl. Aug. 30, 1996) (consent order imposing a $586,750 penalty for failure to obtain required permits, with $311,750 conditionally suspended for compliance with the order); State ex rel. Montgomery v. Rieter Automotive Globe, No. C195-3627 (Lucas Cty. Comm. P1. Dec. 22, 1995) (consent order imposing a $500,000 penalty for air pollution control violations, with $150,000 conditionally suspended for compliance with the order).

[25] Ohio EPA 2002 Enforcement Report (April 2003) at 2.

2000 to 2002.[26] In 2002, the Agency's administrative penalties for 2002 exceeded $2,000,000 for the third consecutive year, and the Attorney General's Office filed fifty-three consent orders assessing $7,608,187 in civil penalties – the second highest total in thirteen years.[27]

Two cases in 2002 are particularly noteworthy. One involved alleged damage to high-quality wetlands in Northeast Ohio; the $1,000,000 penalty was a record amount for a wetlands case.[28] Another was a multi-media case that assessed a total civil penalty exceeding $2,600,000: $1,950,000 for air violations (underreporting and nonrecovery of high emission levels of benzene and volatile organic compounds), $468,000 for hazardous waste violations (illegal storage and disposal of hazardous waste), $150,000 for water violations (discharging effluent without a permit and ground water contamination), and $95,320 for the State's costs to investigate, mitigate, remove, and abate the result of the violations.[29]

4.0 CRIMINAL PROSECUTIONS

The criminal enforcement provisions of Ohio's environmental statutes are set out in the Revised Code at Sections 3704.06 and 3704.99 (air pollution), Sections 3734.10 and 3734.99 (solid and hazardous waste), and Sections 6111.07 and 6111.99 (water pollution). These provisions authorize the Ohio Attorney General to bring criminal actions at the request of the Director of Ohio EPA for violations of the State's pollution control laws.[30]

Criminal liability under Ohio's environmental laws generally extends only to "knowing" violations. An important exception is that a "reckless" violation of the laws governing the emission of excessive air contaminants and the storage, treatment, transportation, or disposal of hazardous waste also incurs criminal liability.[31]

---

26 *Id.*

27 *Id.*

28 State ex rel. Montgomery v. Heritage Dev. & Bainbridge Land Dev., No. 01M000771 (Geauga Cty. Comm. Pl. Jan. 24, 2002) (consent order placing $500,000 of the penalty amount in an escrow account to help the Geauga County Park District acquire and preserve Bass Lake and surrounding wetlands).

29 State ex rel. Montgomery v. New Boston Coke Corp., No. 99-CIG-003 (Scioto Cty. Comm. Pl. Dec. 20, 2002).

30 *See* OAC 3745-49-04.

31 ORC §§ 3704.99, 3734.99.

Violators of air and water pollution control laws may be fined as much as $25,000 per day for each violation or imprisoned for up to one year, or both fined and imprisoned.[32] Violations of solid and hazardous waste laws are subject to maximum penalties of $10,000 or $25,000 and to imprisonment of up to one year or from two to four years, depending on the violation.[33] Second or subsequent convictions under the solid and hazardous waste statutes are punishable by fines of at least $20,000 but not more than $50,000, or imprisonment for at least two years but not more than four years, or both.[34]

A summary of common violations that give rise to criminal liability under Ohio's environmental laws is set out in Appendix A.

The Ohio Attorney General, in concert with Ohio EPA, has voiced a strong commitment to criminal prosecutions for environmental violations. Between 1983 and 1996, the Attorney General obtained 182 criminal convictions for environmental violations. Seventy of those convictions resulted in jail sentences. In 2002, the Attorney General's Office obtained seventeen convictions that included $79,375 in fines, $180,533 in restitution, and sentencing that equated to 3,371 days in jail.[35]

A prime example of the aggressiveness of the State and the willingness of the courts to impose serious penalties is the 1991 conviction of an individual who operated a fraudulent hazardous waste disposal business. The State issued a 219-count indictment – the largest criminal environmental indictment in Ohio's history – that included charges of illegal storage, transportation, and disposal of hazardous waste. The individual's guilty plea resulted in a $2,100,000 fine and an eight-year jail sentence – billed at the time as the stiffest sentence for environmental crimes in the United States.[36]

In 1995, the Attorney General prosecuted a case against Shelby Universal, Inc. for criminal endangerment due to its illegal storage of hazardous waste. The company was ordered to pay a $55,000 fine and to reimburse U.S. EPA $318,000 for cleanup costs.[37]

---

[32] ORC §§ 3704.99, 6111.99.

[33] ORC § 3734.99.

[34] ORC § 3734.99(C).

[35] Ohio EPA 2002 Enforcement Report (April 2003) at 2.

[36] State ex rel. Fisher v. Bohnert, No. B91-2520 (Hamilton Cty. Comm. Pl. Nov. 6, 1991).

[37] State ex rel. Montgomery v. Shelby Universal Inc., No. 94CR548BD (Richland Cty. Comm. P1. Aug. 25, 1995).

Company Chairman Paul Reger also was convicted for abandoning the hazardous waste at the facility. He was ordered to pay a $10,000 fine, to reimburse U.S. EPA $318,000 for cleanup costs, and to serve a prison sentence of three and one-half years.[38]

Ohio generally seeks to tailor criminal settlements and sentences to the seriousness of the violations, the abilities of the violator, and the needs of the State. In addition to involving jail sentences and penalties, many criminal cases have resulted in unusual requirements, such as joining environmental groups, participating in the "Adopt A Highway Program," planting trees, placing ads in newspapers and trade journals, and sponsoring seminars on hazardous waste management. A 1992 action against a company for hazardous waste violations resulted in the establishment of a $1,000,000 environmental trust fund to support hazardous waste cleanup at selected Ohio sites and to expand State training in environmental investigation.[39]

The State has been particularly aggressive about enforcing criminal statutes against corporations and their officers, shareholders, and responsible employees. One of the most notable cases in the development of corporate liability for environmental crimes is *Ohio v. Stirnkorb*,[40] in which Ohio EPA alleged that the operations manager of a hazardous waste landfill acted recklessly when he ordered employees to pump rainwater that had pooled on top of the landfill into a drainage ditch. In 1989, the court convicted the operations manager of eight felonies and two misdemeanors for failure to consult with regulatory officials before taking the action. On appeal, the Clermont County Court of Appeals affirmed, holding that the State's failure to prove any specific environmental harm from the violations was not grounds for acquittal. The court ruled further that Mr. Stirnkorb could be convicted under Revised Code Section 2901.24[41] without being "high managerial personnel." The court

---

[38] State ex rel. Montgomery v. Reger, No. 94CR548AD (Richland Cty. Comm. Pl. Aug. 25, 1995).

[39] State ex rel. Fisher v. Manville Bldg. Materials Corp., No. CR91-12-135 (Athens Cty. Comm. Pl. Dec. 23, 1991).

[40] No. 85-CR-5240B *et seq.* (Clermont Cty. Comm. Pl. May 15, 1989), *aff'd*, 63 Ohio App.3d 778, 580 N.E.2d 69 (Clermont Cty. App. 1990), *motion ovrld.*, 57 Ohio St.3d 718, 568 N.E.2d 690 (1991).

[41] Revised Code Section 2901.24(A) provides that "[a]n officer, agent or employee" of a corporation may be prosecuted for an offense committed by the corporation if he acts with the kind of culpability required for the commission of the offense, and any of the following apply:

(1) In the name of the organization or in its behalf, he engages in conduct constituting the offense, or causes another to engage in such conduct, or tolerates such conduct when it is of a type for which he has direct responsibility;

(2) He has direct responsibility to discharge a duty imposed on the organization by law, and such duty is not discharged.

found, moreover, that the purpose of Section 2901.24 is to impose individual liability for acts committed by corporate employees.

In 1985, Mr. Stirnkorb was a defendant in another case in which he and a colleague were indicted, along with their employer, CECOS International, Inc., and Browning-Ferris Industries (parent company of CECOS), by a Clermont County Grand Jury for illegally discharging hazardous waste from the CECOS landfill into a tributary of Pleasant Run Creek.[42] The trial court's holding that a corporation is criminally liable for acts or omissions of its employees within the scope of their employment was affirmed by the Clermont County Court of Appeals. The cause was then brought before the Ohio Supreme Court pursuant to the allowance of a motion to certify the record. The Supreme Court concluded that "a reasonable and appropriate construction of Revised Code Section 2901.23 indicates a business entity may be found guilty of a criminal offense only if the criminal act or omission was approved, recommended, or implemented by high managerial personnel with actual or implied authority to approve, recommend or implement same. High managerial personnel are those who make basic corporate policies."[43]

As with civil enforcement cases, the State of Ohio sometimes brings a criminal enforcement action jointly with the United States. To facilitate this process, the Ohio Attorney General's Office and the U.S. Attorney's Office for the Southern District of Ohio have formed the Central Ohio Environmental Crime Task Force. One case brought by the task force involved TCW Corp. ("TCW"), a company that had contracted to manage the Muskingum County sanitary engineering department and operate the county's wastewater treatment plants.[44] TCW and a project engineer for the company pled guilty. Ronald Merckle, the owner of TCW, was convicted after a bench trial for submitting false water quality reports to Ohio EPA; he was sentenced to a prison term of twenty-seven months and fined $6,000.[45]

---

[42] State v. CECOS Int'l, Inc., 38 Ohio St.3d 120, 526 N.E.2d 807 (Clermont Cty. App. 1988).

[43] *Id.* at 124, 526 N.E.2d at 811. A good example of a court applying the *CECOS* standard to uphold the conviction of a corporation is found in State v. D.J. Master Clean, Inc., 123 Ohio App.3d 388, 704 N.E.2d 301 (Franklin Cty. App. 1997).

[44] United States v. Merckle, No. CR-2-98-179 (S.D. Ohio, Sept. 20, 1999).

[45] *Id.*

5.0 ENVIRONMENTAL AUDIT PRIVILEGE

In 1996, the Ohio General Assembly enacted legislation that provides a privilege of disclosure in any civil or administrative proceeding for persons voluntarily conducting environment audits.[46] Set out in Revised Code Sections 3745.70 to 3745.73, the law also grants immunity from administrative and civil penalties for voluntary disclosure of information in an audit report that concerns alleged violations of environmental regulations, providing that good faith efforts are made to achieve compliance as soon as practicable.[47]

In order for a facility owner or operator to assert this evidentiary privilege, the environmental audit information must be clearly identified as part of an environmental audit report.[48] For instance, the cover page of the document containing the audit information should display "Environmental Audit Report: Privileged Information" or other comparable language.[49] The owner or operator to whom the privilege belongs may waive the privilege by voluntarily testifying as to the information or by otherwise failing to assert the privilege.[50]

Section 3745.71 (C) of the Revised Code sets forth a number of exclusions from the privilege. For example, information concerning alleged environmental law violations that threaten the public health or safety must be disclosed and may not be the subject of the privilege. [51] Additionally, information required to be reported to a government agency is excluded from the privilege.[52]

To obtain immunity from administrative and civil penalties, the owner or operator must promptly and voluntarily disclose information regarding alleged violations of environmental laws and must make "a reasonable good faith effort ... to achieve compliance as quickly as practicable ...."[53] Both the evidentiary privilege and the immunity provided in

---

[46] HB 138, 121st General Assembly (Eff. Mar. 13, 1997).

[47] ORC § 3745.72(A). This immunity does not extend to the economic benefit component of a penalty if the disclosed violation resulted in "significant" economic benefit. *Id.*

[48] ORC § 3745.71 (C)(12).

[49] ORC § 3745.71(C)(12)(a).

[50] ORC § 3745.71(C) (1) and (2).

[51] ORC § 3745.71(C)(10)(a).

[52] ORC § 3745.71(C)(4).

[53] ORC § 3745.72(B)(1) and (2).

the new audit privilege law apply only to information that is part of an environmental audit conducted before January 1, 2004.[54]

6.0 CITIZEN SUITS AND VERIFIED COMPLAINTS

Although the federal environmental statutes are generous with citizen suit provisions,[55] Ohio laws provide relatively limited opportunity for citizen enforcement. The only citizen suits authorized under State statutes are for alleged hazardous waste violations, after giving at least 150 days notice to Ohio EPA, the Attorney General, and the alleged violator.[56] Because of delegations under federal law, Ohio EPA's regulatory scheme for air and water, including terms and conditions of permits, can be enforced by citizen suits brought in federal court.[57] For other alleged violations, aggrieved or adversely affected persons, including certain government officials, may file an administrative "verified complaint" with Ohio EPA, which forces the Agency to conduct a prompt investigation.[58] Based upon its investigation, Ohio EPA must either dismiss the complaint as unfounded, issue an administrative order to correct any violations found, or request the Attorney General to bring an appropriate enforcement action against the violator.[59] Most verified complaints are resolved within two years of filing.[60]

---

[54] ORC §§ 3745.71(I), .72(F).

[55] *See* 33 USC § 1365 (water), 42 USC § 6972 (solid and hazardous waste), 42 USC § 7604 (air), 42 USC § 9659 (Superfund).

[56] ORC § 3734.101(A) - (B).

[57] *See* 42 USC § 7604, 33 USC § 1365.

[58] ORC § 3745.08(A).

[59] ORC § 3745.08(B).

[60] Ohio EPA 2002 Enforcement Report (April 2003) at 6.

Chapter XIV

ENVIRONMENTAL TORTS

1.0 INTRODUCTION

Ohio courts have not been called upon to deal with environmental issues under tort law to any great extent. However, they have recognized several causes of action in tort that may be used by a plaintiff to recover for environmental claims. Generally, these legal rights are not the product of statute; they are the result of case law granting recovery for claims based upon nuisance, trespass, negligence, and strict liability. This chapter will briefly survey these causes of action in the context of environmentally related activities.

2.0 NUISANCE

The most useful method for establishing tort liability is the nuisance doctrine. Nuisance is not a type of tortious conduct, but rather is a field of tort liability wherein a court will require abatement of certain activities because a defendant's conduct has invaded the legal rights or interests of another with respect to property. The distinction between public and private nuisance is critical in determining whether a party has standing to bring an action. At common law, a public nuisance is an unreasonable interference with a right common to the general public.[1] In addition to common law public nuisances, Ohio has adopted statutes and regulations that define certain activities to be public nuisances.[2] A suit to abate a public

---

[1] Brown v. County Commissioners, 87 Ohio App.3d 704, 712, 622 N.E.2d 1153, 1158 (Scioto Cty. App. 1993) (citing Restatement (Second) of Torts § 821B (1979)).

[2] *Id. See, e.g.*, ORC § 6111.04 (pollution of waterways is a public nuisance).

nuisance may not be brought by a private party unless the injury suffered is different from that suffered by the general public.[3]

A private nuisance is a nontresspassory invasion of another's interest in the private use and enjoyment of land.[4] The typical plaintiff is a property owner suffering injury from a neighbor's use of property. A private nuisance action generally turns on the factual inquiry of whether a particular use of property is reasonable under the circumstances, and whether there is an appreciable, substantial, tangible injury resulting in actual, material, and physical discomfort.[5]

In Ohio, nuisance in the environmental context can be addressed based on common law even though the Ohio Revised Code includes a chapter expressly addressing nuisances.[6] While the statutory provisions address certain environmental harms in very broad terms, the availability of a common law cause of action provides even greater flexibility for prospective plaintiffs.

The modern common law doctrine of nuisance in Ohio is largely the product of the case *Taylor v. City of Cincinnati*,[7] in which the Ohio Supreme Court distinguished an absolute nuisance from a qualified nuisance. In the case of an absolute nuisance or nuisance *per se*, an activity is considered to be a nuisance without regard to the degree of care because the particular activity is inherently injurious.[8] In contrast, a qualified nuisance requires a showing of negligence.[9] A qualified nuisance is any act performed legally but done in a negligent or careless manner, thereby creating an unreasonable risk of harm and causing injury to another.[10]

---

3 Citizens to Protect Environment, Inc. v. Universal Disposal, Inc., 56 Ohio App.3d 45, 52, 564 N.E.2d 722, 729 (Franklin Cty. App. 1988).

4 Brown, 87 Ohio App. 3d at 712, 622 N.E.2d at 1158 (citing Restatement (Second) of Torts § 821D (1979)).

5 Christensen v. Hilltop Sportsman Club, Inc., 61 Ohio App.3d 807, 811, 573 N.E.2d 1183, 1185 (Pickaway Cty. App. 1990).

6 Pizza v. Sunset Fireworks Co., 25 Ohio St.3d 1, 6, 494 N.E.2d 1115, 1120 (1986); ORC Chapter 3767.

7 143 Ohio St. 426, 55 N.E.2d 724 (1944).

8 Metzger v. Pennsylvania, O. & D. R. Co., 146 Ohio St. 406, 66 N.E.2d 203 (syllabus) (1946); Ogle v. Kelley, 90 Ohio App.3d 392, 398, 629 N.E.2d 495, 499 (Hamilton Cty. App. 1993); Conway v. Calbert & Dispatch Consumer Services, Inc., 1997 Ohio App. LEXIS 1672 (Franklin Cty. App. 1993).

9 *Id.*

10 Taylor, 143 Ohio St. at 427, 55 N.E.2d at 725 (syllabus).

In *Taylor*, the court identified certain activities to be absolute nuisances, including pollution of a stream[11] and continual flow of water from a public reservoir onto private lands.[12] Other courts have found noise from a firing range,[13] air pollution,[14] dangerous combustibles, blasting operations, and wild animals[15] to be actionable nuisances.

Chapter 3767 of the Revised Code defines "nuisance" as any act declared by statute to be a nuisance.[16] Certain specific activities or conditions are expressly prohibited, and can be enjoined in an action by the attorney general, a county prosecuting attorney, or a private individual upon payment of a surety bond.[17] "Noxious exhalations or noisome or offensive smells,"[18] the placement of offal or filth in such a way as to damage or prejudice others,[19] obstruction or diversion of a waterway,[20] littering,[21] and the discharge or placement of refuse, petroleum products, or other materials into or along the banks of a waterway[22] are strictly prohibited. The trier of fact generally determines whether an activity constitutes a nuisance.[23] If an activity is found to be a nuisance, the injured party may recover money damages, which may be measured by the cost of restoring the property to its condition before the nuisance.[24] Under certain circumstances, a party also may be awarded equitable relief in the form of an injunction abating the nuisance. A court will issue a permanent injunction only if the injury will be irreparable.[25] In the case of a qualified nuisance, an

---

[11] *Id.* at 433, 55 N.E.2d at 727 (citing City of Mansfield v. Balliett, 65 Ohio St. 451, 63 N.E. 86 (1902)).

[12] *Id.* (citing City of Barberton v. Miksch, 128 Ohio St. 169, 190 N.E. 387 (1934)).

[13] Christensen, 61 Ohio App.3d at 812, 573 N.E.2d at 1186.

[14] Kepler v. Industrial Disposal Co., 84 Ohio App. 80, 82, 85 N.E.2d 308, 310 (Summit Cty. App. 1948).

[15] *See* Curtis v. Ohio State Univ., 29 Ohio App.3d 297, 301, 504 N.E.2d 1222, 1226 (Franklin Cty. App. 1986) (citing Taylor, 143 Ohio St. at 435, 55 N.E.2d at 728-29 (1944)).

[16] ORC § 3767.01(C).

[17] ORC § 3767.03.

[18] ORC § 3767.13(A).

[19] ORC § 3767.13(B).

[20] ORC § 3767.13(C).

[21] ORC § 3767.32(A).

[22] ORC § 3767.14.

[23] Brown, 87 Ohio App.3d at 714, 622 N.E.2d at 1160 (note 3).

[24] Reeser v. Weaver Bros., Inc., 78 Ohio App.3d 681, 686, 605 N.E.2d 1271, 1274 (Darke Cty. App. 1992).

[25] State ex rel. Chalfin v. Glick, 172 Ohio St. 249, 175 N.E.2d 68 (syllabus)(1961).

injunction may attempt to balance the competing interests and permit the wrongful activity to continue under certain restrictions.[26]

Recent environmental nuisance cases have involved actions against licensed pollution control facilities. A license granted by the State of Ohio generally will serve as a defense to a common law action for public nuisance when the action is based upon the same activity for which the permit was granted.[27] As an exception to this general rule, under the provisions of Chapter 3734 of the Revised Code, a person may bring an action for nuisance based upon common law or statute against a duly licensed solid waste landfill.[28] However, the license precludes an action for absolute nuisance or nuisance *per se* because part of the *quid pro quo* for submitting to the comprehensive regulatory oversight of a licensed solid waste landfill is insulation from liability under a theory of strict liability.[29] Similarly, a licensed wastewater treatment plant that emits noxious gases and odors is not an absolute public nuisance under the provisions of Rule 3745-15-07(A) of the Administrative Code, which authorizes an action for public nuisance against sources of air pollution and odors.[30] In the case of an absolute private nuisance, a permit to conduct the activity is a complete defense.[31] In the case of a qualified private nuisance, a license is not a defense, and thus a party may bring a private nuisance action against a licensed pollution control facility.[32]

3.0 TRESPASS

The tort of trespass enables a person to recover for environmental damages to his property caused by the intentional physical invasion of another. In the environmental

---

[26] Christensen, 61 Ohio App.3d at 812, 573 N.E.2d at 1186 (holding that trial court's injunction barring all activity at a shooting range was too broad and should be modified to permit activity to continue under certain restrictions).

[27] State ex rel. Brown v. Rockside Reclamation, Inc., 47 Ohio St.2d 76, 83, 351 N.E.2d 448, 453 (1976).

[28] Atwater Township Trustees v. B.F.I. Willowcreek Landfill, 67 Ohio St.3d 293, 297, 617 N.E.2d 1089, 1092 (1993) (holding that Revised Code Section 3734.10 authorizes an action for nuisance against a solid waste landfill even if the operator was granted a license to operate under Revised Code Chapter 3737).

[29] State ex rel. Schoener v. Board of Commissioners, 84 Ohio App.3d. 794, 801, 619 N.E.2d 2, 6 (Hamilton Cty. App. 1992); *see also* Philips v. City of Garfield Heights, 85 Ohio App.3d. 413, 420, 620 N.E.2d 86, 91 (Cuyahoga Cty. App. 1993). *But see* Collova v. Matousek, 85 Ohio App.3d 440, 445, 620 N.E.2d 104, 108 (Cuyahoga Cty. App. 1993) (holding that issue of whether sanitary landfill is absolute nuisance is question of fact).

[30] Brown, 87 Ohio App.3d at 715, 622 N.E.2d at 1160.

[31] *Id.*

[32] *Id.* at 715, 622 N.E.2d at 1161.

context, the typical claim is for damages for a release of hazardous substances migrating onto adjoining property of the plaintiff.

Trespass differs from nuisance in that trespass involves the invasion of a person's interest in the *exclusive* possession of land whereas nuisance involves a consequential act on land that interferes with the peaceful enjoyment of another's land.[33] For example, if a defendant's air pollution causes discomfort to a neighboring property owner, the action is for nuisance. However, if the pollution becomes deposited upon the neighboring property, the action is for trespass.[34]

An action for trespass requires proof of an unauthorized intentional act and entry upon land in the possession of another.[35] In a recent decision, the Ohio Supreme Court held that a property owner's subsurface rights are not absolute.[36] However, subsurface rights do include the right to exclude invasion of subsurface property that actually interferes with the property owner's reasonable and foreseeable use of the subsurface.[37] Trespass does not require that the intruding substance be tangible or intangible, but that the intrusion interfere with the right to exclusive possession of the property.[38] In one of the few reported environmental cases for this tort, a court awarded damages for a defendant's chemical pollution of a stream that destroyed the agricultural use of plaintiff's downstream farm.[39]

Traditionally, odors from a facility or the invasion of other airborne particles, including dust and smoke, did not create a trespass action.[40] However, in addressing the practice of disposing of hazardous waste byproducts from the manufacture of industrial chemicals through the use of deep well injection technology, one Ohio court has recognized that an invasion of "airborne particles and pollutants on a plaintiff's land" can constitute an action for trespass.[41] In order to recover for this type of invasion, a plaintiff must show an

---

[33] *Id.* at 717, 622 N.E.2d at 1161-62.

[34] *Id.*

[35] *Id.* at 716, 622 N.E.2d at 1161.

[36] Chance v. BP Chemicals, Inc., 77 Ohio St.3d 17, 26, 670 N.E.2d 985, 992 (1996).

[37] *Id.*

[38] Brown, 87 Ohio App.3d at 716, 622 N.E.2d at 1161.

[39] Bana v. Pittsburgh Plate Glass Co., 76 N.E.2d 625 (Summit Cty. App. 1947).

[40] Williams v. Oeder, 103 Ohio App.3d 333, 338, 659 N.E.2d 379, 382 (Clermont Cty. App. 1995).

[41] *Id.* at 339, 659 N.E.2d at 383.

invasion affecting exclusive possession of the property, an intentional act resulting in the invasion, reasonable foreseeability that the act could result in an invasion of the property interest, and substantial damage to the property.[42]

In a trespass case, one may recover money damages for injuries proximately caused. Furthermore, as is often the case in environmental actions, if the trespass is continuing and there is an inadequate remedy at law to compensate for the injury, one may seek injunctive relief to enjoin the trespass.[43]

4.0 NEGLIGENCE

The tort of negligence may provide recovery to a party seeking damages for injury caused by environmentally related activities. As discussed above, a claim for a qualified nuisance merges into a claim for negligence. To recover in a negligence action, the plaintiff must prove that the defendant committed an act, or failed to perform an act that by law the defendant had a legal duty to perform, thereby proximately causing injury to the plaintiff or to his property. The Ohio Supreme Court recently held that in order to recover indirect damages in a negligence action, the plaintiff must prove that the indirect economic damages arose from tangible physical injury to persons or tangible property damage.[44]

The standard of care required of a defendant by Ohio law is to use ordinary and reasonable care. In cases involving dangerous activities or harmful substances such as hazardous waste, the law requires a level of care commensurate with the potential injury that could result.[45]

The violation of a statute imposing a specific requirement upon a person or activity for the protection of others may form the basis for a cause of action for that violation as negligence *per se*.[46] A legislative enactment prescribing a general rule of conduct will not

[42] *Id.* (citing Borland v. Sanders Lead Co., Inc., 369 So.2d 523, 529 (Ala. 1979)).

[43] *See, e.g.*, Lembeck v. Nye, 47 Ohio St. 336, 24 N.E. 686 (syllabus) (1890).

[44] Queen City Terminals, Inc. v. General American Transportation, 73 Ohio St.3d 609, 653 N.E.2d 661 (syllabus) (1995).

[45] *See* Thompson v. Ohio Fuel Gas Co., 9 Ohio St.2d 116, 119, 224 N.E.2d 131, 135 (1967).

[46] Eisenhuth v. Moneyhon, 161 Ohio St. 367, 119 N.E.2d 440 (syllabus) (1954).

suffice.[47] Also, violation of an administrative regulation may not be employed as the basis for a claim based upon the doctrine of negligence *per se*.[48]

5.0 STRICT LIABILITY

Ohio law will impose liability on a defendant for certain activities without reference to the degree of care exercised by the defendant in performing the activity. Known as strict liability, the doctrine applies in products liability cases for defective design,[49] defective manufacture,[50] or failure to give appropriate warnings about inherent dangers that could arise from use of the product.[51] The sections of the Revised Code governing products liability do not supersede or otherwise affect the right of a plaintiff to assert an action for environmental contamination at common law or pursuant to statutory rights.[52] In the context of environmental law, strict products liability has had its greatest applicability to toxic tort cases involving recovery for delayed adverse health effects from exposure to asbestos. As mentioned in the discussion of nuisance, the Ohio Supreme Court has held that a defendant is strictly liable for damages resulting from conducting ultra-hazardous activities on defendant's lands.

6.0 TORT CLAIMS BY A PURCHASER OF REAL PROPERTY AGAINST THE SELLER

Although the tort doctrines discussed above are available to a property owner against persons owning or occupying adjacent or nearby properties, a federal court has concluded that Ohio law does not permit a purchaser of real property to employ the doctrines of negligence, nuisance, trespass, or strict liability to obtain damages from the seller for environmental conditions on the property.[53]

---

[47] *Id.*

[48] Chambers v. St. Mary's School, 82 Ohio St.3d 563, 697 N.E.2d 198 (1998).

[49] ORC § 2307.75; *see* Gilbert v. Bayerische Motoren Werke, A.G., 1993 Ohio App. LEXIS 5966 (Montgomery Cty. App. 1993); *see also* Carrel v. Allied Products Corp., 78 Ohio St.3d 284, 677 N.E.2d 795 (1997).

[50] ORC § 2307.74.

[51] ORC § 2307.76.

[52] ORC § 2307.72(D)(1).

[53] Dartron Corp. v. Uniroyal Chemical Co., 893 F. Supp. 730 (N.D. Ohio, 1995).

Chapter XV

ENVIRONMENTAL CONSIDERATIONS IN REAL ESTATE TRANSACTIONS

1.0 INTRODUCTION

The major environmental statutes enacted over the last three decades were conceived originally to assure that commercial and industrial operations do not harm the environment and that prior harm will be remediated by the responsible parties. As a result of federal and state regulatory developments that followed, the statutes have had an increasingly significant impact on land use planning and development. For example, the Clean Water Act's antidegradation and watershed planning provisions in Sections 204 and 208[1] regulate water discharges, thereby directing growth toward urban areas and political control by the dominant wastewater treatment plant operator, shaping decisions on transportation initiatives, and determining how specific tracts of real estate may be used.

Beyond these mega-trend impacts on real estate, the most significant requirements affecting transactions appear under the Comprehensive Environmental Response, Compensation, and Liability Act ("CERCLA" or "Superfund"),[2] passed by Congress following the 1980 presidential election. Arising out of public concern for the Love Canal and Times Beach events, CERCLA created liability for environmental contamination caused by prior property owners as well as for future owners even though they did not contribute to existing site conditions. This liability scheme spawned substantial litigation over the years as

---

[1] 33 USC §§ 1284, 1288.

[2] 42 USC §§ 9601 - 9675.

individual potentially responsible parties ("PRPs") attempted to shift liability to others and to insurance carriers. Fortunately, recent judicial and legislative trends have ameliorated these impacts.

2.0 CERCLA LIABILITY

CERCLA creates a federal fund, financed by a tax on chemical feedstocks, for use in cleaning up contamination and damage resulting from the release of hazardous substances.[3] Further, it authorizes the federal government to undertake the cleanup of hazardous substances itself or to order a responsible person or company to undertake such a cleanup.[4] If the government undertakes the cleanup or if a private party incurs cleanup costs that are consistent with U.S. EPA regulations governing cleanups (called the "National Contingency Plan" or "NCP"), the government or the private party may recover all the costs of responding to a release of a hazardous substance from PRPs including:[5]

(1) the owner and operator of the facility at which the hazardous substance has been released (*i.e.*, the current owner);

(2) the person who, *at the time of disposal* of any hazardous substance, owned or operated any facility at which hazardous substances were released;

(3) any person who, by contract, agreement, or otherwise, arranged for disposal or treatment of hazardous substances owned or possessed by such person, at any facility owned or operated by another party and containing such hazardous substances; and

(4) any person who accepts any hazardous substance for transport to disposal or treatment facilities selected by that person, from which there is a release of any hazardous substances.

---

[3] A "hazardous substance" includes pollutants, contaminants, and toxic substances identified under other federal environmental laws, hazardous wastes identified under the Resource Conservation and Recovery Act ("RCRA"), and other substances listed by U.S. EPA. *See* 42 USC § 9601(14). Although there is an express exclusion for petroleum products under CERCLA, Congress created a similar strict liability scheme to remedy releases of petroleum from underground storage tanks under RCRA. *See* 42 USC §§ 6991 - 6991k.

[4] 42 USC §§ 9604, 9606. Ohio has not enacted a parallel program to CERCLA. However, if the remedial tools of RCRA – which has been adopted by Ohio – are used at a property, the same CERCLA results can be attained.

[5] *See id.* at § 9607(a) (emphasis added). *See also* City of Toledo v. Beazer Materials & Serv., Inc., 923 F. Supp. 1001 (N.D. Ohio 1996) (holding that three corporations created during reorganization by owner of contaminated property are successor owners and operators of the property); *id.* at 1013 (holding that the City of Toledo may be liable because it was the current owner of the contaminated property regardless of the fact that it was not the current operator).

"Facility" is defined as a "site" or "area" where a hazardous substance has been deposited, stored, disposed of, placed, or otherwise come to be located.[6] As used in the liability provisions of CERCLA, "facility" has been interpreted to include a real estate subdivision where asbestos was determined to be present on the ground.[7] The definition of "operator" has proven troublesome, particularly for insolvent corporations; this definition has allowed many plaintiffs to pierce the corporate veil with increasing success.

In the case of *Donahey v. Bogle*,[8] the Sixth Circuit held that a corporate officer could be held liable for CERCLA liability if he had the authority to prevent the contamination to the property, even though he was unaware of the contamination. The Sixth Circuit, however, did not pierce the corporate veil where a corporation purchased contaminated land, established a subsidiary, and then transferred the land to the subsidiary.[9] The court held that a plaintiff can pierce the corporate veil only where all requirements for doing so have been met. The plaintiff must prove not only that there was unity of interest and ownership, but also that the parent corporation had a fraudulent purpose. The court also cited a public policy concern: imposing liability on the parent would deter future private sector participation in reclamation of contaminated land.[10] In *Kays v. Schregardus*,[11] an Ohio appellate court held that the director of Ohio EPA may order the controlling shareholder of a corporation owning land to clean up land left impaired by a prior tenant, thereby piercing the corporate veil even when the owner did not directly contribute to the impairment.[12]

CERCLA generally exempts from the definition of "owner" any person "who, without participating in the management of a vessel or facility, holds indicia of ownership

---

[6] 42 USC § 9601(9)(B).

[7] United States v. Metate Asbestos Corp., 584 F. Supp. 1143, 1148 (D. Ariz. 1984).

[8] 987 F.2d 1250 (6th Cir. 1993), *vacated on other grounds* 511 U.S. 1201 (1994). The U.S. Supreme Court vacated the judgment of the Sixth Circuit and remanded the case for consideration in light of Key Tronic Corp. v. United States, 511 U.S. 809 (1994) (holding that the "necessary costs of response" included legal costs for the purpose of identifying other parties that may be responsible for the contamination, but did not include legal costs associated with a consent decree).

[9] United States v. Cordova Chem. Co. of Michigan, 59 F.3d 584 (6th Cir. 1995). *See also* Plaskon Materials, Inc. v. Allied-Signal, Inc., 904 F. Supp. 644 (N.D. Ohio 1996) (stating that piercing of corporate veil is dependent on state law).

[10] Cordova Chem., 59 F.3d at 590.

[11] 138 Ohio App.3d 225, 740 N.E.2d 1123 (2000).

[12] *Id.* at 229, 740 N.E.2d at 1126.

primarily to protect his security interest in the vessel or facility."[13] This language generally was thought to protect secured creditors and mortgagees who repossessed or took title to collateral. The federal courts, however, have identified at least two situations in which a secured lender or mortgagee may become an "owner" or "operator" subject to CERCLA liability. If a lender participates in the management of a borrower's business, or controls aspects of the borrower's business relating to the generation or management of hazardous substances, the lender may be deemed to have operated the facility from which the release of hazardous substances occurred, and be subject to liability under CERCLA.[14] Similar protections are afforded under Ohio law in Section 3746.26 of the Revised Code.

Mere financial ability to control waste disposal practices is not sufficient to impose CERCLA liability; rather, some nexus must exist between the actual operation of the facility and the lender, beyond mere participation in the financial aspects of the business.[15] In 1992, U.S. EPA promulgated an interpretative rule focusing on lender and fiduciary liability under CERCLA Section 101(20)(A), the lender safe harbor provision, which excludes from liability "a person, who, without participating in the management of a vessel or facility, holds indicia of ownership primarily to protect his security interest in the vessel or facility."[16] Two years later, the rule was held to be unenforceable by the U.S. Court of Appeals for the District of Columbia.[17] U.S. EPA then issued a guidance document indicating that "EPA and [the Department of Justice] intend to apply as guidance the provisions of the 'Lender Liability Rule' promulgated in 1992."[18] In the 1996 amendments to CERCLA, Congress revised Section 101(20) to create new subsections (E) through (G) which basically enact the extensive lender liability protection principles of the prior U.S. EPA rule.[19] As a part of the

---

[13] 42 USC § 9601(20)(A).

[14] *See, e.g.,* United States v. Mirabile, 23 Env't Rep. Cas. (BNA) 1511 (E.D. Pa. 1985); United States v. Fleet Factors Corp., 724 F. Supp 955 (S.D. Ga. 1988), *aff'd*, 901 F.2d 1550 (11th Cir.), *cert. denied*, 498 U.S. 1046, 111 S. Ct. 752 (1991).

[15] Mirabile, 23 Env't Rep. Cas. (BNA) at 1512 - 1513.

[16] 57 *Fed. Reg.* 18,344 (Apr. 29, 1992). *See* 42 USC § 9601(20(A).

[17] Kelley v. EPA, 15 F.3d 1100 (D.C. Cir. 1994) (holding that U.S. EPA lacks statutory authority to restrict by regulation private rights of action arising under CERCLA).

[18] U.S. EPA Policy on CERCLA Enforcement Against Lenders (Nov. 30, 1995); *see* 60 *Fed. Reg.* 63517 (Dec. 11, 1995).

[19] 42 USC § 9601(20)(E) - (G).

2002 amendments to CERCLA (see discussion below), lender liability protections were created as a matter of law.

In a 1988 Georgia case, a federal district court found that a lender is not liable simply because it provided financial assistance and isolated bits of management advice. However, the court refused to decide, without a factual inquiry, whether alleged releases of asbestos and other hazardous substances during an auction and removal of machinery and equipment were sufficient to result in CERCLA liability.[20] A significant Ohio decision in 1992, however, held that a lender on a defaulted mortgage is liable, even without having taken any active role in corporate management or foreclosing on the property.[21]

In 1994, the Ohio General Assembly provided lender liability protection with enactment of the state's Voluntary Action Program ("VAP").[22] Section 3746.26 of the Revised Code exempts persons holding "indicia of ownership" merely to protect security interests from personal liability for environmental conditions except to the extent that those persons' actions created the impairment or they were responsible for the day-to-day operation of the property. Ohio's statute tracks U.S. EPA guidance and recent changes to CERCLA, and overrules the applicability of the *Pruitt*[23] decision as a matter of Ohio law. With both CERCLA and Ohio law legislatively clarified, both state and federal law are in harmony with the principle that those who hold title to property merely to protect a security interest have no liability for environmental conditions as long as their actions did not give rise to the problem.

Recognizing the results of extensive litigation surrounding interpretation of CERCLA, Congress enacted significant amendments to the statute in 2002. Pursuant to the Small Business Liability Relief and Brownfields Revitalization Act ("Brownfields Revitalization Act"),[24] substantial changes were made, including adoption of a brownfield grants program, clarification of liability under Section 107, and provision of certain liability defenses for cleanup activities conducted under state voluntary action programs, such as the

---

20 Fleet Factors, 724 F. Supp. at 960-61.

21 Ohio v. Pruitt, No. 89-CV-102519 (Lorain Cty. Comm. Pl. June 1, 1992).

22 SB 221, 120th General Assembly (Eff. Sept. 28, 1994), codified at ORC Chapter 3746. For a discussion of the VAP, see Chapter VII, Part 3.0, of this Handbook.

23 No. 89-CV-102519 (1992).

24 Pub. L. 107-118, 115 STAT. 2356 (2002).

one in Ohio. Although not directly available to developers, $200 million was appropriated for federal grants to qualified governmental and nonprofit entities, capped at $200,000 per site, to characterize and develop plans for return brownfield sites to actual use. Grants of similar size are available for cleanup efforts at sites owned by the grant recipient.

Of more importance to real estate development are the clarifications of CERCLA liability extending to contaminants under contiguous properties that were not the source of the contaminants, the prospective purchaser's agreement, and the liability exemption afforded "bona fide prospective purchasers," after they have completed "all appropriate inquiry" into conditions at the site.[25] Congress amended CERCLA Section 107(q) to provide that contiguous property owners would not be liable for contamination that migrated onto their site from third-party source properties.[26] CERCLA Sections 101(40) and 107(r) also were amended to provide that purchasers of properties receiving funding for cleanup activities – although not being directly liable for the costs of the cleanup – would be required to refund to the U.S. government a certain percentage of the increase in the real estate value realized as a result of the benefits of the federally funded cleanup.[27]

3.0 CERCLA DEFENSES

There are three defenses to liability for response costs under CERCLA:[28]

> (1) an act of God;
>
> (2) an act of war;
>
> (3) an act or omission of a third party other than an employee or agent ... or [other] *than one whose act or omission occurs in connection with a contractual relationship*, existing directly or indirectly, with the defendant ... *if* the defendant establishes by a preponderance of the evidence that (a) he exercised due care with respect to the hazardous substance concerned, taking into consideration the characteristics of such hazardous substance,

25 42 USC §§ 9601(40), 9607(q), 9607(r).

26 42 USC § 9607(q).

27 42 USC § 9607(r).

28 *See* 42 USC § 9607(b) (emphasis added). *See also* Velsicol Chem. Corp. v. Enenco, Inc., 9 F.3d 524, 530 (6th Cir. 1993) (stating that because Congress enumerated certain defenses, it intended to foreclose any other defenses to liability).

> in light of all relevant facts and circumstances, and (b) he took precautions against foreseeable acts or omissions of any such third party and the consequences that could foreseeably result from such acts or omissions.

CERCLA defines "contractual relationship" to include land contracts, deeds, or other instruments transferring title or possession, thereby precluding the use of the third party defense.[29] Under the 1986 amendments to CERCLA, however, Congress provided an "innocent purchaser" defense to liability for contamination of real estate prior to the date of purchase. An "innocent purchaser" may assert the third party defense if the purchaser can establish the following:[30]

(1) the property was acquired after the date of disposal or placement of hazardous substances on it; and

(2) the property owner establishes by a preponderance of the evidence that:

   (a) at the time the defendant acquired the facility, he did not know and had no reason to know that any hazardous substance was disposed of on, in, or at the facility; or

   (b) the property owner is a governmental entity which acquired the property by escheat, or through the exercise of eminent domain authority by purchase or condemnation; or

   (c) the owner acquired the property by inheritance or bequest.

In establishing that a property owner had "no reason" to know that any hazardous substances were present on a property, the owner must have undertaken, at the time of acquisition, "all appropriate inquiry" into the previous ownership and uses of the property consistent with good commercial or customary practice in an effort to minimize liability.[31] In determining whether this standard has been met, a court is specifically required to take into account any specialized knowledge or experience on the part of the defendant, the

[29] 42 USC § 9601(35)(A).

[30] *See id.*

[31] 42 USC § 9601(35)(B).

relationship of the purchase price to the value of the property if uncontaminated, commonly known or reasonably ascertainable information about the property, the obviousness of the presence or likely presence of contamination at the property, and the ability to detect such contamination by appropriate inspection.[32] Although many courts have cited to the defense, none have provided a specific definition. One court, however, has noted that a party asserting the defense "would be held to an especially stringent level of preacquisition inquiry – on the theory that an acquiring party's failure to make adequate inquiry may itself contribute to a prolongation of the contamination."[33]

The Brownfields Revitalization Act amended CERCLA by providing significant liability protection for brownfield developers, including prospective purchasers, innocent landowners, and owners of contiguous property. The most significant changes from prior law – which had established joint, several, strict, and retroactive liability – exempt bona fide prospective purchasers of contaminated properties, provided such purchasers do not "impede the performance of a response action or a natural resource restoration."[34] The goal of Congress was to assure that no sham transfers were to occur that shielded prior responsible parties from cleanup obligations through the transfer to shell corporations. Having once purchased the property following completion of "all appropriate inquiry," in order to maintain protection under the amendments to Sections 101(40)(D), 107(q)1(A)(iii), and 101(35)(B)(i)(II), the new owner must immediately stop any continuing releases, prevent threatened future releases, and prevent or limit human, environmental or natural resource exposure to earlier hazardous substance releases.[35] Regulations are currently in process to better define these obligations.[36] The key is that the owner must undertake "reasonable" steps, an equally undefined term but one that implies steady progress in accordance with a

---

[32] *See id.*

[33] Hemingway Transport, Inc. v. Kahn, 993 F.2d 915 (1st Cir. 1993), *cert. denied* 510 U.S. 914 (1993); *see also* In re Eagle Picher Indus., Inc., 164 Bankr. 265 (S.D. Ohio 1994). The Ohio State Bar Association had provided guidance for standard practices in Ohio prior to passage of SB 221, but now has deferred to ASTM standards referenced in that legislation. U.S. EPA currently is completing a negotiated rulemaking to define more comprehensively the elements of "all appropriate inquiry." Promulgation of these new regulations, which will supercede ASTM 1527, is expected in early 2004. *See* U.S. EPA Regulatory Agenda, 68 *Fed. Reg.* 30941, 30959, 31086 (May 27, 2003) (Seq. No. 3357).

[34] 42 USC § 9607(r)(1).

[35] 42 USC § 9607(q).

[36] *See* U.S. EPA Regulatory Agenda, 68 *Fed. Reg.* 30941, 30959, 31085 (May 27, 2003) (Seq. No. 3355).

plan developed by an environmental professional and at least reviewed – if not approved – by a state voluntary action program. As part of these undertakings, the bona fide prospective purchaser, and otherwise innocent and contiguous landowners are obligated under Sections 101(40)(C) and 107(q)(1)(A)(vii) to provide "all legally required notices with respect to the discovery or release of any hazardous substances at the facility."[37] How this obligation relates to CERCLA's "reportable quantity" requirements[38] has not yet been determined. The amendments also provide similar protection to qualified owners of properties contiguous to contaminated sites, removing the owners from CERCLA's definition of a "potentially responsible party."[39] On an interim basis, they also clarify that existing "innocent landowner" defenses allow reliance on ASTM Standard E1527-97.[40]

More significantly, the Brownfields Revitalization Act provides for current owners of real estate, and those purchasers who are not "innocent," with liability protection for conditions at a contaminated site if those parties are proceeding with cleanup of the site under a state's voluntary action program. Previously, parties had to negotiate a prospective purchaser agreement with U.S. EPA prior to receiving such assurance. Under Ohio's flexible VAP, brownfields may be cleaned up more expeditiously, with owners having a better sense of assurance that U.S. EPA will not exercise its authority contrary to the state program. To gain the best protection for a cleanup under Ohio's program, the cleanup probably should be an MOA Track action, as opposed to the original VAP, thereby assuring more active state involvement throughout the process.[41]

---

[37] 42 §§ 9601(40)(C), 9607(q)(1)(A)(vii).

[38] 42 USC § 9602(b).

[39] 42 USC § 9607(q)(1)(A).

[40] 42 USC § 9601(35)(B)(iv)(II). U.S. EPA is expected to promulgate in early 2004 new regulations independently establishing standards for due diligence investigations. *See* U.S. EPA Regulatory Agenda, 68 *Fed. Reg.* 30941, 30959, 31086 (May 27, 2003) (Seq. No. 3357). Subsequent to adoption of the Brownfields Revitalization Act, ASTM again amended the standard from E1527-97 to E1527-02.

[41] For further discussion, see Chapter VII, Part 3.0, of this Handbook.

4.0 FINANCIAL INCENTIVES UNDER OHIO VOLUNTARY ACTION PROGRAM

The interdisciplinary task force that facilitated development of Ohio's VAP laws in 1994 recognized that one of the significant impediments to brownfield redevelopment – over and above the absence of clear generic standards under prior Ohio law – was the economic balancing of brownfield redevelopment versus greenfield development. In order to strike a better balance and to encourage brownfield redevelopment, the General Assembly enacted Sections 5709.87 of the Revised Code, which rewards brownfield redevelopers with tax abatements on increases in real estate values once a Covenant Not To Sue had been issued confirming remediation in accordance with state standards.

Section 5709.88 provides a similar, but not automatic, exemption. As in other tax abatement programs tied to new economic growth, the developer must negotiate a tax abatement agreement, covering both amount and terms, with the local governmental agency having jurisdiction. If the amount of the abatement exceeds seventy-five percent, the developer also must negotiate with the local school board.

A case currently pending before the Ohio Supreme Court raises questions regarding the viability of the automatic exemption.[42] In that case, redevelopers of an inner city hotel site received a Covenant Not To Sue for substantial petroleum and asbestos remediation at the site. At the time the covenant was issued, only a small percentage of remediation was completed, with the balance to be completed pursuant to the terms of the covenant. Once the site was finally remediated, developers sought tax abatements under the automatic exemption. The local board of education challenged the county tax commissioner's approval of the one-hundred percent abatement. In the briefs presented, the board of education argued that the abatement should apply only to the increase in value of the real estate arising from remediation prior to issuance of the covenant and should not apply to the nonenvironmental expenditures associated with complete rehabilitation of the hotel. The developers, to the contrary, argued that without the tax incentive they would not have made any of the balance

[42] Board of Education (Columbus) v. Tax Commissioner, No. 02-1525 (Ohio Unrep. Cas.) (scheduled for oral argument Nov. 4, 2003).

of the expenditures and that the abatement should go to the total value of the project. A decision is anticipated in early 2004.

Chapter XVI

INSURANCE COVERAGE FOR ENVIRONMENTAL LIABILITY

1.0 INTRODUCTION

The need for insurance coverage to address losses arising from environmental liability has triggered the development of a range of insurance products. Following the extensive litigation arising from the pollution exclusion of comprehensive general liability insurance policies issued prior to the enactment of the Resource Conservation and Recovery Act ("RCRA")[1] and the Comprehensive Environmental Response, Compensation, and Liability Act ("CERCLA")[2] in the late 1970s, the American insurance industry has developed policies that serve to protect parties with a stake in an environmental liability claim and to reduce risks associated with releases of pollution.

2.0 POLICIES / COVERAGE

Current environmental policies include pollution legal liability, cleanup cost cap, blended policies that can address more complex transactions, and third party coverage for mortgagees (secured parties). The policies vary in specific makeup, with each policy designed to protect against a different contingency; the terms of the policies, the coverage afforded, and the relative responsiveness to the risks to be underwritten, shift quickly.

---

1 42 USC §§ 6901 – 6992k.

2 42 USC §§ 9601 – 9675.

As of late 2003, two insurance carriers prominent in the market a year earlier are no longer underwriting environmental risks, premiums have increased fourteen percent to twenty-five percent over prior years, policy terms have decreased, and underwriting assessments have become more restrictive.[3] An experienced professional is essential to assist in determining which policy is best suited to a particular environmental operation, and a high degree of sophistication is needed to craft the necessary coverages for complex transactions.

2.1 Pollution Liability Coverage

Pollution legal liability coverage ("PLL") is designed primarily to protect against the widest range of environmental liability. It protects against both known and unknown conditions, natural resource damage, property damage, physical injury, third-party claims for off-site cleanup, transported cargo, and non-owned locations. Overall, this type of coverage encompasses all environmental liability scenarios from pre-existing contamination to newly discovered conditions.

PLL policies provide the most basic and comprehensive coverage for environmental liability issues. Riders are available covering those arising from off-site transportation of hazardous wastes and those that may arise from use of approved third-party waste disposal sites. In addition to capping the costs of known remedial actions, PLL coverage also reduces reliance on indemnification clauses during land sale transactions. These policies have been used successfully in military base closures, Superfund settlements, corporate mergers involving transfers of contaminated properties, brownfields development, and commercial real estate transactions.

2.2 Cleanup Cost Cap

Cleanup cost cap ("CCC") policies protect against cost overruns during remediation activities. Although this type of coverage does not contribute to the main cleanup action, as does a PLL policy, it accounts for changed site conditions, regulatory

---

[3] Insurance carriers in the market in late 2003 include AIG, XL Environmental, Zurich, Chubb, ACE, Gulf, Seneca, Liberty, and Quanta. Of these, AIG, XL and Zurich are the three largest, accounting for an estimated eighty percent of the environmental insurance market.

changes, increased disposal fees, and revisions to remedial action plans to include newly discovered contamination.

The primary advantage of CCC coverage is protection against unexpected cost increases involved with remediation activities. In essence, CCC policies will cover any shortfalls in PLL coverage. Coverage can be obtained to cover "first dollar" liability in excess of anticipated remediation cost or "first dollar" after the insured expends some self-insured retainage. Although it is possible to maintain separate PLL and CCC policies, it is also permissible to combine the two protections into one coverage scheme.

2.3 Blended Policy

A blended environmental liability policy – also known as a "finite policy" – combines the PLL and CCC coverages into a single scheme. The primary advantage of such a policy is that it provides protection under all the scenarios identified above and insures against conditions worsened by remediation activities, such as releasing an initially stationary contaminant. It thus protects against the costs of remediation as well as any cost overruns associated with that remediation. Finite policies often entail use of an escrow or commutation account that leaves with the insurer a large sum of money from which remediation costs are disbursed as remediation progresses.

2.4 Secured Party Coverage

Secured party coverage is structured to protect third parties from incurring liability costs, rather than to protect current landowners or in-house site remediation. It targets secured lenders such as banks and mortgage brokers, consultants, and contractors. Secured party policies also protect lending institutions from "inheriting" environmental liability costs through the default of a borrower. Generally, they reimburse the secured party for the lesser of the actual remedial costs or the unpaid balance of the security instrument. Because these policies do not protect the borrower, no funds are distributed to the borrower in the event of a claim. Coverage for contamination created by consultants and contractors is more generally included within "errors and omissions" policies, which provide protection against the negligent acts of employees as well as conditions arising from contracted services. For consultants, these policies also serve as general professional liability insurance.

3.0 PRE-POLICY INVESTIGATION

Before issuance of any of the foregoing policies, the insurer will require a Phase I environmental investigation. If there was any industrial or commercial use of the property from the time of initial development, the insurer probably will require a detailed Phase II investigation. To meet the insurer's underwriting criteria, these investigations will be extensive and expensive. Gone are the days of investigations by unqualified consultants. In Ohio, use of a certified professional as designated under Ohio's Voluntary Action Program (see Chapter VII of this Handbook) can be expected, and in any event is good practice. From a legal perspective, higher due diligence standards are mandated by CERCLA's requirements for "all appropriate inquiry" as a predicate for use of the "innocent purchaser defense,"[4] for which a definitive federal rulemaking is anticipated in early 2004.

4.0 USE OF ENVIRONMENTAL INSURANCE

Typical examples of the use of environmental insurance coverage are reviewed below.

4.1 The Safe Company

A developer purchases a contaminated piece of land for $1.00, with the accompanying obligation to remediate the land. At the same time, the developer indemnifies the prior owner of any liability resulting from environmental contamination. The indemnity is secured by a first mortgage on the land and includes a right of reversion back to the original owner in the event the prior owner becomes liable for the contamination.

After expending large sums for remediation of the property and upon receiving a Covenant Not to Sue from Ohio EPA (see Chapter VII of this Handbook), which requires long-term monitoring and other controls, the developer wants to sell the remediated property to a company that does not want to assume the indemnity obligations of the developer and is precluded from mortgaging the land, due to the prior owner's first mortgage.

At this point, the prospective purchaser secures environmental liability insurance both to indemnify the prior owner from any costs associated with the

[4] 42 USC § 9601(35).

contamination, thereby allowing release of the mortgage, and to protect the developer and new buyer from any future liability costs. By fully indemnifying the prior owner with an insurance policy, as opposed to relying on the promises (solvency) of the developer or future buyer, the original owner will be comfortable in releasing any security interests, thereby allowing free transfer of the property to the new buyer.

4.2 The Reserve Company

A large manufacturing company owns several plants, all with similar environmental issues. The company hires a consultant to study each of the plants and develop reliable risk assessment and remedial cost estimates. The estimated costs are well under the amount of cleanup reserves on the company's books, which had been estimated originally in the mid-1980s prior to risk-based standards becoming acceptable. The cleanup will take several years and will be paid for out of the reserve funds.

By using environmental insurance, the consulting company can take "ownership" of the contamination along with corporate guarantees backed by a CCC policy to protect against any overruns. The consultant then purchases PLL environmental policies or a finite policy to protect against cost overruns. As a result, all parties are protected against cost overruns and future liability. The company then can release excess reserves on its books, bringing them into profits, and be assured that its ongoing liability for these prior conditions has been discharged adequately.

4.3 PRP Release Site

A Superfund site has a large number of *de minimis* potentially responsible parties ("PRPs"), none of which has more than two percent liability exposure. The absence of any large number of PRPs precludes the establishment of an effective steering committee as all the *de minimis* players shrink from the table. While the state environmental agency knows and accepts the remedial plan and estimated costs, the transactional costs of proceeding are excessive, given the number of PRPs. Moreover, the agency wants immediate cleanup and cannot deal effectively with all the PRPs to reach a settlement.

Following the agency's formal acceptance of the remedial plan, a consulting firm may receive funds from settling PRPs in an amount necessary to cover all costs, take title to the site, purchase environmental insurance – thus providing financial assurance to the state that the remediation will be completed – and assure the PRPs that they will have no ongoing liability. The cleanup proceeds without the time or expense involved in either the agency reaching a settlement with each individual PRP or typical, massive litigation among the PRPs as each tries to prove its nonliability.

4.4 Urban Redevelopment Site

A developer purchases an impaired property "as is." Remediation is required to assure lenders that the site is safe for a loan. If construction financing can be expedited, remediation and development can proceed concurrently.

Using any number of environmental insurance policies – PPL, CCC, secured lender protection – the developer can secure a loan from the construction lender, using the company to guarantee remediation sufficient to obtain a Covenant Not To Sue later in the process. As a result, the developer can receive a loan more quickly and begin remediation activities sooner. The combination of these actions results in a shorter "time to market" for the entire property.

5.0 RECENT INSURANCE LITIGATION

As is generally the case with large entities carrying environmental liability insurance, there is usually more than one policy covering the same contingencies. The question then becomes, "Which insurance company is liable to pay on its policy when one event triggers multiple policies?" The Supreme Court of Ohio answered this question in 2002 when it decided *Goodyear Tire & Rubber Co. v. Aetna Cas. & Sur. Co.*.[5]

In this case, the plaintiffs had obtained multiple insurance policies that were then simultaneously triggered by the same pollution event. As a result, Goodyear attempted to collect on its various policies, but each insurance carrier claimed that it was not primarily responsible to pay the full amount of the policy, given the existence of additional, overlapping policies. Goodyear argued that it should be permitted to choose which single policy to invoke, up to that policy's limits, from all the triggered policies (the "all sums"

[5] 95 Ohio St.3d 512, 769 N.E.2d 835 (2002).

approach).[6] Conversely, the insurance carriers argued that each policy is triggered in pro rata amounts, correlated to the amount of overlap between the pollution event and the corresponding policy (the "pro rata" approach).[7] In the end, the court agreed with Goodyear and adopted the "all sums" approach to insurance carrier liability.[8]

The "all sums" approach provides that when a party holds overlapping policies that are simultaneously triggered by the same event, the policy holder may choose which policy to invoke, up to that policy's limit. In the event that the chosen policy does not completely cover the costs of the damage, the holder may choose another triggered policy to cover any remaining costs. This scheme can repeat itself until either the liability costs are accounted for or the holder exhausts the triggered policies. Then, each selected insurance provider may look to the other triggered policies for contribution based on the insurance treaties in place for all carriers. It is the responsibility of each selected carrier – not the policy holder – to look for contributions. The only limitation placed on the policy holder in selecting carriers to cover the liability is that the holder must give notice to all carriers without significant delay. Although the amount of delay in notifying an insurance carrier is interpreted in light of all the facts, it is important to make notification "as soon as practicable."[9]

6.0 THIRD-PARTY RECOVERY ACTIONS

In some instances, an environmental incident on one property may allegedly impact neighboring properties even through there has been no physical impact. This is sometimes referred to as "stigma" damages. In these situations, third parties may attempt to recover for an alleged drop in property value on the basis of contaminated adjacent land, without any physical impact on that land.

Ohio courts have ruled that when there is no property damage associated with the alleged diminution of the neighboring property value, a neighbor cannot maintain an action

---

6 *Id.* at 515, 769 N.E.2d at 840.

7 *Id.*

8 *Id.* at 516, 769 N.E.2d at 841.

9 *Id.* at 517-518, 769 N.E. 2d at 842-843 (quoting Ormet Primary Aluminum Corp. V. Employers Ins. Of Wausau, 88 Ohio St.3d 292, 725 N.E.2d 646 (2000)).

to recover from the site owner or from an environmental insurance policy covering the site.[10] Specifically, the Ohio Court of Appeals for the Fifth District found that because "there was … no property damage caused by an 'occurrence' [as defined in the policy at issue] … [the neighbor] was not entitled to coverage under such policy."[11] In essence, the court concluded that neighboring property must be actually damaged by migrating pollution in order for a third-party landowner to recover on the insurance policy.

---

[10] Environmental Exploration Co. v. Bituminous Fire & Marine Ins. Co., No. 1999CA00315, 2000 Ohio App. LEXIS 4985, at *23 (Ohio App. 5th Oct. 16, 2000).

[11] *Id.*

Chapter XVII

POLLUTION PREVENTION

1.0 INTRODUCTION

Pollution prevention continues to reshape the way that business and industry conceptualize environmental management. As distinguished from more traditional pollution abatement initiatives, which relied on media-specific "end-of-pipe" control, pollution prevention focuses on the use of source reduction techniques and environmentally sound recycling to reduce risk to public health and safety and the environment. It uses a multi-media approach to managing all types of waste and environmental releases to the air, water, and land.

2.0 FEDERAL POLLUTION PREVENTION SCHEME

U.S. EPA established an Office of Pollution Prevention in August 1988. However, it was not until Congress passed the Pollution Prevention Act of 1990 ("Act"),[1] that pollution prevention was established as a distinct component of environmental regulation. The Act is premised on several specific Congressional findings that are set out in the statute.[2]

First, the United States annually produces millions of tons of pollution and spends billions of dollars controlling it. Second, there are significant opportunities for the reduction and prevention of pollution at the source through cost-effective changes in production, operation, and raw materials. Third, the opportunities for source reduction often are not

---

[1] Sec. 6601, Omnibus Budget Reconciliation Act of 1990, PL 101-508, 104 STAT. 1388-321(1990), codified at 42 USC §§ 13101 - 13109.

[2] *See* 42 USC § 13101(a).

realized because existing regulations focus on treatment and disposal and do not emphasize multi-media management of pollution, and businesses lack information and technical assistance. Fourth, source reduction is fundamentally different and more desirable than waste management and pollution control. Fifth, the country needs a national source reduction program.[3]

Based on its findings, Congress declared a national policy on pollution prevention that recognized a four-tiered priority scheme:[4]

> [P]ollution should be prevented or reduced at the source whenever feasible; pollution that cannot be prevented should be recycled in an environmentally safe manner whenever feasible; pollution that cannot be prevented or recycled should be treated in an environmentally safe manner whenever feasible; and disposal or other release into the environment should be employed only as a last resort and should be conducted in an environmentally safe manner.

At the heart of the Act is a requirement that each facility subject to the Toxic Release Inventory ("TRI") reporting provisions of Section 313 of the Emergency Planning and Community Right-to-Know Act ("EPCRA" or "SARA Title III")[5] include in the TRI report information on source reduction and recycling for each toxic chemical listed, as follows:[6]

> (1) the quantity of the chemical entering any waste stream prior to recycling, treatment, or disposal during the calendar year, and the percentage change from the previous year;
>
> (2) the amount of the chemical that is recycled during the year, the percentage change from the previous year, and the process of recycling used;
>
> (3) the source reduction practices used with respect to that chemical during the year at the facility;

---

3 *Id.*

4 42 USC § 13101(b).

5 42 USC §§ 11001 - 11050. For a discussion of EPCRA and TRI reporting requirements, see Chapter X of this Handbook.

6 *See* 42 § 13106(b)(1) - (8).

(4) the amount expected to be reported under (1) and (2) for the next two years, expressed as a percentage change from the amount reported in (1) and (2);

(5) the ratio of production in the reporting year to production in the previous year;

(6) the techniques that were used to identify source reduction opportunities;

(7) the amount of any toxic chemical release that resulted from a catastrophic event, remedial action, or other one-time event, and not associated with production processes; and

(8) the amount of the chemical that is treated during the calendar year and the percentage change from the previous year.

The focus of U.S. EPA's Office of Pollution Prevention is to ensure that prevention becomes the preferred approach to protecting the environment. A wide range of tools – including market incentives, public education and information, and small business grants, as well as the more traditional tools of regulation and enforcement – are being used to promote and integrate a pollution prevention ethic that cuts across all U.S. EPA programs.[7]

3.0 OHIO POLLUTION PREVENTION PROGRAM

The pollution prevention program in Ohio, established in 1990 under existing authorities of the State's air and water pollution control and waste management schemes, is administered by the Ohio EPA Office of Pollution Prevention ("OPP").[8] The goals of the program are to:[9]

(1) reduce the amount of pollution generated in Ohio by providing pollution prevention assistance to business, government, and other organizations; and

(2) integrate pollution prevention principles into Ohio EPA programs to reduce the amount of pollution generated in Ohio.

---

[7] *See* http://www.epa.gov/ebtpages/pollutionprevention.html.

[8] *See* http://www.epa.state.oh.us/opp.

[9] *See* http://www.epa.state.oh.us/opp/more_about.html.

Pollution prevention and reduction initiatives can change frequently, depending on federal and state priorities. Examples of initiatives underway in Ohio include the following:[10]

(A) Ohio Materials Exchange ("OMEx") – OMEx disseminates information on surplus and waste materials that are available from or wanted by industrial and commercial entities. By facilitating the beneficial reuse of waste materials, the exchange helps to reduce the need for landfill space and encourages the proper management of solid and hazardous waste. More than twenty categories are used for listing materials available and materials wanted. OMEx services are free to all users.

(B) Pollution Prevention Technical Assistance – OPP provides a number of nonregulatory technical assistance services to help Ohio business prevent pollution in a cost-effective manner. Included are on-site pollution prevention assessments, information on prevention opportunities, and assistance targeted toward compliance needs.

(C) Pollution Prevention Loan Program – Jointly administered by Ohio EPA and the Ohio Department of Development, this program provides low-interest capital improvement loans for the purchase of equipment and/or construction to complete pollution prevention activities at small and medium-sized facilities in the State.

[10] *Id.*

APPENDIX A

CIVIL AND CRIMINAL PENALTIES UNDER OHIO'S ENVIRONMENTAL STATUTES

CIVIL AND CRIMINAL PENALTIES UNDER OHIO'S ENVIRONMENTAL STATUTES

AIR
(ORC Chapter 3704)

VIOLATION	CIVIL PENALTY	CRIMINAL PENALTY
Emission of air contaminant in excess of emission standard, without a variance/permit, § 3704.05(A)	Penalty of up to $25,000 for each day of each violation, § 3704.06(C)[1]	For reckless violation, fine of up to $25,000 or imprisonment for up to one year, or both, for each day of each violation, § 3704.99(A)
Emission of air contaminant in excess of emission standard, with a variance/permit, § 3704.05(B)	"	"
Violation of permit term or condition, § 3704.05(C)	"	"
Failure to install and maintain monitoring devices or to submit required reports and information, § 3704.05(D)	"	"
Refusal of entry to OEPA or hindering of OEPA investigation, § 3704.05(E)	"	"
Failure to submit required plans and specifications, § 3704.05(F)	"	"
Falsification of plans, specifications, data, reports, records, or other information, § 3704.05(H)(1)	"	For knowing violation, fine of up to $10,000 for each day of each violation, § 3704.99(B)
False statement on forms, notices, or reports required by Title V program, § 3704.05(H)(2)	"	"
Rendering inaccurate any monitoring device required by Title V permit, § 3704.05(H)(3)	"	"
Falsification of inspection certificate, § 3704.05(I)	"	For reckless violation, fine of up to $25,000 or imprisonment for up to one year, or both, for each day of each violation, § 3704.99(A)

1 This does not apply to any requirement regarding prevention or abatement of odors.

Appendix A – Civil and Criminal Penalties Under Ohio's Environmental Statutes

WATER
(ORC Chapter 6111)

VIOLATION	CIVIL PENALTY	CRIMINAL PENALTY
Pollution of waters of the state by discharge of sewage, industrial waste, or other waste, without a permit, § 6111.04(A)	Penalty of up to $10,000 per day of violation, § 6111.09	Fine of up to $25,000 or imprisonment for up to one year, or both, § 6111.99(A)
Pollution of waters of the state by discharge of sewage, industrial waste, or other waste, in excess of permitted amounts, § 6111.04(C)	"	"
Violation of national effluent limitations, national standards of performance for new sources, or national toxic and pretreatment effluent standards, except in compliance with permit terms and conditions, § 6111.042	"	"
Drilling of new well or conversion of existing well for underground injection of sewage, industrial waste, or other waste without a permit, § 6111.043(C)	"	"
Use of a well for underground injection of sewage, industrial waste, or other waste without a permit, § 6111.043(E)	"	"
Refusal of entry to OEPA or hindering of OEPA investigation, § 6111.05(B)	"	"
Violation of order, rule, or permit term or condition, or failure to perform a required duty, § 6111.07(A)	"	"
Failure to submit required information or records, § 6111.07(C)	"	Fine of up to $25,000, with no imprisonment, § 6111.99(C)
Knowing submission of false information or records, § 6111.07(C)	"	"

NOTE: There also are penalties under Ohio's nuisance statute for corruption of a stream or body of water. *See* ORC §§ 3767.13(C) and 3767.14. Penalties range from a fine of $500 to $1,000 or imprisonment of 60 days to 6 months, or both, depending on the type of misdemeanor. *See* ORC §§ 3767.99(A), (C) and 2929.21(B), (C).

SOLID AND HAZARDOUS WASTE
(ORC Chapter 3734)

VIOLATION	CIVIL PENALTY	CRIMINAL PENALTY
Establishment or modification of solid waste facility or infectious waste treatment facility without a permit, § 3734.02(C)	Penalty of up to $10,000 for each day of each violation, § 3734.13(C)	Felony fine of at least $10,000 and up to $25,000 or imprisonment of 2-4 years, or both, for each day of each reckless violation, § 3734.99(A)
Operation of a solid waste facility for which a permit has been denied, after date prescribed for commencement of closure, § 3734.02(C)	"	"
Establishment or operation of hazardous waste facility or use of solid waste facility for storage, treatment, or disposal of hazardous waste without a permit, § 3734.02(E)(2)	"	"
Filling, grading, excavating, building, drilling, or mining on land where a solid or hazardous waste facility was operated without prior OEPA authorization, § 3734.02(H)	"	"
Emission of particulate matter, dust, fumes, gas, mist, smoke, vapor, or odorous substance that unreasonably interferes with personal enjoyment of life or property in the vicinity of a hazardous waste facility or that is injurious to public health, § 3734.02(I)	"	"
Knowing acceptance of certain infectious wastes for disposal in a sanitary landfill, § 3734.02(K)	"	"
Transportation of infectious wastes that have not been treated to render them non-infectious without certificate or license, § 3734.022(A)	"	"
Disposal of solid or infectious waste by open burning or open dumping, § 3734.03	"	"

Appendix A – Civil and Criminal Penalties Under Ohio's Environmental Statutes

Failure to submit an explosive gas monitoring plan for a sanitary landfill or to monitor and report on explosive gas, § 3734.041	"	Felony fine of at least $10,000 and up to $25,000 or imprisonment of 2-4 years, or both, for each day of each violation, § 3734.99(B)
Operation of solid waste facility without a license, § 3734.05(A)(1)	"	Felony fine of at least $10,000 and up to $25,000 or imprisonment of 2-4 years, or both, for each day of each reckless violation, § 3734.99(A)
Operation of infectious waste treatment facility without a license, § 3734.05(B)(1)	"	"
Falsification of or failure to keep or submit plans, specifications, data, reports, records, manifests, or other required information regarding solid waste facilities, § 3734.05(G)	"	"
Refusal of entry to OEPA or local board of health or hindering investigation by either entity, § 3734.07(D)	"	"
Violation of permit or license terms and conditions, § 3734.11(B)	"	"
Operation of solid waste facility within the boundaries of a state or national park, § 3734.11(C)	"	"
Violation of rules governing storage and disposal of PCBs and PCB-contaminated materials, § 3734.122(B)	Penalty of up to $25,000 for each day of each violation, § 3734.13(C)	Fine of up to $25,000 for each day of each violation or imprisonment of up to one year, or both, for knowing violation, § 3734.99(D)
Violation of enforcement order terms and conditions regarding solid or hazardous waste, § 3734.13(D)	Penalty of up to $10,000 for each day of each violation, § 3734.13(C)	Felony fine of at least $10,000 and up to $25,000 or imprisonment of 2-4 years, or both, for each day of each violation, § 3734.99(B)
Transportation of hazardous waste without registration and permit, § 3734.15(A)	"	Felony fine of at least $10,000 and up to $25,000 or imprisonment of 2-4 years, or both, for each day of each reckless violation, § 3734.99(A)
Acceptance for treatment, storage, or disposal of any hazardous waste from an unregistered transporter, § 3734.15(C)	"	"

Acceptance for transportation, treatment, storage, or disposal of any hazardous waste from a generator who is in violation of hazardous waste rules, § 3734.17	"	"
Failure to collect and forward fees for disposal of hazardous waste, § 3734.18	"	Fine of up to $10,000 for each day of each violation, with no imprisonment, § 3734.99(A)
Failure to collect and forward fees for disposal of solid waste, § 3734.57	"	"
Manufacture or distribution for use in Ohio of certain plastic containers without appropriate labeling, § 3734.60(B)	Penalty of up to $250 for each day of each violation, § 3734.13(C)	"

APPENDIX B

GLOSSARY OF ACRONYMS

GLOSSARY OF ACRONYMS

AAC	Acute aquatic criterion
ACE	Any credible evidence
APA	*Administrative Procedure Act*
BACT	Best available control technology
BAF	Bioaccumulation factor
BAT	Best available technology
BCF	Bioconcentration factor
BCT	Best conventional technology
BMP	Best management practice
BPT	Best practicable technology
BUSTR	Bureau of Underground Storage Tank Regulation
CAA	*Clean Air Act*
CAC	Chronic aquatic criterion
CAM	Compliance assurance monitoring
CCC	Cleanup cost cap
C&DD	Construction and demolition debris
CEM	Continuous emission monitoring
CERCLA	*Comprehensive Environmental Response, Compensation, and Liability Act*, aka *Superfund*
CFR	*Code of Federal Regulations*
CO	Carbon monoxide
CSO	Combined sewer overflow
CWA	*Clean Water Act*, aka *Federal Water Pollution Control Act*
EIS	Environmental impact statement
EMF	Electromagnetic field
EMP	Enhanced monitoring program
EPA	Environmental Protection Agency
EPCRA	*Emergency Planning and Community Right-to-Know Act*, aka *SARA Title III*
EPRI	Electric Power Research Institute
ERAC	Environmental Review Appeals Commission
FWPCA	*Federal Water Pollution Control Act*, aka *Clean Water Act*
GLI	Great Lakes Initiative
HAP	Hazardous air pollutant
HB	House bill
HWFB	Hazardous Waste Facility Board

Appendix B – Glossary of Acronyms

ICS	Individual control strategy
I/M	Inspection and maintenance
JCARR	Joint Committee on Agency Rule Review
LAER	Lowest achievable emission rate
LSC	Legislative Service Commission
MACT	Maximum achievable control technology
MAGLC	Maximum acceptable ground level concentration
MCL	Maximum contaminant level
MCLG	Maximum contaminant level goal
MOA	Memorandum of agreement
MRF	Materials recovery facility
MSDS	Material safety data sheet
MS4	Municipal separate storm sewer system
NAAQS	National ambient air quality standard
NCAPS	National Corrective Action Prioritization System
NCP	National contingency plan
NEPA	*National Environmental Policy Act*
NESHAP	National emission standard for hazardous air pollutant
NFA	No further action
NIEHS	National Institute of Environmental Health Sciences
NO_x	Nitrogen oxide
NOI	Notice of intent
NOV	Notice of violation
NPDES	National Pollutant Discharge Elimination System
NPL	National Priorities List
NSPS	New source performance standard
NSR	New source review
OAC	*Ohio Administrative Code*
OMEX	Ohio Materials Exchange
OPP	Ohio Rapid Assessment Method
ORAM	Office of Pollution Prevention
ORC	*Ohio Revised Code*
PCB	Polychlorinated biphenyl
PLL	Pollution legal liability
PM	Particulate matter
$PM_{2.5}$	Particulate matter of 2.5 microns or less in diameter
PM_{10}	Particulate matter of 10 microns or less in diameter
POTW	Publicly owned treatment works

PPA	Projected project accomplishment
PPM	Parts per million
PRG	Preliminary remediation goal
PRP	Potentially responsible party
PSB	Power Siting Board
PSD	Prevention of significant deterioration
PTE	Potential to emit
PTI	Permit to install
PTO	Permit to operate
PUCO	Public Utilities Commission of Ohio
PWS	Public water system
RACM	Reasonably available control measure
RACT	Reasonably available control technology
RAGS	Risk Assessment Guidance for Superfund
RAP	Remedial action plan
RCRA	*Resource Conservation and Recovery Act*
RI/FS	Remedial investigation/feasibility study
RMP	Risk management plan
SARA	*Superfund Amendments and Reauthorization Act*
SB	Senate Bill
SDWA	*Safe Drinking Water Act*
SERC	State Emergency Response Commission
SFM	State Fire Marshal
SIC	Standard industrial classification
SIP	State implementation plan
SO_2	Sulfur dioxide
SPCC	Spill prevention, control, and countermeasures
SWMD	Solid waste management district
SWP3	Storm water pollution prevention plan
TCLP	Toxicity characteristic leaching procedure
TLV	Threshold limit value
TMDL	Total maximum daily load
TPY	Tons per year
TRI	Toxic release inventory
TSD	Treatment, storage, and disposal
TSP	Total suspended particulates
UIC	Underground injection control
USC	*United States Code*
UST	Underground storage tank
VAP	Voluntary action program
VOC	Volatile organic compound

SUBJECT INDEX

Subject Index

CASES

Subject Index

Subject Index

CASES

WEBSITES (http://)

Subject Index

CASES

Cincinnati ex rel. Crotty v. Cincinnati, 50 Ohio St.2d 27, 361 N.E.2d 1340 (1977)
Citizens Com. To Preserve Lake Logan v. Williams, 56 Ohio App.2d 61, 381 N.E.2d 661 (1977)
Citizens Lobby for Environmental Action Now v. Schregardus, Nos. EBR 092958-092961 (Oct. 19, 1993)
New Boston Coke Corp. V. Tyler, 32 Ohio St.3d 216, 513 N.E.2d 302 (1987)
State ex rel. Maynard v. Whitfield, 12 Ohio St.3d 49, 465 N.E.2d 406 (1984)
State ex rel. Williams v. Bozarth, 55 Ohio St.2d 34, 377 N.E.2d 1006 (1978)
Warren Molded Plastics, Inc. v. Williams, 56 Ohio St.2d 532, 384 N.E.2d 253 (1978)

CASES

Atwater Township Trustees v. B.F.I. Willocreek Landfill, 67 Ohio St.3d 293, 617 N.E.2d 1089 (1993)
Bana v. Pittsburgh Plate Glass Co., 76 N.E.2d 625 (Summit Cty. App. 1947)
Brown v. County Commissioners, 87 Ohio App.3d 704, 622 N.E.2d 1153 (Scioto Cty. App. 1993)
Carrel v. Allied Products Corp., 78 Ohio St.3d 284, 677 N.E.2d 795 (1997)
Chambers v. St. Mary's School, 82 Ohio St.3d 563, 697 N.E.2d 198 (1998)
Chance v. BP Chemicals, Inc., 77 Ohio St.3d 17, 670 N.E.2d 985 (1996)
Christensen v. Hilltop Sportsman Club, Inc., 61 Ohio App.3d 807, 573 N.E.2d 1183 (Pickaway Cty. App. 1990)
Citizens to Protect Environment, Inc. v. Universal Disposal, Inc., 56 Ohio App.3d 45, 564 N.E.2d 722 (Franklin Cty. App. 1988)
Collova v. Matousek, 85 Ohio App.3d 440, 620 N.E.2d 104 (Cuyahoga Cty. App. 1993)

Subject Index

Subject Index

Subject Index

Government Institutes Mini-Catalog

PC #	ENVIRONMENTAL TITLES	Pub Date	Price*
949	ABCs of Environmental Regulation, Second Edition	2002	$79
812	Achieving Environmental Excellence	2003	$79
898	Book of Lists for Regulated Hazardous Substances, Tenth Edition	2001	$99
846	Clean Water Handbook, Third Edition	2003	$125
822	Environmental Compliance Auditing & Management Systems (ECAMS)	2001	$1,395
897	EH&S CFR Training Requirements, Fifth Edition	2001	$125
4300	EH&S Daily Federal Register Notification Service (e-mail)	2003	$150
890	Environmental Biotreatment: Technologies for Air, Water, Soil, and Wastes	2002	$149
4045	Environmental, Health & Safety CFRs on CD-ROM, single issue	2003	$450
825	Environmental, Health and Safety Audits, 8th Edition	2001	$115
4900	Environmental Law Expert, CD-ROM	2003	$695
955	Environmental Law Handbook, Seventeenth Edition	2003	$99
688	Environmental Health & Safety Dictionary, Seventh Edition	2000	$95
956	Environmental Statutes, 2003 Edition	2003	$125
957	Fundamentals of Environmental Sampling	2003	$79
689	Fundamentals of Site Remediation	2000	$85
907	Hazardous Materials Transportation Training, Student's Manual	2002	$89
958	Information Technology Solutions for EH&S Professionals	2003	$115
823	Integrating Environmental, Health, and Safety Systems	2001	$495
588	International Environmental Auditing	1998	$179
819	ISO 14001: Positioning Your Organization for Environmental Success	2001	$115
936	Managing Your Hazardous Wastes	2002	$89
830	RCRA CFRs Made Easy	2002	$115
841	Risk Management Planning Handbook, Second Edition	2002	$115
816	Stormwater Discharge Management	2003	$89
946	Wastewater and Biosolids Treatment Technologies	2002	$129

PC #	SAFETY and HEALTH TITLES	Pub Date	Price*
697	Applied Statistics in Occupational Safety and Health	2000	$105
893	Beyond Safety Accountability	2001	$79
894	Building Successful Safety Teams	2001	$79
843	Emergency Preparedness for Facilities	2003	$125
904	Ergonomics: A Risk Manager's Guide	2002	$159
949	Excavation Safety	2003	$85
663	Forklift Safety, Second Edition	1999	$85
814	Fundamentals of Occupational Safety & Health, Third Edition	2003	$79
818	Job Hazard Analysis	2001	$79
888	Keys to Behavior Based Safety	2001	$85
662	Machine Guarding Handbook	1999	$75
838	Managing Chemical Safety	2002	$95
889	Managing Electrical Safety	2001	$69
4800	OSHA Compliance Master CD-ROM	2003	$375
668	Safety Made Easy, Second Edition	1999	$75
947	Safety Metrics	2003	$85
815	So, You're the Safety Director, Third Edition	2003	$89

Government Institutes
4 Research Place, Suite 200 • Rockville, MD 20850-3226
Tel. (301) 921-2323 • FAX (301) 921-0264
Email: giinfo@govinst.com • www.govinst.com

Please call our customer service department at (301) 921-2323 for a free publications catalog.

CFRs now available online. Call (301) 921-2323 for info.

*All prices are subject to change. Please call for current prices and availablity.

Government Institutes Order Form

4 Research Place, Suite 200 • Rockville, MD 20850-3226
Tel (301) 921-2323 • Fax (301) 921-0264
Internet: http://www.govinst.com • E-mail: giinfo@govinst.com

4 EASY WAYS TO ORDER

1. Tel: **(301) 921-2323**
Have your credit card ready when you call.

2. Fax: **(301) 921-0264**
Fax this completed order form with your company purchase order or credit card information.

3. Mail: **Government Institutes Division**
ABS Group Inc.
P.O. Box 846304
Dallas, TX 75284-6304 USA
Mail this completed order form with a check, company purchase order, or credit card information.

4. Online: **Visit http://www.govinst.com**

PAYMENT OPTIONS

❑ **Check** *(payable in US dollars to* ***ABS Group Inc. Government Institutes Division****)*

❑ **Purchase Order** *(This order form must be attached to your company P.O. Note: All International orders must be prepaid.)*

❑ **Credit Card** ☐ VISA ☐ MasterCard ☐ American Express

Exp. ___ /____

Credit Card No. ______________________

Signature ______________________

(Government Institutes' Federal I.D.# is 13-2695912)

CUSTOMER INFORMATION

Ship To: (Please attach your purchase order)

Name ______________________

GI Account # *(7 digits on mailing label)* ____________

Company/Institution ______________________

Address ______________________
(Please supply street address for UPS shipping)

____

City ____________ State/Province ____________

Zip/Postal Code ____________ Country ____________

Tel ( )______________________

Fax ( )______________________

E-mail Address ______________________

Bill To: (if different from ship-to address)

Name ______________________

Title/Position ______________________

Company/Institution ______________________

Address ______________________
(Please supply street address for UPS shipping)

____

City ____________ State/Province ____________

Zip/Postal Code ____________ Country ____________

Tel ( )______________________

Fax ( )______________________

E-mail Address ______________________

Qty.	Product Code	Title	Price

30 DAY MONEY-BACK GUARANTEE

If you're not completely satisfied with any product, return it undamaged within 30 days for a full and immediate refund on the price of the product.

Subtotal ________
MD Residents add 5% Sales Tax ________
Shipping and Handling (see box below) ________
Total Payment Enclosed ________

SOURCE CODE: BP03

Shipping and Handling

Within U.S:
1-4 products: $6/product
5 or more: $4/product

Outside U.S:
Add $15 for each item (Global)

Sales Tax

Maryland 5%
Texas 8.25%
Virginia 4.5%